MORE ANALYSTS AT WORK

MORE ANALYSTS AT WORK

Edited by
Joseph Reppen, Ph.D.

JASON ARONSON INC.
Northvale, New Jersey
London

The editor gratefully acknowledges permission to reprint sections of *Shot in the Heart* by Mikal Gilmore. Copyright © 1994 by Mikal Gilmore. Used by permission of Arthur Pine Associates, Inc. and of Doubleday, a division of Bantam Doubleday Dell Publishing Group, Inc.

Production Editor: Elaine Lindenblatt

This book was set in 10 pt. New Baskerville by Alabama Book Composition of Deatsville, Alabama and printed and bound by Book-mart Press of North Bergen, New Jersey.

10 9 8 7 6 5 4 3 2 1

Library of Congress Cataloging-in-Publication Data

More analysts at work / edited by Joseph Reppen.
p. cm.
Includes bibliographical references and index.
ISBN 1-56821-857-5 (softcover : alk. paper)
1. Psychoanalysis. I. Reppen, Joseph.
[DNLM: 1. Psychoanalysis. 2. Psychoanalytic Therapy—methods.
3. Psychoanalysis—case studies. 4. Psychoanalysis—personal
narratives. WM 460 M835 1996]
RC509.M665 1996
616.89'17—dc20
DNLM/DLC
for Library of Congress 96-13800

Printed in the United States of America. For information and catalog write to Jason Aronson Inc., 230 Livingston Street, Northvale, New Jersey 07647-1731. Or visit our website: http://www.aronson.com.

Contents

Contributors

Victor Manuel Aiza, M.D., practices psychoanalysis in Mexico City, where he is a member of the Mexican Psychoanalytic Association and the International Psychoanalytical Association.

Maurice Apprey, Ph.D., is professor of psychiatry and associate dean, University of Virginia School of Medicine, Charlottesville, Virginia. He is the English language translator of Georges Politzer's *Critique des Fondements de Psychologie*; co-author of *Intersubjectivity, Projective Identification and Otherness;* and, with Howard F. Stein, co-author and co-editor of the three-volume series *Ethnicity, Medicine and Psychoanalysis.* He is a member of the Association for Child Psychoanalysis and the Division of Psychoanalysis of the American Psychological Association.

Harold P. Blum, M.D., is clinical professor of psychiatry and training analyst, Psychoanalytic Institute, New York University Medical Center; executive director, Sigmund Freud Archives; past editor of the *Journal of the American Psychoanalytic Association*; a vice president of the International Psychoanalytical Association; and author of *Reconstruction in Psychoanalysis* and numerous papers.

Paul A. Dewald, M.D., is training analyst (emeritus) and supervising analyst, St. Louis Psychoanalytic Institute, and clinical professor of psychiatry, St. Louis University School of Medicine. He is the author of *Psychotherapy: A Dynamic Approach, The Psychoanalytic Process: A Case Illustration, Learning Process in Psychoanalytic Supervision: Complexities and Challenges*, and numerous papers.

Steven J. Ellman, Ph.D., is past-president and Fellow of the Institute for Psychoanalytic Training and Research, a member of the International Psychoanalytical Association and the American Psychological Association, and author of *Freud's Technique Papers: A Contemporary Perspective.*

Arnold D. Richards, M.D., is training and supervising analyst at the New York Psychoanalytic Institute and assistant clinical professor of psychiatry at New York University Medical Center. He is the past editor of *The American Psychoanalyst*, and currently editor of the *Journal of the American Psychoanalytic Association*; co-editor of *Psychoanalysis: The Science of Mental Conflict—Essays in Honor of Charles Brenner; Fantasy, Myth, and Reality: Essays in Honor of Jacob A. Arlow*; and author of numerous papers. He is a member of the New York Psychoanalytic Society, the American Psychoanalytic Association, the International Psychoanalytical Association, and the Division of Psychoanalysis of the American Psychological Association.

David Rosenfeld, M.D., practices psychoanalysis in Buenos Aires, where he is a member of the Buenos Aires Psychoanalytic Association. He is a past vice president of the International Psychoanalytical Association and author of *The Psychotic Aspects of the Personality.*

Andrew Samuels is a training analyst of the Society of Analytical Psychology, London, where he is in private practice, and a scientific associate of the American Academy of Psychoanalysis. He is a member of the Registration Board of the United Kingdom Council for Psychotherapy and a member of the executive committee of the International Association for Analytical Psychology. He is the author of *Jung and the Post-Jungians, The Father, A Critical Dictionary of Jungian Analysis, The Plural Psyche, Psychopathology, The Political Psyche,* and numerous papers.

Joseph W. Slap, M.D., is training and supervising analyst with the Philadelphia Association for Psychoanalysis and clinical professor of psychiatry at the Thomas Jefferson Medical School. He is the co-author of *The Schema in Clinical Psychoanalysis.*

Ron Spielman, M.D., B.S., FRANZCP, practices psychoanalysis in Australia, where he is a member and training analyst of the Australian Psychoanalytical Society, having completed his psychoanalytic training with the Sydney Branch of the Society.

Jaime P. Stubrin, M.D., practices psychoanalysis in Buenos Aires, where he is a member of the Argentine Psychoanalytic Association and the International Psychoanalytical Association. He is the author of *Sexualities and Homosexualities.*

Introduction

When plans were under way for the reprinting of *Analysts at Work* (1985) in the Jason Aronson Master Work Series, I thought it was time for a sequel to that work—one that would include a new group of psychoanalysts writing about how they work and think. Perhaps this time, I thought, it should be more international in scope.

I wrote to a number of analysts in the United States and abroad, many of whom I knew personally, and the eleven chapters by eleven analysts who agreed to contribute are presented in *More Analysts at Work.*

I asked each contributor to provide a personal and informative communication with you, the reader, to describe in a candid manner how he practices, thinks, and works, and to describe those theories that inform his thinking. Most important, I stated that they all should offer the reader a picture of what goes on in day-to-day practice.

The contributors are almost equally divided between the United States and abroad. Two analysts are from Argentina, one from Mexico, one from England, one from Australia; six are from the United States.

Each contributor chose to interpret my request, which was open-ended, in his own way. Some wrote about how they work, others about what is currently of interest to them in research; some included personal memoirs, others described a case. The result is a variegated picture of analysts at work and personal portraits of eleven creative psychoanalysts.

One analyst presents a fascinating case that has within it all the elements of a mystery novel while at the same time demonstrating enormous tact and treatment skill. Another chose applied psychoanalysis or psychobiography in understanding the history of a family that had produced a serial killer. One analyst who has published widely presents a case in which the patient's silence is a major factor in treatment. Another senior analyst describes his professional journey through training and teaching and concludes with wise comments about his present vision of psychoanalysis.

An analyst with considerable teaching and research experience demonstrates how he works, emphasizing the value of trust in the therapeutic relationship; still another presents a professional journey, from an interest in psychoanalysis during childhood to the editorship of a major analytic journal. There also is the treatment through interpretation of a psychotic patient, a treatment heavily under the influence of Melanie Klein's theories. Another analyst who has written extensively on politics and its place within the psychoanalytic frame explores in a cogent way the role of politics and how it challenges analysts to integrate politics in their work. The history and frustration of introducing a new model or paradigm and the intellectual journey that led to that conclusion, and its personal consequences and reactions, are highlighted in another chapter. An analyst from Australia tells us something about what it is like to practice in that faraway country and presents fascinating case material. Last, an analyst who has written extensively on sexuality, influenced by the work of Joyce McDougall, offers us a humane plea for the understanding of "deviant" sexual orientations.

Each contributor clearly chose to interpret my request in his own way. Thus we have a picture of what excites each psychoanalyst, whether it is telling a life story, a piece of research, applied psychoanalysis, or a case presentation. We are also informed about how diverse analysts are in their interests, personalities, and values. There is certainly no one analytic personality and clearly no one way to be a psychoanalyst. These eleven chapters present a bold statement of that individuality.

Perhaps in another few years I may edit a book called *Still More Analysts at Work.* In the meantime I trust that this volume will give you portraits of eleven "more" analysts and their personal psychoanalytic journeys.

Joseph Reppen, Ph.D.

1

"The Village Doll" Pregenital Trauma: Its Influence on the Definition of Gender Identity

Victor Manuel Aiza

We analysts are increasingly fortunate to explain at congresses and scientific meetings as well as in publications what we really do in our consulting room. That is why I feel gratified to belong to the group of colleagues who collaborated on *More Analysts at Work* to show how we work, our countertransferential reactions, and our doubts and anxieties upon confronting specific material, and to communicate the inability that arises from the unique, particular, and special relationships that develop in the analytical situation.

I believe that a communication barrier between analysts is the a priori disqualification of theoretical positions of others, depending on personal preferences and prejudices. Another important aspect of poor communication has been the subordination of theoretical differences to the constitution of political groups searching for power (a problem that has affected more than one institution in all areas where psychoanalysis is practiced) and the ideological utilization of the theories for founding schools and institutions that compete for dominance.

These concerns came to me while thinking about the technical aspect of the treatment of the patient I will present, who, experiencing pregenital pathology, shows a regression that restates the most primitive object relations and shows the most archaic fantasies. Such regression in the service of analysis supposes an intense transferential relation of symbiotic nuance. The therapeutic symbiosis, therefore, represents the repetition of a stage of development (Mahler 1968, Mahler et al. 1975), which simply is a stage and condition of object relations, indispensable in laying a foundation for an appropiate psychological development in and out of the analytical situation and which permits, among other things, the achievement of true intimacy and a feeling of basic confidence.

This point of necessary symbiotic reiteration demands, nevertheless, interpretative explanations that permit the patient to gradually define what is his own and what corresponds to a transferential distortion that opposes the strengthening of the ego.

Patients with pregenital pathology show delay in their development at a previous point in the acquisition of object constancy; that is, when the process of separation-individuation has not been adequately completed. They present a level of immaturity in their narcissism (Kohut 1971, 1977); in other words, they suffer from a grandiose self and omnipotent objects; they employ defensive primitive mechanisms previous to the repression, such as projective identification, massive regression, negation, and acting out (Klein et al. 1952); they maintain object relations of a partial kind; and they find themselves functioning at a preoedipal level. They suffer from a fundamental split ego. As a defensive maneuver the ego divides itself to handle the original catastrophic experience. An archaic portion separates itself from the stream of development and remains at a primitive level; it does not reach evolution because it lacks a facilitating environment (Winnicott 1965, 1971,

1975). The other side continues its partial development with damage to its integrity and strength, achieving at best a fragile and unstable adaptation. Those who experience this split, therefore, are full of critical periods and pass through an atmosphere of existential anxiety and the permanent threat of solitude and emptiness.

Winnicott has described this as the growth of a false self, which harbors a true primitive self waiting for its own conditions for its development.

These are patients who suffer from a basic fault, described by Balint (1965), that relates to the narcissistic personality disorders, with the borderline organization and with the disorders caused by the delay in development. It is of fundamental importance, therefore, to help them control envy, hate, anxiety, and the depression that unlink the loss of feeling of omnipotence reestablished in the symbiotic transferential womb.

This is a highly painful process, gradual and prolonged, that for the first time inscribes in the patient the experience of separation-individuation (Boyer and Giovacchini 1967). Its absence constitutes the disorder in development that causes this fundamental deficiency.

The pregenital patient has been described by multiple authors, such as Kohut (1971, 1977) and Kernberg (1975) in the narcissistic disorders of the personality and borderline conditions, and Masterson (1981) and Meissner (1980) in those who because of delay in the development suffer from this particular disorder.

Each of these authors explains the metapsychology of the pregenital conflict in a different manner. For Kohut (1971) the immature damaged ego of these cases is the result of the transmutative internalization of the subject in his relationship with the objects of the self, made possible through the gradual imperfections of the empathic and idealizing function of such objects. The gradual deidealization makes the idealization of the superego structure possible (that is, its investment with narcissistic libido). The psychic structures would require the maturity of the vicissitudes (ups and downs) of the narcissism, which start from a grand self to a mature self, creative and wise, with a sense of humor and the ability to accept its purpose.

In his description of borderline patients, Kernberg (1975) specifies that they utilize primitive defensive mechanisms, described by M. Klein and colleagues (1952), and their aggression is uncontrollable, impulsive, and indiscriminate.

Freud (1915a,b, 1924) stated that the narcissistic libido of the organism moves the destructive instinct outward so as not to be destroyed by it; the relationships of the individual with his objects are based on this process and the mechanism of projection is created. Furthermore, he stated that there is another part of this aggressive instinct that does not move outward but stays inside the organism, finding itself there charged with libido and accompanied by sexual excitement; this part he called "primary erogenous masochism."

We could say that the destructive impulses emerging in the child and causing severe anxiety follow two different courses: one makes him feel the panic of being destroyed by these impulses—that is, relating this fear to the instinctive internal danger; the other focuses this fear on the outer object, toward which the child directs his sadistic feelings as the origin of the danger.

The immature ego finds the desired protection by being able to destroy the outer object.

Abraham (1920, 1921–1925, 1955) demonstrates the relationship between this sadism and its expression during the urethal stage of development, in which the penis becomes an instrument of cruelty and, when urinating, is a medium to express aggressive and hostile impulses.

The intensity of the impulse seems to be the key to the problem, because what gives rise to the sadism is a frustration of libido in the first place, of sadistic oral desires, which increase and stimulate the aggression of all the subsequent stages. Consequently, we can see this aggression appear in the phallic stage or, according to Mahler's (1968) outline, in the culmination of the period of separation-individuation.

Abraham (1921–1925) also tells us that envy on oral levels is one of the factors that influence the child to take everything he can from his mother, even though later on these destructive impulses cease to be directed solely toward her; they spread toward the father and toward the objects that stem from her: the siblings. The vagina also becomes an aggressive instrument. Freud describes this clearly when he speaks of the mortal vagina—of a trap that seizes and does not allow escape (vagina dentata). Because this fantasy is a satisfaction of unconscious desires of an aggressive nature, the child develops guilt for the attacks his parents direct at each other, but this guilt and anxiety also help to intensify his aggression and to increase his impulse to destroy the dangerous object. In this way his sadistic and destructive desires increase against the parents; at the same time he fills himself with a panic intensified by the hostile entity represented by them.

The rage and hate that accompany the fantasies of the parental coitus develop guilt and anxiety that are difficult to handle. In early genital masturbation the sadistic fantasies directed against the parents are reason for remorse and shame. If we establish that these masturbatory fantasies contain the essence of the oedipal conflict, we could say that the incestuous situation carries not only the feeling of guilt, but also those aggressive impulses that have formed part of these incestuous desires because they initially appear in the child.

Freud (1915a) restated that in the development of the individual the feelings of hate precede those of tenderness and love, diverting this hate from the rejection that the primary narcissistic ego has for the outer world. "The ego hates, abhors and pursues with intent to destroy all objects that cause him pain, without taking into account whether they mean a frustration of sexual satisfaction or of the satisfaction of self-preservative needs" (p. 138). He further states (1915c) that the instinct of aggression can be found in the basis of all love affairs and loving relationships between human beings.

In the formation of the superego Freud (1924) follows two lines of thought, one complementing the other: first, the severity of the superego depends on the severity of the parents, who repeat orders and forbiddances; second, the parents' strictness and severity depend on the destructive impulses of the child. Considering the second point, we conclude that the superego, formed as a result of the child's impulses, is highest in its criticism and is precisely in this early pregenital period the instrument from which come the first instinctive inhibitions. As a result of the guilt and anxiety and the hostile and aggressive impulses, the child is incapable of handling this anxiety, which paralyzes him and becomes an inhibitive factor of his maturity, limiting the development of the ego and the possibility of reaching a normal sex life.

By virtue of these aggressive impulses the individual creates a distorted figure of his objects, not only causing the objects to exert a different influence on the formation of his superego, but increasing the importance of this formation to his object relations and to all his ego functions. By liberating himself from his object, he is able to silence the demands of the superego, but when the primary situations of anxiety are too powerful and traumatic, such as in the clinical case that follows, they will oblige the subject to keep defensive mechanisms of this sadistic period characterized by a great fear of the superego retaliation. The panic is handled either by surrendering to the relentless demands of the superego or, to the contrary, by trying to destroy it, which would cause the development of a criminal type of conduct. In other words, upon projecting this threatening superego into his objects, the individual increases his hate and at the same time his fear of them. If the anxiety and aggression are excessive, the outer world is perceived as a place of terror and the objects as enemies. The subject will be persecuted on both fronts: his outer world and his bad introjected imagoes. His relationship with the object will be at a primitive and elementary level, where the representative split and alternate systems show themselves in a narcissistic behavior, omnipotent-paranoid, in which the aggression hinders an adequate relationship. Transferential narcissistic relationships are established according to Kohut. Guntrip (1969) describes them as of a schizoid type, Mahler (1968) as symbiotic, and Winnicott (1971) as regressive.

The patient presented shows this type of pregenital pathology aggravated by a real trauma that has left on him an indelible mark through all of his psychological development and shows itself in severe and uncontrollable homosexual behavior.

CASE HISTORY

C is an individual of medium height and weight and slightly bald. He seems to be a little older than his chronological age of 28 years, has a pleasant appearance, and always looks clean and well dressed. His speech is fluid and clear, with a slight foreign accent. C was referred to me by a colleague, and it was not until the third session that he told me the nature of his problem:

> I have been a homosexual since I was 6 years old. My life is an inferno because I want to get married and establish a home, but I know that I can't. . . . You are the only person who can do something for me. . . . It is my last attempt, because if not, I will commit suicide, I know that I cannot go on living like this. . . . I can say that I freeze when I try to solve my problem. . . . My family constantly pressures me to look for a girlfriend and to get married, and I don't know how to answer them. . . . My mother cries and she drives herself to despair because she says I am getting old and have not established a home. . . . Many times I have thought of committing suicide, and if I don't get well, I believe this is the only solution left for me.

The patient says that he has practiced homosexuality since he was 6 years old when he was seduced by a carpenter in his home town, a small town in a central European country. This experience was pleasant and consisted of anal contact, with a passive attitude, which he has continued to practice until now, always with a semi-erection, anal orgasms, and the impossibility of playing an active role in the homosexual relationship for lacking an erection. This practice continued until he came to Mexico and has continued more or less regularly until now. As a measure to avoid homosexual relationships he masturbates compulsively, which is accompanied by a slight feeling of guilt. He has masturbated since childhood, when he discovered the pleasure derived from manipulating the genitals.

C's current masturbatory fantasies consist of previous anal experiences, especially with individuals of a much lower social level, such as workers under his supervision in the shop he runs. He is mainly attracted to dark-skinned people with muscular arms and chests, and does not put much importance on the size of the penis. He suffers sporadically from episodes of depression caused by homosexual experiences in which he obtains profound satisfaction and enjoyment. These depressions consist of crisis in crying, personal degradation, and the contemplation of suicide, whether by ingesting barbiturates or some poison that would kill him instantly, but he has never attempted to carry it out.

Seven years before beginning the current treatment, when he was 21 years old, the patient consulted a psychiatrist who administered two electroshocks; when he found out about the doctor's doubtful professional reputation, however, he left him. He consulted another psychiatrist who administered a total of twelve electroshocks with truly sad results. Aside from increasing his emotional confusion, and due to the organic disorder, the patient missed work, which caused his family to interfere, which put him in a state of panic and caused him to abandon all types of treatment. Two years later he underwent psychotherapy that lasted approximately two years. In the beginning he had three sessions per week, but at the patient's request and in agreement with the therapist sessions were reduced to two and finally to one per week or even less. This frequency turned out to be so irregular that it was the patient who indicated the date of the appointment. He felt this was not beneficial and his symptoms became worse. He decided to abandon therapy, and consulted many endocrinologists with the idea that his suffering was of organic origin because the "analytic" treatment had not helped him at all.

C describes his life and family history as "unpleasant, painful, and full of injustice." Elements of aggression, coolness, and rejection filled the atmosphere of his home. He always perceived indifference and resentment by his mother toward his father and a lack of understanding between them; the relationship between his parents was of a sadomasochistic nature, in which the father always submitted to the imperative demands of the mother. He remembers with anger this passive parental attitude, which confused him and prevented him from understanding his fondness or hate for either one.

His childhood memories of his father are of a good, prudent, and affectionate man, who with uncommon patience tolerated his mother's constant criticism. When he was 6 years old he casually overheard in a conversation that his father had been married before and the marriage had produced three daughters and a son who was only four or five years older than he. Two years after becoming a widower the father married his mother who was twenty years younger: he was 38 and she was 18. It was a marriage "arranged" by his maternal grandparents who felt honored that such a prominent and rich man in the small community would pay attention to their daughter. They never noticed that she never accepted him but resented him until the day he died. A motive for resentment toward the father was his passiveness and inability "to be more of a man." Since birth the patient had shared the bedroom with his parents; when he was about 12 years old he woke up one night and heard his mother, with authority and hostility, throw his father out of the room because he had asked her to have sex. "I have never felt I had a father, only a weak and dominated shadow."

C describes his mother completely differently from the father and does it in a paradoxical and contrasting manner. He remembers that she always had him close to her, and did not allow him to go out to play with other children his age in the neighborhood. She curled and fixed his hair with such interest it was almost devotion, and did not allow it to be cut until he was 7 years old. She dressed him in tight-fitting feminine pants that embarrassed him, but did not let him change them until he was 7. She took him on visits to friends' homes—and he remembers vividly how she sat him down at the visits and ordered him with her eyes to sit properly and not to move. This brought on the flattery and admiration of these women, who called him "pretty," "well behaved," and an "ideal child," which made him the center of attention then and desired when he was grown-up. "The friends envied my mother for having a child such as I, and I clearly remember how when I was 5 years old she told me that I was 'the village doll.'"

She always tried to keep him away from the father and when he was about 8 years old, when they operated on his father, she did not allow the boy to see him in spite of his insisting and crying. When he was 7, his younger brother lost some money his mother had entrusted to him. He was physically punished in such a brutal manner that the neighbors had to intervene: "If not, she would have killed him." He remembers the panic toward his mother when this happened, which paralyzed him and prevented him from uttering a sound. He remembers crying with his other brother because of the thrashing inflicted on the younger brother. "She used to protect me to such an extent that until now she has built an armor plate around me." When he was 12 his mother told him that his father was going to die and that he would be the head of the household, which he resented and considered an injustice and one more demand from her. At the death of the father they returned to their maternal home, where some distant relatives were set up as ideals of success and morality. These relatives had emigrated to Mexico and achieved economic and social success by establishing a business that produced great wealth. A year later, as a consequence of the repeated pleadings of the family members in town, who were truly threatened in their survival, the patient's family asked the family living in Mexico for help to emigrate, which happened successfully.

His early memories of school are full of shame and humiliation because of his homosexual problem. He remembers when he was 6 that some children, 3 or 4 years older than he, came up close behind him in the school bathroom. Even though he did not know what they pretended to do, he did not separate himself from them because he felt pleasure. Then they called him "faggot," which caused him such shame that he stayed hidden behind a toilet for 3 hours.

He was sent to a boarding school in the capital where he could get an education according to his traditions. Even though some of the teachers were of other nationalities, he could communicate and take refuge with them with great confidence. He wanted to study in order to have a career, but changed his mind because he wanted to make a fortune and emigrate to America. His education was limited to completing middle school. His homosexual activities increased at the boarding school. Each time someone approached him to have intercourse, he submitted passively, without objection, whatever the time or place: in the bathrooms, classrooms, or dorms. They called him "the whore of the school." His companions, who avoided his friendship, made him an object of derision and cruelty. On many occasions they slapped and humiliated him; he received the insults "like a punishment for my sin." One year before graduation his behavior became so notorious that the principal found out and, using the excuse that his grades were poor, called his mother to say that he was going to dismiss him. The patient panicked, fearing that his mother would learn about his homosexual behavior, and for the first time he thought about suicide. The principal and teachers were discreet, however, and did not mention it. A few months later the family left their country to live in Mexico.

His slight physique and feminine way of speaking made him a figure of ridicule, particularly in the family social circle. This always pushed him to seek homosexual experiences, six or seven, and on occasions 10 to 15, times a day. This inflamed his rectum so severely that at times he was unable to sit down. At the age of 18, to prove to himself that he could be a man, so that his family would not suspect that he was a homosexual, he started to frequent brothels with a cousin of the same age. The outcome was constant failure as opposed to his cousin's successes. This pushed him to look for partners, always of a lower class, at the movies and in the street.

His social life became a little livelier after treatment started, due to the ample circle of relatives in his community. He discreetly took care not to seduce or come on to anybody, even though the temptation was strong, mainly with people who innocently wanted to cultivate his friendship. The fear of being discovered and the consequences to his mother and brothers hindered him from establishing any kind of relationship.

At the initial therapeutic sessions the patient always showed clear signs of resistance. He started asking if I had family members who might know him. I did not, but the possibility was nonetheless used as a weapon to restrict the spontaneity of his communications. He told of his homosexuality with great anguish. Although he did it openly, one sensed distance and suspicion that put him "on guard"; he emphasized in a sad and monotonous tone his shortcomings and his poor self-esteem, always relating to his sexual problem. Immediately after, he would take the words back to emphasize his brilliant commercial ability and skillfulness in manipulating others to his advantage. He referred to himself as "two men in one": one a dark, abnormal, sexual animal he could not control, which put him in the position of being the screwed one; the other, brilliant, able, but so lost to the sick one that he was unable to find and use it.

C demonstrated ego splitting, and the initial period of his treatment was characterized by massive projections and a paranoid suspicion manifested in the transference relation. A repetitive subject was that he did not trust me because this was the first time someone else had such profound knowledge of the nature of his problem. He did not know what I might do with the information. For months this subject was the essence of his communication. His special concern was that my own unconscious would betray me, and that I would be indiscreet and expose him at a social gathering. His fear, as I interpreted it to him, was directed at my having a special power over him by sharing his secret and by being able to dominate and destroy him at will, whereby he would be found out. This made him react with tremendous violence; he openly threatened to kill me or to ruin my professional reputation by telling others that I was a charlatan, that I used this false accusation to blackmail and exploit him. The therapeutic situation focused on helping him, making him see the conflict his concept of being abnormal and inferior caused in the relationship to me, whom he saw as a relentless persecutor who sought only to humiliate him and swindle him as had happened in all his previous relationships. This calmed his anxieties temporarily.

At the end of the second year of treatment C explained the concept he had of marriage: the man should be in control, dominate like a master, making the woman humiliate herself and obey unquestionably. Then he pressured me to tell him if I was married or single because he did not want his ideas to interfere with or influence my conjugal adaptation and my relationships with women. This was interpreted as his wanting to show me that his ideas were sufficiently strong to have an impact on my behavior, thus putting himself in a position of equality and rivalry with me. He reacted to this interpretation with a submissive and seductive attitude, saying: "You are the first sympathetic person I have known in my life. At the same time you are sufficiently discreet, because if other people found out about my problem they would say that I am perverted, degenerate, and incapable of getting a woman to marry me." This accommodating behavior was pointed out to him: feeling threatened renourished his paranoid nucleus and impelled him to calm and please me. He replied, "Yes, I am afraid of you, very afraid of you and of my mother and the whole family circle surrounding me because I have to bear this. If not, I would cause my mother great sorrow and she would never forgive me." I showed him how his behavior was like that of a submissive child, describing his necessity to hide his hostility toward me because of fear of reprisal. Again, paranoid accusations appeared, his threats related to this repetitive projective identification in the transference.

Later C presented a dream I think very relevant to his conflict:

> Two ladies went for a walk, one of them was quite pleasant, attractive. I laid down face up with a complete erection. The prettier one said to me, "I don't want to sleep with him because he has the smaller penis. I'd rather go with this one," taking the arm of the other person, unknown to me, a tall one, dark, with small eyes, mustache, a bit ugly, not very pleasant, and then I said to myself, "Why didn't she sleep with me if I have an erect penis and am better than he?"

His associations were almost nonexistent. He asked me if I was preparing the terrain for blackmail and then said:

> I only want to warn you that you should take care, because if you try to destroy me, and in case you should succeed, there would be someone who could carry on with my work. I would tell my brothers to kill you. Besides, when I left here after the last session I got the idea that you have a hidden microphone under the chair to record what I say so as to have more palpable proof against me. I think a person could hide there under the couch or behind the plants, as a witness, to corroborate your accusations. I believe this person could be that friend I said might know you.

The main problem, as well as the nature of the transference, is clearly shown in the contents of the dream and the session: obsessive rivalry and competition with the analyst, just like his fear of castration and the hostility toward me, are revealed in his paranoid projections of destruction and blackmail. The patient sees the therapist as an assaulting aggressor whom he constantly has to protect himself from and whom he wants to destroy because of his envy and feelings of rivalry. This helped to bring us closer to the tranference relationship, mainly, the hostile and destructive feelings that tortured and filled him with panic because he was thinking of an unacceptable and hostile attitude on the part of the analyst. This was corroborated after two sessions by the contents of the following dream:

> I really wanted to defecate. I did it on the floor, an exaggerated amount. I eliminated a tapeworm and other parasites. There were seven to eight pounds of excrement. Afterwards I felt nimble and light, as if a weight had been taken off me. I thought, How could I have had this inside me for such a long time? I went to look for a shovel and I threw it away. I walked lightly, and felt rested and tranquil.

The massive projective identification on some occasions limited my interventions when I felt invaded by his continuous internal projections that made me a depository of his pathology. On more than one occasion I felt the necessity to interrupt the analysis because, contratransferentially, I found myself angry and tired of being the object of his persecutions, which at times seemed to diminish but more often made the progress of the treatment more difficult because the patient was prevented from truly understanding the contents of the interpretations and repeated the same pattern of aggression-submission again and again.

Nevertheless, despite the seriousness of his pathology, something pushed me to continue. His history was so dramatic and full of deficiencies: his discreet flexibility to tolerate the depression and the regression, his disposition to accept the analytical framework four times a week on the couch, but above all his motivation and sincere desire to resolve his conflict, to reach a level of health that would permit him, as he had said, "to be like everybody else." To have endured so much, and to keep trying with all the odds against him, awakened countertransferentially in me the desire to want to help him in spite of his resistance and paranoid defenses, so often repeated and threatening.

During the course of analysis, the patient became calmer in his projections and started to relate in detail with more clarity and less guilt the nature of his homosexual relationships. He described his passive homosexuality by relating how at first, to excite himself, "I 'pet' the partner, his chest, shoulders, and arms, and then I turn around so they [sic] can penetrate me. I almost immediately have an orgasm, without caring whether the other individual satisfies himself or not." Once gratified, as I interpreted it, he could be the rejecting object, the one who sucks and gives nothing. His inability to share was exposed by his attitude and concept of the world and his surroundings: "The one who fucks and destroys first is the one who wins and stays on top."

Transferentially, he felt that I was getting everything out of him, money and information, and for that he resented and envied me. In reality he wanted me to give him "something magical" so he could have an erection, be capable of having heterosexual relationships, resolve his problem, and not need me any more. When I made these interpretations, the patient smiled and called me clever, capable of manipulating people to get, suck from them whatever I wanted.

C saw the sessions as a battleground, where he always tried to catch and defeat me, whether with ambiguous communications or criticism of the treatment. It was interpreted that his necessity to "rob" was to obtain a security he felt he was missing before. He would obtain it by pestering or exploiting friends or relatives, which gave him the satisfaction of feeling more intelligent and masculine; in his sexual relationships he obtained it by taking the penis and making it his, introducing it into his rectum, and in the transference taking, demanding, and threatening all that he considered necessary: "To be the loser drives me crazy and infuriates me. I can't tolerate it and it doesn't matter what I have to do, but I always have to come out winning." He transformed himself into my analyst, observing me and playing the part thus to learn more from me. He was made to see how in reality he was an intermediary so that he could act his limitations with my identification. In the sexual area he wanted to take my power and be capable of realizing the sexual act. C started to communicate his interest in me; an intense fondness and affection developed, along with the respect and confidence I had inspired in him. His identification with me increased and he showed his desire to look like me, act like me, and possess and have the things I have.

In the second year of treatment C began to tell me about the existing relationship between his early experiences and his current situation—rebelling against his mother's overprotective and domineering behavior as if he were expressing with aggression and rage his feeling of being "swallowed up by her," an experience of the childhood frustration of being intimidated and totally controlled by her. This frustration indicated his complete submission to a symbiotic relationship with his mother, which included unpredictable reactions of rejection and deprivation on her part; this perpetuated his fear of any feminine figures, experienced as castrating and destructive. This is the same old dramatic story of the pregenital patient: when there is convergence of a necessity and an object of unpredictable behavior, even though preponderantly frustrating, the ambivalent bond acquires excessive intensity based on the hope of a satisfaction that increases when the frustration is greater. In other words, a painful attachment to the bad objects became more obvious. He made his anus an unsatiable mouth of intense oral necessities, with consequent resentment if these necessities were not satisfied immediately. On the other hand, the masculine figures are experienced as competitors for power, who can be used to get from them what he fears losing: the penis. He thus avoids their being able to take away from him the source that satisfies all his necessities. At the same time he feels resentment and hate for women, because in his opinion they are ferocious beasts who can only exploit; thus the only way to defend himself from them is to keep at a distance and to take away from them their love object.

Initiating his third year of analysis, the patient came to the session disturbed and obviously anguished, as indicated by the way he constantly rubbed his hands, his restlessness on the couch, and his profuse perspiration. Babbling, he started to tell me something that was barely audible until he finally decided to use his normal tone of voice:

> Today I have to tell you something that only God and I know. I am a criminal, a murderer, because I killed my sister. . . . It is an image that in my 30 years I have not been able to forget. . . . I remember everything as if I were living it and it

> was happening at this moment. . . . The two of us were alone in the bedroom . . . she was in the crib, she was barely a few months old, I don't know if I was 5 or 6. I must have been about 2½ years old, I was only 2 years older than her. I remember she was crying and didn't hush up. She screamed and her screams bothered me; seeing that she did not quiet down made me angry or perhaps impatient, I don't know, all these thoughts rushed through my mind. The only thing I wanted to do was to hush her up; I was eating one of those hard rolls. I remember that I split it and put it in her mouth, thus she instantly hushed up. . . . I bent over to see her and to observe how she gasped. A few minutes later I noticed that she didn't respond and my mother and my aunt came in; on seeing the girl they started to scream and call my father. All asked me at the same time what I had done; they cornered me. . . . It appears that I am seeing myself surrounded by all of them screaming at me at the same time. . . . I cried and covered my face, I ran out and crawled under the bed. . . . Do you see it? Do you realize what kind of a monster I am? I know that I can escape from human justice, but not from divine justice. God has punished me by making me a homosexual and pervert. To this day my mother cries and laments for not having had a daughter, she feels alone not having the companion I took away from her and I haven't been able to replace, not even through marriage.

The anguished unloading was so intense that in this session I could only give him the required support, trying to alleviate a little the tortured guilt he had carried all his life and at the same time lessen his intense feeling of loneliness and abandonment.

This material gave us the opportunity to interpret the necessity to submit to the unjust demands of the mother, which were now more clearly understood. The submission then extended to almost all objects with which he established a relationship, and in the same way led him to become feminized as he tried to repair with his own self the loss of the feminine object. In other words, his sadistic impulses of an oral nature kill when feeding, and in fear of the severe trauma he submits to a relentless superego that makes him renounce all satisfaction, serving only to gratify the desires and demands of the outer world, symbolized in its early period in his mother's personality. C was incapable of adequately differentiating or separating the experiences of guilt and persecution: "Before I thought that I had inherited homosexuality, now I see it isn't so; I always kept everything quiet, I prostituted and permitted to destroy myself and be destroyed." As the treatment progressed he started to realize his great repressed hostility, but above all his great panic of showing it and the passive feminine techniques he used, compelled by his fear not only of castration but of total destruction.

A month later he related a dream that explained the confusion of sexual objects. He perceived the woman as sadistic and the man as masochistic and incapable:

> I am in Brazil. I am going to marry a cousin I have there, but I cannot do it because she is too young. On top of her breast she had a big penis, very erect. It frightened me and I wanted to keep on running away. The girl's mother looked at me angrily; her father looked lame and idiotic, sitting there doing nothing. I was worried because the mother did not pay any attention to me. Only the mother was important to me and not the father.

His associations revealed resentment and hate toward the mother, perceived now as insatiable and above all as someone who had never given him anything, despite his (useless) efforts to please and calm her. He saw her as a woman with a threatening breast-penis, an enemy, a projection of his guilt produced by the pregenital trauma. By wanting to feed, he had killed, just as his mother did with her hostile and masculine breast that became the strongly feared persecutor.

The explanation of his homosexuality and its use as a pacifying and calming mechanism of the superego could be clearly seen in the contents of the following dream:

> The butcher's son, who by the way I liked very much although I had not had any sexual relations with him, is next to the shop where I work. He and I had killed a woman. Another man had seen us do it. We wanted to kill him as well, so he wouldn't say anything, but a beating was enough. The police came to investigate the crime. Only one of them stayed, a clean and well-dressed man. I took him to my house—in my dream it was a very luxurious mansion. I acted pleasant and seductive. I gave him a chair and told him to make himself comfortable. I convinced him I hadn't killed anyone. Suddenly I found myself with my pants down. I felt the contact with his legs and the warmth of his breath, but we did not culminate the act. I felt sure of myself, content, the clever boy who solves all his problems, as if after intercourse I would not feel guilty or troubled.

In this dream he may show the fear he had of me, represented by the policeman to whom he had told the secret of his crime. The patient could see his passiveness and his masochistic behavior in the sexual act, which on many occasions made him the object of ridicule and humiliation and put him at risk of discovery. His sexual behavioir is thus at the service of a major atonement. For the first time he set free all this indignation and rage in the face of his submissive and feminine behavior.

We do not believe that a single interpretation or isolated act of treatment is meaningful by itself. The process demands a well-reiterated elaboration. It is expected that one covers the same defensive routes many times and explores the contents over and over again before bringing substantial changes.

About a month later, at his first session of the week, C said he had looked for feminine companions who would not reject him. His former behavior had been to court women he knew beforehand would repudiate him. To be accepted by a woman filled him with surprise and disbelief; at the same time he felt an almost paralyzing panic. His ambivalence was obvious: although it pleased him to feel accepted, the company of a woman frightened him; he did not feel capable of satisfying her (in non-sexual terms). He continued to see feminine objects as ferocious beasts, insatiable, similar to the cold and rejecting mother who devoured all and gave nothing, just as can be seen in the following dream:

> I was in a shop, I think it was my brother's. A gigantic cat was making fun. It was a beautiful animal. When I approached it, it transformed itself into a wild and ferocious woman. She had a familiar face, but I could not remember her. She tried to attack me . . . at that moment I awoke perspiring profusely and filled with terror.

C's behavior began to change. His relationship with his mother experienced dramatic change, characterized by his desire to become independent and rebel against orders and "advice." He extended this behavior toward women he came in contact with. He saw them as castrating objects, like the mother in his childhood fantasies who had robbed the father of his penis and made it a part of herself to use as a powerful, destructive weapon. Interpretations were based on his inability to conceive of love, caring, and tenderness in relationships between man and woman. He saw coitus as an act of aggression in which the man had to rip and tear, introducing the penis "well inside" to satisfy himself. This thinking had the habitual content of his masturbating fantasies. Coitus also inspired fear of the damage he could inflict by doing it. He unconsciously associated the vagina, an orifice, with the mouth and introduction of a hard object, and was thus afraid of suffocating, drowning, and destroying the woman the way it had happened in his traumatic childhood experience.

By learning to accept his aggressions and hostility, along with the intense guilt associated with them, he could manage his impulses at more mature and real levels with subsequent lessening of the anxiety.

He started to court a girl who accepted him. The experience is tinged by ups and downs of suspicions, submission, aggression, and love. These feelings were analyzed and the patient could relate them to his past and traumatic childhood experiences. The "then and there" became the "here and now" in a gradual and constructive way.

In presenting this case I have tried to demonstrate the development of severe pathology shown in a confused sexual identity and overt promiscuous homosexual behavior as a result of a real childhood trauma. Murderous impulses came to realization with subsequent failure in an ego unable to handle a punitive superego aggravated by a psychotic mother who used the patient in a symbiotic relationship to realize her unconscious, forbidden feelings against the masculine figure symbolized in the patient. The intense transference–countertransference relation in the treatment helped the patient to communicate his feelings and the tremendous secret that had damaged his life. This permitted a long process of elaboration and analysis throughout his twelve years of treatment.

REFERENCES

Abraham, K. (1920). The narcissistic evaluation of excretory processes in dreams and neurosis. In *Selected Papers of Karl Abraham*, ed. E. Jones, pp. 318–322. London: Hogarth, 1949.

——— (1921–1925). Psycho-analytical studies on character-formation. In *Selected Papers of Karl Abraham*, ed. E. Jones, pp. 370–417. London: Hogarth, 1949.

——— (1955). *Clinical Papers and Essays on Psycho-Analysis.* London: Hogarth.

Balint, M. (1965). *Primary Love and Psycho-Analytic Technique.* London: Tavistock.

Boyer, L. B., and Giovacchini, P. L. (1967). *Psychoanalytic Treatment of Schizophrenic and Characterological Disorders.* New York: Science House.

Freud, S. (1915a). The instincts and their vicissitudes. *Standard Edition* 14:109–140.

———(1915b). Repression. *Standard Edition* 14:143–158.
———(1915c). The unconscious. *Standard Edition* 14:161–215.
———(1924). The economic problem of masochism. *Standard Edition* 19:157–170.
Guntrip, H. (1969). *Schizoid Phenomena Object-Relations and the Self.* New York: International Universities Press.
Kernberg, O. (1975). *Borderline Conditions and Pathological Narcissism.* New York: Jason Aronson.
Klein, M., Heimann, P., Isaacs, S., and Riviere, J. (1952). *Developments in Psycho-Analysis,* ed. J. Riviere. London: Hogarth.
Kohut, H. (1971). *The Analysis of the Self.* New York: International Universities Press.
———(1977). *The Restoration of the Self.* New York: International Universities Press.
Mahler, M. S. (1968). *On Human Symbiosis and the Vicissitudes of Individuation Vol. 1: Infantile Psychosis.* New York: International Universities Press.
Mahler, M. S., Pine, F., and Bergman, A. (1975). *The Psychological Birth of the Human Infant: Symbiosis and Individuation.* New York: Basic Books.
Masterson, J. (1981). *The Narcissistic and Borderline Disorders.* New York: Brunner/Mazel.
Meissner, W. W. (1980). The problem of internalization and structure formation. *International Journal of Psycho-Analysis* 61:237–248.
Winnicott, D. W. (1965). *The Maturational Processes and the Facilitating Environment: Studies in the Theory of Emotional Development.* New York: International Universities Press.
———(1971). *Playing and Reality.* London: Tavistock.
———(1975). *Through Paediatrics to Psycho-Analysis.* New York: Basic Books.

2

Transforming the Injunction to Die: Transgenerational Transmission of Aggression in Mikal Gilmore's Biography

Maurice Apprey

The question of how one works as a psychoanalytic practitioner is a very difficult one to address because one does not hold a stable position strictly all the time. In my discovery-oriented phenomenological research I take the view that phenomenology is a necessary preliminary approach for psychological theories that seek to explain human phenomena. I consider phenomenology a precondition for the formation of psychoanalytic theories; otherwise the formation of theories would remain essentially incomplete. In this chapter I want to show how I use one phenomenological praxis to unpack a phenomenon that I am interested in. In the past I have used infant and child observation to sharpen my understanding of conscious and unconscious phenomena. When I use phenomenological praxes, I continue that sharpening of observational skills.

In addition, I increase my ability to describe in ways that ensure that I see both what has always been there and stares me in the face and structures that require systematic discovery and explication. This chapter is a shorter version of a more complete study that is forthcoming.

INTRODUCTION

A family story is necessarily multifaceted. Many characters interact to tell one story or another and each story has various subtexts and it is difficult to privilege one subtext over another. Accordingly, I am interested in a family created by a Mormon woman who tried all her life to break away from her family by marrying a Catholic who lived in anger all his life because he perceived himself to have been fathered and rejected by a magician of a father. She struggled with a protracted case of postnatal psychotic depression; he was a criminal imposter who heaped physical and psychological abuse upon his family. Such a family produced a very well-known American homicidal criminal who begged to be executed and was. In writing about such a complex family, how does one select one subtext over another? I have chosen then to examine one family member who survived to tell the tragic story. I have chosen also to determine what his dreams can tell us. Above all, what can we learn about the infusion of destructive aggression that manifests itself as hatred in the family, and what transformations are feasible? How does the transmission of hatred show itself, and what form does the overturning of the received poison take?

The Mormons have a legacy from Joseph Smith and early Mormonism that is known as Blood Atonement. It says that when one kills, one's blood must be shed in restitution and when one's blood is shed onto the ground the killer will have apologized to God.

Mikal Gilmore's (1994) biography of his family provides a window for us to see how one family attempted to transform the violence of early Mormon history through such practices as Blood

Atonement and holy murders in Utah. Current Mormon practices do not include Blood Atonement, which was motivated by vengeance. Rather, the Mormon Church sees the shedding of Christ's blood as atonement for Christians and therefore replaces vengeance with redemption as the motivating force behind how one accounts for one's sins. The official account, says Gilmore, is that "there are some sins [however] that are so grave—and murder is one—that if you commit these deeds you have placed yourself beyond the power of Christ's atonement" (p. 17). How then may one hope for redemption? The only hope for redemption "is to have your blood shed—and even that may not be enough to earn forgiveness in the next world. But for this form of Blood Atonement to be properly carried out, we must wait for a better world when the civil and spiritual laws are administered by the same government, and such a time has not yet come" (p. 17).

Given the willingness to see vengeance as a motivated error and an ambivalence in seeing redemption as its replacement, one wonders how much of human destructive aggression remains sequestered. How much of it gets tamed and transformed in subsequent generations? How much of it is transferred with only a slight modification in appearance? How much human destructive aggression gets detoxified in ways that engender a sublimatory aim and positive direction? The purpose of this chapter, then, is precisely the following: What form of sequestration of destructive aggression occurs in a family member who survives death and destruction in his family and what is the fate of such a psychological toxin, as it were? To this end I shall first and only briefly follow the account of Mikal Gilmore, the survivor who lives to tell his family's story with the aid of a surviving brother, Frank Gilmore Jr. Next, I shall enter the private world of Mikal by submitting his seven dreams and one night terror to a detailed phenomenological analysis. Third and last, I shall dialogue the results, that is, the structures of experience of the survivor, with the impact of his Mormon ancestry. In the interest of methodological accuracy the survivor's dreams were analyzed before the rest of the book was even read. In this way the central question of how violent aggression is stored and/or transformed remains uncontaminated by the author's research on his family and his construal of what his findings meant to him.

RESIDUES OF A VIOLENT MORMON PAST IN THE GILMORE FAMILY

Mikal Gilmore has a story to tell about his family and its violent ancestry:

> IT IS A STORY OF MURDERS: Murders of the flesh, and of the spirit; murders born of heartbreak, of hatred, of retribution. It is a story of where those murders begin, of how they take form and enter our actions, how they transform our lives, how their legacies spill into the world and the history around us. And it is a story of how the claims of violence and murder end—if indeed, they end. [p. x]

Perhaps the most famous member of his dying family is Gary Gilmore, who murdered innocent men and gained his fame in 1976 by refusing his right to appeal his death sentence and so faced the firing squad in Utah. About Gary's death, Mikal surmised that his brother was essentially saying that "*there is nothing you can do to punish me, because this is precisely what I want, this is my will. You will help me with my final murder*" (p. x; italics in original).

Another member of this family, and perhaps we should say "psychological member," is the famous Harry Houdini, born Erich Weiss. Mikal's research disputes the assumption by his father's mother and by his father that Houdini fathered Mikal's own father, Frank. Frank Sr. and his mother, Fay, told the story that Houdini fathered Frank and rejected him. As a result, "Frank shared his mother's hatred of the dead man. The two of them would get drunk and call Houdini the worst names. *It was their strongest bond*" (p. 63; italics added).

Mikal's father, Frank Sr., received the name Gilmore from one of his mother's husbands who did not stay in her life very long and disappeared. The fiction that ties Frank and his mother to Houdini is that Frank's father died from a blow to his stomach. This is the reference to Houdini's death from peritonitis following a challenge during one of Houdini's magical performances when at age 48 he "allowed an overzealous fan to deliver some hard blows to his midsection as a proof of the magician's undiminished stamina and strength" (p. 67). Houdini subsequently died from his irreparable injury.

Fay's advice to Bessie, Mikal's mother, when she married Frank was based on the bitterness that attended Houdini's fictive rejection of Frank, which apparently caused him to be a troubled and restless man who in his turn as father could not stay true to children. For he had married six or seven times before under several assumed names, fathered several children, and like a magician, disappeared from the families he formed. This time, says Fay to Bessie upon their marriage: "If you have children with him, Bessie, make him stay true to them. That's the only thing that will ever bring him peace. It's too late to be Houdini's son. The only thing he can do now is to be a father to his own sons" (p. 68).

Will having children and staying true to them bring him peace? He fathered Frank Jr. and just as quickly got on the road with his acrobatic shows and later with his cheating scams, which from time to time got him jailed and which ensured that some stranger or another was always following him to catch him.

He fathered Gary next while on the run, originally naming the child Faye Robert Coffman. The name Faye is from Frank's mother, Fay, and Robert is the name of his son from a previous marriage whom he knew for one year before disappearing for eighteen years. Coffman is an assumed name Frank chose to ensure that he eluded his pursuers.

Frank's wife, Bessie, objected and chose for her second child the name Gary over Frank's objection that the name Gary was much too close to Grady, the name of a man whom he found in bed with one of his ex-wives. Every time he saw the child Gary he remembered the man who had stolen his wife's heart. In Mikal's words, Gary "has just been born of two people who carry their own bad legacies and who are presently in flight from certain unknown demons. If a parent's fear can be passed on to a child at its birth, then Gary began life as a bundle of insecurity" (p. 87). To Mikal the name switching from Faye, after a mother who could not love her son, Frank, to Gary, which by association to an unfaithful wife and her transgressor invokes bitterness, can only constitute the following: "*Gary was never born; he would only die*" (p. 87). None of his names would ensure love and a welcome to this world. In a drunken bout Frank Sr. would point at Gary and say, "*This isn't my son*" (p. 87). It is Robert's, he would charge—Robert, Frank's son, whose mother had an affair with Grady. Robert was raised by Frank's mother after Frank disappeared. Eighteen years later, Frank met Robert in Fay's house where Fay, a psychic and spiritualist minister, was to conduct the marriage of her son Frank to Bessie.

Gary's younger brother, Gaylen, came next and this time also Frank ensured that his family could be uprooted and transplanted at any time and on very short notice either to carry out a scam or to elude a pursuer. Gaylen as a young adult was eventually killed in the Chicago criminal subculture.

After the birth of Frank Jr., Gary, and Gaylen, Bessie insisted that the family take root in one place so that Frank Sr. could develop a legitimate advertising business. He reluctantly agreed. Upon settling down, Mikal, the now journalist and author, was born. He would not be part of the life on-the-run. He would not be a constant spectator to the battering of his mother by his father or to the physical abuse of the other three boys. His life would come to seem very different. He wanted to be included by the children in play when they did not want him to play a part; he even wanted to be included in the madness of his family. But little did he know that he was *already* included. Shortly after his birth, following a bout of untreated puerperal psychosis, his mother attempted to smother him with a pillow. He was rescued by his father but his conflicts continued. In Mikal's own words:

> My father feels so close and yet so far. He's the biggest enigma in this history, and I am worried that I can't solve him—if I can't uncover his secrets and explain his fears—I have no right telling this story. Maybe to know my father, I am going to have to examine my own heart and face up to the part of him that dwells there. At the same time, my greatest fear is that I am too much like the man, that *I already own his sins.* [p. 93; italics added]

Mikal wants to transform his legacy and insists that the stories from his mother of Mormon ghosts, supernatural spirits, and death are too much for him. Thus, and with courage, he concludes:

> There are memories of rage and loss and longing that are so ruinous and transforming, you can carry them to your grave before they will leave you alone. It is easy to be frightened of the unknown, and it is also easy to give superstition the power to rule you. By contrast, it is much harder to confront the real demons—the faces of all those people, those loved ones and others, who shaped your character or your history. Dealing with the memories and legacies of those fears, I figured, could be haunting enough. I did not need any other ghosts. But I allowed my mother her stories. She came from another time and another culture, and maybe those beliefs helped make sense of just how much had been lost or destroyed over the years. [p. 116]

This is the resolve of a man who was saved from smothering by the very person who severely injured the rest of his family by physical and psychological injury. This is also the son whom, by compromise, his mother was to raise to become a Mormon. The story behind the compromise is that Bessie, Mikal's mother, wished to raise at least one son as a Mormon. Frank, a Catholic, wanted nothing to do with the Mormon faith. He simply wanted a child. Mikal tells us that his parents struck a deal: "If my mother could safely bear one more child, my father would let her raise it as a

Mormon" (p. 110). However, when Bessie tried to kill her son, Frank used that incident as an opportunity to renege on his part of the shared promise, the compromise, with these words: "The day he is baptized a Mormon, I'll throw you both out on the street" (p. 112).

What then is this fear of Mormons? Mikal's account of his family has a generous infusion of legends and stories about murder and massacre in Mormon history. Mikal speaks of these legends that he heard from his mother as inheritance that she passed on to him and his brothers. There is a long line of Mormon heritage on Mikal's mother's side of the family. In his biography he tells us that his mother's mother was Melissa Kerby who was the granddaughter of Francis Kerby and the great-granddaughter of Emmanuel Masters Murphy. The Murphys and Kerbys settled in the Provo region of Utah. We are told that Provo was the second city that Brigham Young ordered organized in the late 1840s and that Provo had a most violent history. Named after Etienne Provost, there is the history of his exploration party being slaughtered by Snake Indians, several battles between the settlers and local Indians over the use of the land and cattle grazing. It is reported that more often than not the Indians died during these skirmishes. Provo was also the site of the first recorded execution. There is the story of the Ute Indian, Patsowits, who, following a version of Blood Atonement for killing a local settler in 1850, was disemboweled, had his abdomen filled with rocks, and thrown into a lake.

Mikal Gilmore tells us that there were several Mormon superstitions admixed with various Indian tales and in most of these stories Provo was *the* haunted place. Stories told of ghosts moving through the hills and around the farm at night. Tales were told of spirits of humans who had died violently at the hands of Mormons and their new and very strange rituals.

There is the story of Mikal's mother, Bessie, playing with a Ouija board that conjured up the spirit of a dead Indian who subsequently was alleged to have caused the death of Bessie's sister Alta and the paralysis of her sister Wanda.

Given the limitations of space, let me simply say that there were countless experiences of death and dying in early Mormon history, and several reports of sightings of vengeful ghosts, which put children and adults on their guard. The early Mormon Church, with its penchant for ritual and atonement by the shedding of blood, played a significant role in how people viewed the world in which they lived and *how they conceptualized the border between the domains of life and death.*

Let us now go to the preconceptions in the phenomenological presence that I bring to this study.

Given this precarious border between life and death in the early Mormon view of the world, we should be curious to know just how a survivor of this frightening world negotiates this prior history and fails or succeeds in transforming it in the world he now creates. Before discovering this we must go to the preconceptions the researcher has in view of the phenomenological presence that he brings to this study of the Gilmore family as seen through the eyes and reflections of the biographer, Mikal Gilmore.

PHENOMENOLOGICAL PRESENCE

The phenomenological presence I bring to this study begins with one premise from phenomenological philosophy that suggests that all perception is perspectival. Roman Ingarden (1975) provides a vivid spatial metaphor of the premise that perception is one-sided, partial, and perspectival.

> Every particular outer perception (e.g., seeing) is in its essence "partial" (in parts) and not adequate to what is given in it. It is one-sided and partial apprehension of the perceived object and the "other side"—which is turned away from the perceiving subject—and the interior of the thing is only co-given or co-meant. . . . Only in the further course of the experience (encounter), i.e., in other perceptions of "the same" thing, can the back become the front and then it is

> given effectively, *explicitly*. We can also in certain cases "peep" into the "interior"—by cutting or making the thing transparent, etc. These later perceptions of the same thing can corroborate the result of the actual perception. [p. 14]

Accordingly, when we analyze the dreams of the author, Mikal Gilmore, we will be given one perspective. When we return to the story of the family with its infusion of family history and so on, we will be given another partial discovery. When we come to dialogue our results with the family's history, we may discover yet one more perspective. All these perceptions may constitute the "peep" into the interior that may tell us just how humans transmit destructive aggression from one generation to the next. More correctly, if any form of transmission is in the data, the phenomenological unpacking will bring it out.

Let us now bracket, that is, suspend, our phenomenological presence and begin the study.

THE PHENOMENOLOGICAL METHOD DEMONSTRATED

In his preface to *The Phenomenology of Perception*, Maurice Merleau-Ponty (1962) explained that

> phenomenology is the study of essences, and according to it, all problems amount to us finding definitions of essences: the essence of perception, or the essence of consciousness, for example. But phenomenology is also a philosophy which puts essences back into existence, and does not expect to arrive at an understanding of man and the world from any starting point other than that of their "facticity." [p. vii]

Giorgi (1979, 1985) grounded this philosophy into a psychological research praxis.

I shall now illustrate how Giorgi's phenomenological praxis works.

Step 1 requires that the researcher collect the data from which new discoveries are to be made by using a transcribed audiotaped text acquired by means of an interview. Or, as in the case of Mikal Gilmore, the subject of this study, we may use his own words from his biography, *Shot in the Heart*, written in 1993. I shall use only the seven dreams and the one night terror that he provides as the data for our naive description in Step 1. In Step 1, then, the researcher reads the text to get the sense of the whole.

In Step 2 we read the very same description more slowly. Each time there is a change of thought, meaning, or idea, we draw a slash. By the end of the second reading we would now have separated the text into several meaning units, which would become the objects of analysis in Step 3. Each meaning unit is numbered.

In Step 3 each meaning unit is individually interrogated and unpacked, so that we could arrive at the deeper meaning for the subject in very concretely expressed terms. In this step each meaning, when relevant, may be expressed in both concrete terms and in a psychologically meaningful language.

In the final step, Step 4, all the separate meanings and essences are collapsed into a total structure of experience for the subject. We enter into the phenomenological world of the subject to see how he or she situates himself or herself in the world.

The structures then are the results of the study, which must now be considered in a dialogue with the rest of the biography and scientific literature to explicate specific knowledge or further our fund of knowledge with new discoveries. It is crucial to bear in mind that in a phenomenological study we do not, as in natural science verification-oriented studies, make a reduction toward closure of the phenomenon under the study into a narrowly conceived hypothesis. Rather, we proceed with the open and discovery-oriented position that we want to know more about some phenomenon. We proceed with the study until we have arrived at consistent descriptions of the structure of the phenomenon in ways that synthesize and integrate the essences in the motivational and phenomenal world of the subject. For detailed descriptions of Giorgi's method, one should consult his 1979 and 1985 publications. Owing to the limitations of space I shall unpack Dream 1 by using and showing all four steps in this paper and delete steps 1, 2, and 3 for Dreams 2–8.

Steps 1 and 2: Native Descriptions and Meaning Units (Dream 1)

I have dreamed a terrible dream.

[1]In this dream, it is always night./[2]We are in my father's house/[3]—an old charred-brown, 1950s-era home. Shingled, two-story, and weather-worn, it is located on the far outskirts of a dead-end American town, pinioned between the night-lights and smoking chimneys of towering industrial factories./[4]In front of the house, forming the border to a forest I am forbidden to trespass, lies a moonlit stretch of railroad track./[5]Throughout the night of the dreams, you can hear a train whistle howling in the distance, heralding the approach of a passenger car from the outside world./ [6]For some reason, no train ever follows that signal. There is only the howl./

[7]In the house, people come and go, moving between the darkness outside and the darkness inside. These people are my family, and in the dream, they are all back from the dead./ [8]There is my mother, Bessie Gilmore, who lived a life of bitter losses, who died spitting blood, calling the names of her father and her husband—men who had long before brutalized her hopes that she had so long feared./ [9]There is my brother Gaylen, who died young of old wounds, as his new bride sat at his side, holding his hand, watching the life pass from his sunken face./ [10]There is my brother Gary, who murdered innocent men in rage against the way life had robbed him of too much time and too much love, and who died when a volley of bullets tore his violent, tortured heart from his chest./ [11]There is my brother Frank, who turned increasingly

quiet and distant with each new death, who was last seen walking down a road nearby the night-house of this dream, his hands rammed deep into his pockets, a look of uncomprehending pain seizing his face./ [12]And there is my father, Frank Sr., who died from the ravages and insults of cancer./ [13]Of all the family members, he is in these dreams the least, and when he is there, I end up feeling guilt over his presence:/ [14]I am always happy to see him, it turns out, but nobody else is. That's because, in the dreams, as in life, there is the fear that my father will spread anger and ruin too far for his family to survive that he will somehow find a way to kill those who have already been killed,/[15]who have already paid dearly for his legacy./ [16]When he appears, sometimes the point of the dream is to convince him that the only care for all the bitterness, for all the bad blood, is for him to return to death. Lie down, Father, we say. Let us bury you again./

[17]Finally, there is me. I watch my family in these dreams and seem always to feel apart from the fraternity—as if there is a struggle here for love and participation that, somehow, I always fail. And so I watch as my brothers come and go./ [18]I look out the windows and see them move in the darkness outside, through the bushes, across the yard, toward the driveway. I watch cars cross the railway tracks. I watch them come and take my brothers and deliver them back, and I know they are moving to and from underworlds that I cannot take part in, because for some reason I cannot leave this house./

[19]Then, one night, years into these dreams, Gary tells me why I can never join my family in its coming and goings, why I am left alone sitting in the living room as they leave: It is because I have not yet entered death. I cannot follow them across the tracks, into the forest where their real lives take place, he says, until I die./ [20]He pulls a gun from his coat pocket. He lays it on my lap./ [21]There is a door across the room, and he moves toward it. Through the door, there is the night. I see the glimmer of the train tracks. Beyond them, my family. "See you in the darkness beyond," he says./

[22]I do not hesitate. I pick the pistol up. I put its barrel in my

mouth. I pull the trigger. I feel the back of my head erupt. It is a softer feeling than I expect. I feel my teeth fracture and disintegrate and pass in a gush of blood out of my mouth. I also feel my life pass out of my mouth, and in that instant I feel a collapse into nothingness. There is darkness, but there is no beyond./ [23]There is never any beyond, only the sudden, certain rush of extinction. I know that it is death I am feeling—that is, I know this is how death must truly feel—and I know that this is where beyond ceases to be a possibility./

[24]I have had this dream more than once, in various forms./ [25]I always wake at this point, my heart hammering hard, hurting for being torn back from the void that I know is the gateway to the refuge of my ruined family. Or is it the gateway to hell? Either way, I want back into the dream, but in those haunted hours of the night, there is no way back. [Gilmore 1994, pp. ix–x]

Step 3: Eidetic Abstractions (Dream 1)
(25 Meaning Units)

1. Subject (S) recognizes that there is *a presentation* of a dream world *that is invariably nocturnal.*
2. S sees himself and his *family presented in these nocturnal scenes in his father's house.*
3. S describes father's house as located in some *dead-end* place and conceptualizes the house as located in an imaginary space between *night*-lights and *smoking* chimneys.
4. S perceives the *facade* of his father's house as *a border* to a forest *that he must not overstep* and the *railroad track must not take him beyond that dimly lit threshold.*
5. S suggests that *the train announces an overstepping of the border* by passengers from the outside world.
6. S recognizes that *what the train announces only ends in a howl.*
7. S recognizes that, in his father's house, *there is a gateway* between *an outside darkness* and *an inside darkness* that *his*

family members can cross and do cross when they all return from the dead.

8. S perceives his now deceased *mother* as one who *longs for* and *submits to* the *same father and husband whose violence she feared* and who are linked to her experience of violent losses.
9. S perceives his now deceased brother Gaylen as one who died young and violently and therefore could not *enter* a new world of marriage away from home and consequently could not escape the family's violence.
10. S perceives his now deceased brother Gary as one who died violently, in retribution for *exchanging his experience of violence* in his father's house *with the perpetration of violence and murder by his own hand* on innocent people.
11. S perceives his living brother Frank as one who withdrew after seeing violent deaths in his father's house as puzzled and pained in his retreat from murders.
12. S perceives his father, Frank Sr., as one whose violent death came from cancer.
13. S recognizes conflict in his experience of his father's presence.
14. S perceives that other *family members know* from firsthand experience *that their father kills people* and so when he appears his family members anticipate death whereas he, the subject, has yet to suffer death or violence from his father.
15. S perceives that *father transmits a legacy of death* to his own family members.
16. S perceives further that the family would like to return the transmission of death back to the dead father by giving him a fresh burial as though a fresh burial would conjure up a fresh start in life without violence.
17. S perceives that he has failed to fit into the family pattern of experiencing violent deaths and so cannot cross the same border with the family.
18. S perceives that *to be spared from dying means that he cannot*

cross the border between life and death and so *all he can do is observe death and destruction in a house where he is both spared and trapped with his father's violent legacy.*

19. S receives confirmation from his murderous brother Gary that *to have died is* the way *to gain access and to cross the track into the dimly lit forest.*
20. S sees his murderous brother Gary show him *a gun as an instrument of death* and as a visa into the dark forest.
21. S sees himself as now prepared to have access into the domain of death.
22. S sees himself as accepting the opportunity to cross the gateway into death when he dreams of firing Gary's gun and so *for the subject suicide constitutes membership into the family of death, provides an indirect recipient of father's legacy of death, and access into the dark domain of death,* but *his dreamed death does not deliver the promised access* to the world of his dead family members.
23. S perceives that *the oneiric experience of death does not constitute belonging to his violence-prone family.* Rather, *he awakes to the possibilities of living* in spite of his family's fate.
24. S recognizes that this dream of wishing to join his violence-ridden family and his struggle to grasp the possibilities of living shows itself with regularity and import.
25. S knows now that he struggles to die with his family and to survive them but *he lives on.*

Step 4: Structure of Experience (Dream 1)

Darkness opens a door to *the domain of the dead.* In that world those who have died in the external world can appear as those who have access back and forth across a gateway to one side or the other. *To the one who does not inhabit the domain of the dead, there are only howls as signal* when the dead are approaching. Those dead include a mother who submits to the very violent men who caused her to experience violent losses; a brother who died young before he could escape his violent family by getting married and moving away; a brother who exchanged his experience of violence in his father's house with the perpetration of homicide on innocent people outside his family; a brother who withdrew from the family unable to bear the pain of watching violence in his father's house; a father who himself submitted to the cancer that caused his death. In this violent world father, in life, caused violence, and in death left a legacy that poisons and kills his family and its survivors. In this world to be spared from dying means that one cannot cross that imaginary border between life and death and therefore must be left with howls, signals, and only observe how father's legacy of killing traps those he affects. The mandate to kill may not be heeded by all family members. Some survive even when they know that suicide is one way of joining the homicidal dead and others. Although the struggle to submit to and fight the mandate to die is an abiding one, one can reject that injunction and live.

Step 4: Structure of Experience (Dream 2)

Darkness can house identifiable or unidentifiable monsters that threaten life when they eat up a child or appear as featureless vapors that can inhabit and kill family members. Sometimes it is too late to waken family members because they are already dead. The surviving one who warns belatedly may himself be a host of that poison that prompts one to kill. As if the surviving member had escaped the legacy and mandate to kill, he may continue to observe and investigate killings thought to be perpetrated by an Other. However, the killer may be the very one who investigates others. That killer may proceed to murder witnesses to his crime or children who like him have been witnesses to murder. In this world, then, killer, accomplice, investigator, and infants who are witnesses and are without words to speak are all interchangeable and subject to the injunction to kill or to seek one's own death.

There is no reprieve from this fate once the poison has taken an abiding hold on its host.

Step 4: Structure of Experience (Dream 3)

There is a compelling force that drives one to revisit the home of one's youth even if one fled this place once before. Whereas a reentry promises the discovery of secrets, lost things one had, lost parts of oneself, the actual experience is that the home is a haunted house where endless tales of sadness are told and where its dead inhabitants contrast with the living outside it. By a ruse, one may reenter but when one does not heed the warning to avoid staying till dark, evil presence comes through the darkness to meet him. This presence appears at night in dream as it is felt upon awakening so that escaping it is nearly impossible.

Step 4: Structure of Experience (Dream 4)

Things are not what they look like. A dead father may actually be alive elsewhere or exist in another form. A son may seek to know his father's identity and be disappointed to learn that the opportunity to know him does not exist. It is as if one may never truly know who one's father is. To cry about one's lost father is to search for his true but elusive identity.

Step 4: Structure of Experience (Dream 5)

A brother who has already died may be reexperienced as facing a firing squad. Worse, one's own brother may be asked to carry out such a weighty responsibility as executing a brother. Protests do not make a difference. No reprieve will remove the mandate. One must carry out the execution to awaken from the thick and malicious fog of a dreamworld. There is the hope that, awake, one may be more in control of his role in familial executions. Nevertheless, awake or asleep, the reexperience of an already dead brother's demise is parallel to the execution of another brother who was jailed and sentenced to death by firing squad for committing homicide. To a mother, nevertheless, she must outlive two deceased sons.

Step 4: Structure of Experience (Dream 6)

Trapped in an endless journey toward a death or execution one may fight one's situation with confusion, going round in circles to avoid the eventuality of death. In place of potential death, a censor might give new aim and direction, but ruses and/or substitutions cannot prevent a mother's or family member's execution. One can only mask the trip to the execution with incest, carousal, eating, and imaginary substitutions of women more attractive than those in one's own life and yet the eventual death can be deferred for only so long. It must happen.

Step 4: Structure of Experience (Dream 7, A Night Terror)

The reality of multiple deaths in one's family can be replaced by the specter of one's own death and that foreshadowing specter may be so vivid and haunting that it may be perceived as a real death.

Step 4: Structure of Experience (Dream 8)

In a world of transgenerational haunting, a parent's sentence to die amounts to the child's pronouncement of death. When he wants to die, she dies along with him because the border between him and her is imprecise or nonexistent. Given such a mandate to hasten one's own demise, protest is in vain. A mandate is a fait accompli. The mandate amounts to the execution itself. To pronounce it is to have accomplished it. It is a deed that has already happened and its announcement is but delayed. The responsibility of the man who hastens his own death is entirely his own because he failed to transform his history of abuse, rejection, and abandonment by his own father.

TRANSGENERATIONAL HAUNTING AND THE TRANSMISSION OF HOMICIDAL IMPULSES

1. Imprecise boundaries lead to perceptions of darkness, confusion, threat to identity of self, and so on. The threat is misread as an impulse toward one's own death and/or others'.
2. Dread of potential death is misread as a mandate to be carried out or as a legacy to be passed on.
3. The rule or economy of the mandate is misread as urgent, peremptory, and without reprieve so that a perceived pronouncement amounts to a fait accompli.
4. Suicide and homicide are forms of hastening one's precipitous and peremptory urge to submit to death in this system.
5. The infusion and reception of legacy barely spares a survivor or two who (i) live with guilt as though they were accomplices who unwittingly effected a death or, (ii) in the course of their survival impotently look on while an innocent child is contaminated and murdered as a consequence of the contamination. The one(s) that survive(s) must heed the unspoken injunction to separate the toxic infusions of childhood from the adult responsibility to transform the received.

CONCLUSION

I use this conclusion to refer back to Gilmore's (1994) biographical account and to see what revisions in our results are called for and at the very end link these results to three prior but related studies.

Our results have shown that Subject as survivor is not without guilt. Now we know that he very narrowly escaped death when his mother almost smothered him in the crib during her bout of *puerperal psychosis.* Subject may dismiss this piece of history as merely some chemical reaction to childbirth and spare his mother of attempted infanticide. Nevertheless, Subject's longstanding wish to be included in this family and his relative exclusion from their madness points to his experience of himself as a survivor who is a criminal by omission, leading to his sense of guilt. To survive therefore is to commit unwitting criminality, by not participating in the imperative to hasten one's own or others' deaths; hence, the guilt that follows. In surviving, Subject remains torn, even tortured, in receiving the psychological toxin but not utilizing it to cause death. Close to consciousness, Subject links his role of not propagating family madness and homicidal delinquency to his childlessness as follows:

> If I did have kids . . . I feared I would end up committing the same arrogant error my father had committed: waiting too late in life to have children that I would never live long enough to love and protect properly. I hated realizing that truth about my life and I hated seeing knowledge of it on my face—it made me look empty and old and ugly—and I never wanted anyone in the world to see me with that look. [p. 92]

Close to consciousness, then, fear of becoming as troubled as his father shows. However, according to Subject's older brother, the cross that Subject had to bear was choosing between a mother who threatened to kill his father in his sleep or a father who participated generously in his mother's hurt and injury. Toward which potential assassin must Subject lean? This is Subject's answer:

> This is the way I learned how to love: choosing between two loves that I could not live without and that I could never hope to reconcile. I learned that, in some ways, loving could be like killing—or that at least a certain kind of choosing was like murdering. I knew I had to hurt my parents by choosing to abandon one or the other, by being forced to declare which one I preferred over the other, which one I loved more than the other. In effect, I would kill the heart of one of them by revealing this truth, and for the most part, it was my mother's heart I had to kill. (No wonder I feared her.) [p. 177]

Subject's torment continues. Torn between two potential assassins, he could become an assassin himself because, for him, to love one parent is to kill the other.

To survive the killing madness in Subject's family is to come to terms with one's own potential to be an assassin, real or imagined.

The specter of Mormonism over Subject's family presents an interesting irony. Subject's Catholic father did all he could to prevent his family's acceptance of Mormonism, fearing as he did the visitation of evil upon his family, and yet his daily actions ensured that creation of the very injury, death, and devastation that he feared. In the Mormons were housed his own potential to commit harm and injury. The Mormons, with their own violent history, provided Subject's father with a suitable place to deposit and potentiate his own poison. He came from a Catholic family to marry a Mormon with a long history of involvement with the church and its legends. When he brought his own poison it seemed familiar to his in-laws, who recognized before the fact that he was bound to get involved in criminal activity. The in-laws' rejection of him and his new wife served only to provoke the misery and criminality they feared.

To make the transcendental turn, the reader will realize by now that the vehemence with which religious laws and constraints promise to "protect" humans from temptation may turn out to be the very carrier of the evil temptations those church laws were meant to prohibit or prevent. In this respect early Mormonism is like any other religious group or religious practice that knows no moderation. For as Maurice Merleau-Ponty and Freud would tell us, all extreme behaviors are the same as their opposites. Each extreme end thoroughly conceals the other. Merleau-Ponty would call this phenomenon "psychological rigidity"; Freud, "reaction formation." What is unique, however, is that the special emphasis in Mormonism on transgenerational transmission, concerns about violence, the history of violent retributions known as holy murders all contributed to shape lives lived in terror and thus created the anxieties that eroded boundaries between self and other, one generation and another, and so on, and thus made it possible to confuse one's crime for another person's.

Continuing to make the transcendental turn, the existence of tendencies by families to sacrifice a specific member or members is not unique to Gilmore's family or any family with a generous infusion of criminal history. Small doses of derivatives of infanticidal impulses exist in many families.

Some versions end in anorexia nervosa. Other versions result in transsexualism. Some others end in schizophrenia. In the midst of one's attempt to change one's life there is a central concern about coming to grips with one's potential toward a creative and constructive life or a skid toward one's demise. Sometimes there is a compromise that sustains an impulse to die and a concurrent submission to die. Within this horizon, where one may yield to an impulse to die and another may contest such an impulse or compromise the two tendencies, some distinctions of what entities are horizonal, but not interchangeable, must be made.

There is the paradigm of the person who construes a nameless dread in her family and receives it as an injunction to die and proceeds just as quickly to protest against the mandate. The compromise becomes her choosing to live but on the brink of death. Such an individual is our sufferer of anorexia nervosa (Apprey 1991).

There is the paradigm of an individual who construes a real or imagined loss in the family as a mandate to die. Somebody must die. It is an errand that must be completed. Who will appropriate it? When he decides he must submit to the injunction, he proceeds just as quickly to find a strategy of stealth or ruse to die in one form but live in another. Such is the trick of our transsexual. The result is that he obeys, protests, and transforms (Apprey 1992).

There is a third paradigm of an individual who receives the injunction to die but forms a complicit compromise with a parental figure to feign a death and feign a repair. The result is that they make a shared promise to maintain the injunction with its perceived power and a simultaneous and carefully conceived strategy to create a mental paralysis that is followed by a promised but often unfulfilled restoration of the self. Such a sufferer is our schizophrenic (Apprey 1994).

There is now, following this study, a fourth paradigm of our sufferers who share the same horizon with our anorexics, transsexuals, and schizophrenics and yet are not interchangeable with them. These individuals in our fourth paradigm *receive the injunction to die but only hasten their demise.* Slavoj Žižek (1992), a Lacanian cultural theorist, has briefly observed this phenomen in Hitchcock characters in his studies on film. These individuals who precipitously seek their demise are often agents of homicide. Here we have determined the structure of such an *agency of the transmission of homicidal impulses* and have provided an intersubjective constitution of such an agency through the naive and uncontaminated descriptions of a surviving subject's dreams.

REFERENCES

Apprey, M. (1991). The intersubjective constitution of anorexia nervosa. *New Literary History* 22:1051–1069.

——— (1992). Dreams of urgent/voluntary errands and transgenerational haunting in transsexualism. *Melanie Klein and Object Relations* 10:129.

——— (1994). *On the sense of disappearing in schizophrenia: a phenomenological reading.* Paper presented at the International Symposium for the Psychotherapy of Schizophrenia, Washington, DC, June 12.

Gilmore, M. (1994). *Shot in the Heart.* New York: Doubleday.

Giorgi, A. (1979). The relation among level, type, and structure and their importance for social science theorizing: a dialogue with Shutz. In *Duquesne Studies in Phenomenological Psychology*, vol. 3, ed. A. Giorgi, R. Knowles, and L. Smith, pp. 81–96. Pittsburgh: Duquesne University Press.

Giorgi, A., ed. (1985). *Phenomenology and Psychological Research.* Pittsburgh: Duquesne University Press.

Ingarden, R. (1975). *On the Motives Which Led Husserl to Transcendental Idealism.* The Hague: Martinus Nijhoff.

Merleau-Ponty, M. (1962). *The Phenomenology of Perception*, trans. C. Smith. New York: Humanities Press (1945).

Žižek, S. (1992). *Looking Awry.* Cambridge, MA: M.I.T. Press.

3

Silence, A Telling Nightmare, and Agents of Change

Harold P. Blum

The psychoanalysis of the relatively silent patient presents some of the most difficult, trying, perplexing, provocative treatment situations. This chapter will not attempt to deal with the general problem of silence, but with a specific form related to early traumatization and its effects on subsequent development, ego function, and object relations. The silence and absence of dreams was changed with the report of a "telling nightmare," and these phenomena are the primary subjects of this clinical essay. The silence to be described was not associated with enjoyment, love, or positive affective experience. It was the silence of mutism and melancholia, the silence of traumatic ego regression and a state of relative helplessness with severe impairment of communication. In analysis the silence was associated with frequent lateness and absence, an inability to free-associate, delinquency toward basic analytic rules, and a fundamental mistrust that undermined the analytic alliance. The silence of psychotic depression or schizophrenic withdrawal serves very different functions than the soothing silence of normal mourning or fatigue. The lack of verbal communication does not, of course, preclude other modes of communication that are nonverbal. The absence of verbalization may represent suffering in silence, sleep or death, forms of sulking, revenge, and traumatic loss, and so on. Zeligs (1961) noted that silence is a complex psychic state with many interrelated meanings and functions. It may represent a fixation, or disturbance, at any level of development, is usually vastly overdetermined, and tends to be unique to each particular analytic patient and analytic dyad. The transference–countertransference field is extremely important, because a dominant silence presents a most formidable resistance, and because continuing silence is antithetical to the very nature of a "talking treatment." The silence of the patient will have its own effect on the patient, the analytic process, and the analyst. The chronic silences may appear in a variety of patients and diagnostic categories, but are more likely to occur with severely traumatized, severely disturbed patients.

The patient described here falls into the category of a borderline personality with obsessive facade, severe narcissistic and masochistic features, ego constriction, defective object relations, and a tendency toward basic mistrust. The silence was associated with other conflicts and problems inside and outside the analysis. Despite some degree of hope for symptom relief, attenuation of conflict, and emotional growth, analysis was regarded by the patient as highly dangerous with underlying fears of primitive love and hate. He was afraid of failure, but he also needed to fail. He failed to maintain a consistent and cohesive analytic relationship as well as a positive sense of self. I consider the silence as attempting in particular to perpetuate an object relationship (and a specific set of identifications) (Arlow 1961, Loomie 1961), but also representing trauma, object loss, and enfeebled efforts at the mastery of traumatic loss. The silence was a communication that attempted to preserve the relationship while signifying its threatened dissolution with overwhelming hidden grief and rage.

In addition to silence, the patient presented the formidable problem of not remembering any dreams. A patient who "never dreams" might not be analyzable (Blum 1976). The patient did not report any dreams until almost two years of analysis, although he did report fantasies, daydreams, and the history of childhood nightmares. His first dream was a nightmare, which indicated the beginning of recovery from traumatic disorganization and ego helplessness to newly gained or regained efforts at mastery. By this time analysis had loosened his defenses, and he was less terrified of being retraumatized in the analysis and confronting his unconscious fantasies. The appearance of the nightmare was not directly comparable to those patients who have nightmares at the beginning of analysis. In his case his capacity to remember and report a dream was a sign of analytic progression rather than initial fear of free association and regression. Given his traumatic history and vulnerability with ego fragility, the silence of the analyst was a particular threat and goad. The patient used the analytic silence to extract more comments and questions from the analyst, challenging the analyst to greater verbal communication, but also inviting the analyst to join in silence and passive withdrawal.

The silence also represented specific pathogenic identifications. The identifications were part of the patient's structure and character and were also, in part, consequences of severe traumatization (Freud 1937, Blum 1987). Silent traumata continued through the patient's early development and adolescence, with developmental disturbance. His silence represented a reactive bulwark to the threatened breakthrough of unacceptable impulse and dysphoric affect, and a pathogenic adaptation to developmental challenge. He lived in a "chronic traumatic" situation and acted out derivatives of his trauma and associated unconscious fantasies. His silence was not associated with a particular traumatic event or acute shock, but more with chronic strain, empathic failure, object loss, and neglect.

The lack of verbal communication taxed the resources of the

analyst and the limits of the analytic process. Such a severe developmental disturbance also raised questions concerning the role of uninterpreted factors in the analytic situation—the analyst's empathy, patience, and tact; the patient's identifying with the analyst's ego and analyzing functions; and the patient's use of the analysis. Did the patient have a need to complete development through analysis? Was the analysis used not only for clarification and interpretation but for new object relationship and new experience, which facilitated ego and developmental reorganization? Can retarded development in an adult be rectified with developmental progression in the context of interpretive analytic work? Despite the long, intermittent silences and sessions of silence, the patient appeared to use the analyst and analysis for stability, reliability, the internalization of patient inquiry, and so on.

CASE HISTORY

At the time he began analysis, the patient was in his twenties and having difficulties with his studies. He was the child of immigrant parents and reported being slow in language communication with early school maladjustment. He was twice left back in grade school and was a discipline problem. He had temper tantrums and nightmares as a child, checked the gas jets before going to sleep—a symptom that continued in mild form into his adult life. He indicated a history of juvenile delinquency, including instances of house and auto theft, but the more extensive nature of his delinquent violence did not emerge in the initial interviews. He had feelings of inadequacy as a male, anxieties about homosexuality, and was concerned about compulsive masturbation and a tendency to avoid sexual intercourse with his wife.

He did not give clear pictures of either his wife or his parents, and acknowledged tending to withhold information and to ruminate about particular thoughts, feelings, and fantasies. He reported blocking on the recall of names and concentrated on visual images of persons and percepts that were isolated from other thoughts. He was not silent with his wife, but she took the initiative in communication and social activity.

From the inception of analysis there were long, stubborn silences, repetitive lateness, and absences with and without prior notice of cancellation. There were delaying as well as fragmenting tactics in which he would start but not complete a train of thought. The anal-phase quality of his communications and his style of speech and silence were evident in his obstinacy, withholding, and need to dig up or squeeze out material. His difficulties with schedule and lateness were so chronic that when he came on time several days in a row, he commented that he had "set a record." He had often given hints concerning his lateness or absence and other forms of enactment, but, particularly in the early phase of analysis, it was not possible to understand and utilize the patient's hints in the analytic work. He acknowledged that his silence involved suppression and conscious evasion, but it was also apparent that aspects of his silence were not completely under conscious control. He was not aware of its deeper motives, functions, and goals. He could speak of evasion and camouflage, but his silence also communicated a lack of comprehension and a confusion about his evasive behavior.

He was usually dressed in rather adolescent fashion: rather sloppy but not slovenly attire, with open shirt and unpressed pants. He would lie on the couch and occasionally rub his eyes or tweak his nose, sometimes lying still and sometimes moving about restlessly. He was grappling with feelings of impotence and inadequacy and feeling deficient in both intellectual and sexual ability. When he did talk, his language frequently betrayed mechanized, machinelike preoccupation with sexual/intellectual equipment and sadomasochistic imagery. Slowly, despite intense shame and self-denigration, guilt, and self-reproach, analysis revealed his fear of aggression and hostility.

The patient had engaged not only in theft but in the torment and murder of pets. He had thrown a cat off the roof and drowned a dog in a pond. As a child he had set a fire within his own home.

Of great importance, he referred to a "psychotic mother," probably manic depressive, who was periodically severely disturbed. She had required shock treatment during his childhood and, as we would later learn, required it again during his analysis. He was unaware of his identification with his mother and denied being afraid of insanity. However, the denial and evasion coexisted with fears of going crazy and driving the analyst crazy. He was inwardly frightened of losing control and of behaviors that would confirm some form of insanity. On beginning analysis the patient castrated his cat.

He continued to be deeply ashamed and disturbed by his few adolescent homosexual experiences. He had no further homosexual experience or homoerotic fantasy as an adult. He was nevertheless fearful of his masculinity and afraid of a feminine side of his personality. Related to these fears, he revealed that he preferred oral sex in fantasy and behavior to sexual intercourse with women and, currently, with his wife. He compulsively masturbated with oral heterosexual fantasies, which had a tranquilizing, anxiety-relieving effect. His hunger for love was hidden within his silence, symptoms, and fantasies.

The patient recalled no dreams during the first two years of treatment. Instead, he remembered childhood dreams of falling and of being unable to pull the trigger when he was just about to shoot a lion. This was related to his numbness and sometimes paralyzing anxiety associated with both oral and written examinations. His examination anxiety was also described as "nightmarish," and was one of the major conscious motivations for his being in analysis. As the analysis proceeded, he began to masturbate prior to coming to his session. Deeper feelings of being defective and castrated as well as fears of homosexuality came to the surface. His frightening images of seeing himself as having the face of a woman wearing cosmetics were immediately dismissed. He was afraid he would be a failure in school and in life, which he equated with castration, rejection, and abandonment. He felt he lived under a cloud because of the pet murders, and that he would eventually be severely punished. He was pessimistic, with depressive trends, and much of the rage that had previously been enacted in his delinquency was now turned against himself.

In the transference he struggled between silence and speech, between allowing himself to become dependent and enacting a narcissistic self-sufficiency in which he did not need the analyst or anyone else. At times his silence represented a type of narcissistic reverie, but at other times it was a defense against unbearable thoughts and feelings. He suffered in silence, wanted the analyst to suffer, and, in a protracted, negative, therapeutic reaction, attempted to wreck any analytic success. He tried to provoke the analyst to reject him as a final punishment. When these issues were explored along with his need for omnipotent control and his homosexual retreat from male competition, there was considerable improvement in his verbal communication and a reduction in his lateness and absence. Signs of a strengthened, positive transference and analytic alliance indicated that the patient was better able to participate in the analytic work. At this point he could discuss his circumlocution and censorship of thought and avoidance of conscious transference-derived feelings.

He was now able to develop insight into his separation anxiety and his rage at the analyst's cancellations or vacations. It was in relation to separation that he was finally able to discuss his homosexual experiences in adolescence. In reaction to rectal intercourse at age 17, he had hurled a cat from a height to its death. This was really what he wanted to do to his homosexual partner and unconsciously to himself. He would later see his identification with his mother and his derivative, warded-off thoughts of being criminally insane. His compulsive masturbation represented the doing and undoing of his castration fantasies and his reassurance that he was adequate, potent, and masculine. His delinquency had denied in action his passive, dependent, and feminine wishes and expressed his defiant rage and his sadomasochism. Many of his adolescent friends were tough delinquents who rationalized arrogant, contemptuous attitudes toward authority and society.

The patient's tendencies toward difficulty in cognition and abstraction, his numbing and isolation of affects, gradually gave way in the very difficult, painstakingly slow analytic work that had been punctuated with silences. He recalled a reading disability where he blocked on words like "cat" and "rat." The cat, his totem animal, figured as a representation of himself and his parents. The cat predominantly and classically represented his mother and the female genitals, and thus his homosexual partner. The murder of the cat was unconsciously a disguised form of matricide. With those issues under analysis, the patient was able to begin to talk about the severe disappointment and disturbance in his relationship with his mother, both parents, and between the parents.

His mother suffered from severe depression and episodes of withdrawal. She then enacted fantasies of starvation through anorexia and vomiting if she attempted to eat. Not only was she silent but she frequently, like the patient, cancelled appointments with psychiatrists. His father had beaten his mother when she cancelled an appointment and had to pay for the missed session. The patient aimed at "absolute zero" in his emotional life and felt utterly alienated from his devalued parents. He was not able to discuss his needs to mother his mother, to provide ego support for her, and wanting his analysis to protect him and her from her manic-depressive psychosis. His self-denigration and self-hate matched his unconscious denigration and ambivalence toward his damaged, psychotic mother. On the weekends he was especially solicitous of his cat, whom he could overfeed. He would sexually unite with his wife to deal with the weekend separation from the analyst. He recalled having followed a friend in putting his penis into a dog's mouth and could recognize that his homosexual fantasies were linked to counterphobic behavior, which would deny the danger of castration while simultaneously inviting castration. At this time there were numerous fantasies of abandoned pets, animals and people injured in auto accidents, and machinery and equipment that showed signs of damage, fatigue, and failure. Could he be repaired and could the split in his identity between delinquent and scholar as well as his homosexuality be healed?

As his aggression and hate surfaced, his matricidal fantasies became available in the analysis. He would destroy the analyst in the analysis as he had wanted to do with his mother. He then first described her frenzied, manic behavior. When his mother was manic, he would be filled with worry and fury. She would run around the room in her pajamas, overstimulating the patient both sexually and aggressively. She would burst into song, making buzzing noises with her fingers only to fall into protracted silences. She became depressed following narcissistic slights such as not being invited to a Christmas party. This accounted for the patient's peculiar behavior during holidays, and he could see more clearly the reverse transference in which he behaved like the mutant negativistic mother, turning the analyst into the traumatized child. He had been frightened that his mother actually would die as a result of his death wishes and her declarations that she was going to die. He deeply resented her hostile withdrawal from him and maintained their relationship through identifying with her. He also realized that he did not have the experience of parents who maturely cared about each other. They did not have an affectionate, friendly relationship. His participation with his delinquent friends was an adolescent search for a new family and a hostile devaluation of parental authority. He had reproached the analyst/parent for being neglectful, and at the same time experienced the analyst as neglectful and the analysis as a deprivation. He had thought of breaking off the treatment, but that would be "suicide." He recalled that his mother had threatened suicide by jumping out a window. This again confirmed his killing of a cat as a displaced derivative of matricide.

It was in this context of matricide and the recognition that it would be "suicide" for him to break off the analysis that he remembered and reported his first dream—a terrifying nightmare. He had been late and silent in the previous session and thought of his mother moaning. He wondered how the analyst tolerated his lateness, silence, and absence. He could not have brought himself, in the past, to give advance notice of lateness or a cancellation. His parents could not communicate with each other, and he thought of his mother moaning in bed in the depth of depression. It was an awful thing to see. He then told the analyst of his terrifying dream from which he woke in tremulous anxiety and sweating; "I was taking a bath, the water was cloudy. As I got out of the tub I saw the water moving and something moving under the surface. There was a cloud of blood as though something had ripped a creature. A head appeared that was part lizard and part feline." He left the bathroom and returned to find that his cat had gotten into the dangerous tub. There had been a fight, and he had found his cat dead with no head. He wanted to take revenge on the lizard—to cut it up into pieces. The lizard was lying motionless, but then it was aroused and attacked him. He was full of bites and claw injuries from the battle with the lizard. He killed the lizard, but then he was frightened by the thought of rabies. He would need immediate inoculations to prevent a painful death. In his imperative need for revenge he was terrified of contracting a fatal rabies illness or being decapitated like the headless cat.

The patient and analyst pondered the patient's severe developmental disturbance in the light of his mother's psychosis. She had been under psychiatric treatment during his analysis, and one of the precipitants for his nightmare may have been her slipping into a stage of psychotic decompensation. How much could the early structural damage be repaired in analysis? Would the patient lose his head and be irreparably damaged like his mother? Would analysis be helpful or harmful, a recurrent concern? Had he inherited the genes with the predisposition to manic-depressive psychosis? Could his disturbances in early attachment and object relations, his severe ambivalence, and his fragile object constancy be repaired and restored in the analytic work? Was his nightmare related to a sense of analytic failure or the beginning of developmental reorganization and analytic reintegration? While the nightmare had its profoundly regressive dimensions, it appeared to signal the awakening of new efforts at mastery of trauma. His report and vivid recall of the nightmare heralded a change from silent trauma to analytic communication, clarification, and verbal comprehension. What the patient could not express in words, and what he had formerly acted out in delinquent attacks on animals, he could now begin to bring into the analytic dialogue. This first dream after two years of analysis was therefore the outgrowth of progressive analytic work and it indicated the patient's greater readiness to deal with unconscious fantasies.

His nightmare dealt with partially encapsulated trauma. In avoiding the nightmare and the analysis of the underlying conflicts embodied in his frightening fantasies, the patient avoided dependent as well as loving relationships and denied both his feelings of helplessness and his desperate search for help. His repeated traumatization, intense oedipal and preoedipal conflicts, narcissistic injuries, and withdrawal had not been assimilated and attenuated in the course of development. He had "succeeded" in avoiding dreams and nightmares in the prior analytic work. But this avoidance did not permit the integration of his fantasy life with his ordinary waking life. He did not seem to be overtly hypervigilant. Yet he was easily either emotionally hypersensitive or relatively numb. His affective and cognitive disturbance left him prone to action rather than reflection. He was fixated toward trauma and infantile patterns while at the same time vulnerable to retraumatization and regression. The nightmare depicted the most frightening aspect of his self and object representations and was made available in the safety of the analytic situation. While nightmares frequently appear at the onset of mental or physical illness, they also commonly appear in children and adults meeting developmental challenges and attempting to master prior traumatic experience (Mack 1970).

It may be noted here that the patient did not simply drop the nightmare into the analyst's lap like a "hot potato," nor did he treat the nightmare as if it were reality or an unacceptable part of himself—a meaningless fantasy to be dismissed or a foreign body unrelated to himself. He was not in a nightmarish state in the form of a hangover or "daymare" in the aftermath of the nightmare. Furthermore, after remembering and reporting the nightmare, he was able to associate to it and to participate in the analytic work in which the nightmare figured. While he was frightened of his relationship and identification with his psychotic mother, he showed evidence of identification with the analyst's analyzing functions and in analytic attitude. He had become aware of the analyst's empathy, sensitivity to his fragility, and sometimes the analyst's countertransference reactions. Now there was much greater, though cautious, interest in the analytic process and efforts to understand himself and others. His curiosity and introspection retained a tentative quality, as though he could easily retreat from his new position.

Giving voice to what were previously inchoate, fragmented, thoughts and feelings, the patient actively associated to the nightmare. Upon reflection he could connect some of the associations to each other and to the transference and his life.

It should also be noted that his frightening dream did not depict a continuing state of helplessness. He could be immunized against rabies, which indicated that a fatal madness could be avoided by appropriate treatment. He associated to his fear of madness in identification with his mother. His anxiety that free association could lead to psychotic productions was interpreted again and again. The fear of body damage and of bodies being torn as well as brain damage was apparent. He was afraid of his mother's fragmentation, his father's rages, and his own impulses, which he had previously acted out. His frequent silences had led to fragmentation of sessions. "Chopping the session to bits" defended against murderous transference wishes while representing "killing time" and destroying or sabotaging analytic work. The transference was a battleground, and for this patient it was hardly ever a playground. In the transference struggle the nightmare, associations, and choice of metaphor and symbol were shaped mainly by the patient. This patient recognized aspects of the transference and his life history in the analytic process and that the analyst had not suggested or provoked the mutilating, murderous nightmare. If the analyst had been unempathic, critical, or otherwise hurtful, the patient observed that his transference reaction had little relation to the reality of the analytic situation. The disguised recapitulation of preadult trauma and childhood fantasy was highly individual and selective. The countertransference in work with a fragile, frightened, silent patient with a nightmare is very significant. Impeding and facilitating analytic understanding, the countertransference here was not regarded as co-creating the transference or the patient's dream and associations. The omnipresent transference to contertransference matrix or potential are not, however, the focus of this study.

For the patient, silence was repeatedly sleep and death but also an incestuous sleeping together and a soothing, comforting fantasy enactment of a symbioticlike union with the preoedipal mother. He had fantasies of merging with and murdering the preoedipal mother. An oral triad (Lewin 1946) of eating, being eaten, and dying did not emerge clearly. He also associated to his need for revenge, which had an imperative quality in the dream. Narcissistic injury and castration/mutilation anxieties led to vindictive attitudes concurrent with fears of retaliation. His fear of retaliation and rejection was exemplified in his fantasy of being cast out by the analyst and left to starve in the cold like his starving mother or stray animals. His delinquent acts had had a strong vindictive component, and for the first time the patient could discuss both his love and his hate for his mother. When she was well, between bouts of psychosis, she was a different person who was able to be affectionate and nurturing. He hated his sick mother and had to admit to himself that he hated the same person when she was well. He was afraid both of his incestuously loving thoughts toward her and the murderous rage against her that broke into his awareness. He had a fantasy that his cat would be burned on a hot stove but would be saved by a vet and then left badly scarred. This was his psychological portrait of himself as well as his mother. Could he become rabid again, a madman? This was similar to later fantasies in which he was the hero and saved the girl in a burning building. His wounds required the continued treatment of analysis during which he would get a new mother and a new identity. He could recognize that he was rescuing his mother from her own psychotic "demon" as well as undoing and mourning her lost availability and the damage of his earlier delinquent acts.

This was then the beginning of the patient's bringing dreams into his analysis and being able to restore and make new connections between fantasy and reality, present and past. Lions were declawed and changed into friendly cats. He could befriend and comfort his parents. He had more open fantasies of affectionate and exciting sexual contact with still-forbidden women and he thought of impregnating a woman who represented both his wife and his mother as a composite. This was followed by thoughts of the possible execution of a juvenile murderer. His guilt over his oedipal impulses was associated with omnipotent punishment, but the patient could now allow for merciful reprieve and the rehabilitation of the young criminal.

As Freud (1918) remarked in the case of the Wolf Man, such a severe developmental disturbance cannot be fully reversed or rectified by analysis. In such cases, perhaps with an inherited constitutional predisposition, the systematic analysis of unconscious conflict may not necessarily correct developmental disturbance, structural damage, and ego defects. The developmental disturbance encompassed cognition, affect regulation, and object relations. His oedipal development was impaired by antecedent and preoedipal narcissistic problems. Untamed aggression and infantile omnipotence left him with a severely sadistic superego that at the same time tolerated impulsive behavior. His object representation and his own self-representation were severely devalued and damaged, and ambivalent conflicts reigned supreme. A preconscious dread of homosexuality was bound up with his unconscious retreat from a frighteningly aggressive masculinity, fear of castration, and a hidden hunger for maternal love and nurturance.

His narcissism was entrenched, and he readily regressed to narcissistic withdrawal and to a relationship with narcissistic objects. True object constancy had not been achieved, leaving the patient vulnerable to regressive separation anxiety, with collapse of self-esteem and self-confidence. He recognized, in the analysis, a defective sense of himself identified with a devalued "other." His personality was not fragmented, but neither could he be described as a well-integrated or "together" person. Analysis has resulted in considerable improvement in his overall personality, functioning, and organization. Psychoanalysis provided new opportunities for the attenuation of conflict and the mastery of trauma. From a structural and developmental point of view, there were many problematic residua.

Trauma is represented and repeated in nightmares, in transference, acting out, and many other forms and derivatives. Some gifted individuals are able to use nightmares in the overall process of sublimation. Like the underlying trauma, nightmares may have both a disorganizing and a subsequent organizing effect upon development. In uncommonly gifted individuals, putting aspects of their nightmarish traumatic experience into words serves a purpose similar to psychotherapy. Writers such as Robert Louis Stevenson and Mary Shelley were able to transform their traumatic experience and immediate nightmares into literature. Mary Shelley modeled Frankenstein after a demon image in a nightmare; Stevenson used the paradigm of a polished aristocrat turning into a mad monster in a nightmare for his creation, upon awakening, of Dr. Jekyll and Mr. Hyde. The attempt to master trauma that Freud (1920) inferred in the nightmare may be successfully carried forward in advanced, consciously organized psychic activity. Remembering, drawing, reporting, and talking about the nightmare all help to transform the unthinkable and unspeakable into what can be accepted and assimilated, clarified, and eventually understood. Opposite to his tendency to retreat into silence, the patient described here was inwardly pressured to describe his nightmare.

The nightmare vividly brought out the patient's fears about being criminally insane and "going to pieces" like his mother. The criminal was also his father who had mistrusted and neglected his mother. He thought of himself as a genetic defective, but there were obvious problems of both nature and nurture. His mother may have had serious problems in attachment to her child and in the affective mother–infant communication. The patient had all the problems of relating to and identifying with the mother whose care was so disturbed and distorted by her episodic psychosis. Was she able to empathize with her child, was she sensitive to his needs and feelings, and could she provide consistent and reliable care? Could she use good judgment even during her nonpsychotic periods? The nightmare may also deal with preverbal trauma. Such trauma either does not receive verbal representation, or the verbal representation derives from later-phase transformation of the preverbal trauma and organismic distress.

The nightmare telescopes instances of shock trauma and long periods of cumulative trauma and developmental strain. In patients such as this, with long periods of developmental disturbance, the pathogenic development along with the associated trauma has influenced both symptoms and character. In these patients the experience of the analyst's tolerance, tact, and empathy and the experience of the analyst as a new, clarifying, and understanding object are very important. The analytic experiences may facilitate developmental progression. The application of insights to their unconscious conflicts and traumata, inside and outside the analytic situation, proceeds with the facilitating, noninterpretive factors in the analytic situation. It is probable that in such a patient the analytic experience itself has a facilitating effect, synergistic and concurrent with gaining insight into unconscious infantile conflict (Blum 1992, Pulver 1992, Sandler 1992). It is of theoretical interest that although he had recalled childhood nightmares, he did not have a nightmare again until well into his psychoanalysis. This implies a loosening of his defenses and the threat of regression, but also an enriched ego capacity to confront his frightening memories and fantasies. The analytic process permitted a reconstruction of his childhood and the persisting existence and influence of that childhood in his present life. His dreams proved to be useful in the recapture of his actual and internal childhood experience. The expectation that the analytic process with the revival and reconstruction of past traumata would tend to elicit further nightmares was not borne out in the analysis. Other symptoms either persisted or recurred, but nightmares, as opposed to mild-anxiety dreams, were rare analytic occurrences. The absence of nightmares may have represented a positive analytic development or possibly a limitation of the analysis. His childhood nightmares were probably prototypes for the analytic nightmare, but with later, different meanings, alternatives, and effects.

Did analysis permit and facilitate more than the mastery of trauma and the attenuation of unconscious conflict? Adult development cannot be on a par with developmental processes of childhood linked to biological maturational progression and phases. It is possible to think of earlier fixations being loosened and some forward development occurring, pari passu with the analysis of intrapsychic conflict. Some nightmares in analysis may then be regarded as Janus-faced, a revival of the frightening dangers of the past and a harbinger (among others) of analytic progress and developmental challenge and change. The analytic movement demarcated at the time of the nightmare should not minimize or overstate the limits of analysis and the limitations of analytic change with a severely traumatized, developmentally disturbed patient.

REFERENCES

Arlow, J. (1961). Silence and the theory of techniques. *Journal of the American Psychoanalytic Association* 9:44–55.

Blum, H. (1976). Dreams and free association. *International Journal of Psycho-Analysis* 57:315–324.

——— (1987). The role of identification in the resolution of trauma: the Anna Freud memorial lecture. *Psychoanalytic Quarterly* 56:609–627.

——— (1992). Psychic change: the analytic relationship(s) and agents of change. *International Journal of Psycho-Analysis* 73:255–265.

Freud, S. (1918). From the history of an infantile neurosis. *Standard Edition* 17:3–122.

——— (1920). Beyond the pleasure principle. *Standard Edition* 18:364.

——— (1937). Constructions in analysis. *Standard Edition* 23:255–269.

Lewin, B. (1946). Sleep, the mouth, and the dream screen. *Psychoanalytic Quarterly* 15:419–434.

Loomie, L. (1961). Some ego considerations in the silent patient. *Journal of the American Psychoanalytic Association* 9:56–78.

Mack, J. (1970). *Nightmares and Human Conflict.* Boston: Little, Brown.

Pulver, S. (1992). Psychic change: insight or relationship. *International Journal of Psycho-Analysis* 73:199–208.

Sandler, J. (1992). Reflections on developments in the theory of psychoanalytic technique. *International Journal of Psycho-Analysis* 73:189–198.

Zeligs, M. (1961). The psychology of silence: its role in transference, countertransference, and the psychoanalytic process. *Journal of the American Psychoanalytic Association* 9:7–43.

4

A Psychoanalytic Retrospective

Paul A. Dewald

After majoring in psychology at college, I entered medical school in 1942 intending to become a psychiatrist. Psychiatry at that time was a small subsection of the department of medicine, and in my medical school career it consisted of a weekly one-hour, third-year, lecture-demonstration series at the local state hospital, at which time psychotic patients were described and then demonstrated to us. In my senior year we had a one-hour weekly conference with a faculty psychiatrist who discussed more typical neurotic patients. That, in essence, was my medical school experience.

World War II had decimated residency training programs, and as undergraduate students we had unusually high levels of clinical exposure and experience with hands-on procedures and responsibility for patient care. This excitement and clinical responsibility (after the preclinical years) had led me to abandon my original goal, and in succession I was going to become a surgeon, a plastic surgeon, a general internist, or a specialist in some form of internal medicine. Medical school's four years were covered in three, with only a brief vacation between academic years; during those interludes I served as an extern on services that I would otherwise not have experienced.

All of us were already members of the armed forces and attended various military exercises in preparation for ultimate service in one of the branches of the military. My internship was already arranged by the time I was halfway through my third year of medical school, and the internship when it occurred lasted nine months, followed by military induction.

World War II ended shortly after my graduation from medical school; therefore the risks of exposure to combat in military service were eliminated. Demobilization of the armed forces led to a significant return of the young physicians whose careers had been interrupted and the ranks of residents rapidly filled with these people, so that the previous level of responsibility and initiative was sharply reduced. These men returned with a variety of accounts of their military service and of the importance that they had recognized in regard to psychiatric casualties and the role of psychological and emotional factors in their experience.

Immediately following basic training, I was sent to Germany as part of the Army of Occupation. For the first nine months I served as a general batallion surgeon, after which I was assigned to a station hospital. The commanding officer had asked what my preferred assignment was, and I said I was curious to explore the possibilities of psychiatry. I was placed on general medical wards.

After about three months the psychiatrist in charge asked if I were interested in seeing some psychiatric patients, which I was eager to do. He interviewed a few of the inpatients with me sitting in, and after asking if I had any questions (I didn't know enough to have questions), he said, "That's fine, because I'm going home on rotation, and from now on you're going to be the psychiatrist in charge."

For the next year I served as the only psychiatrist for a community of 30,000 soldiers and civilians—wives, children, and employees of the military—and it became a struggle for survival and a self-learning process based on trial and error and on reading the few army manuals at my disposal. I found it a stimulating area of interest, but following discharge I elected to take a residency in internal medicine at the medical school where I had graduated.

When I returned, I found the situation in regard to psychiatry had changed totally from when I had been a student. John Romano, George Engel, and a group of junior associates had arrived to organize and develop a freestanding department of psychiatry and to build an inpatient and outpatient unit to care for psychiatric patients. An extensive medical school curriculum in psychiatry was being devised as well as a residency training program: there was a sense of excitement, enthusiasm, new perceptions, and development of a cadre of psychiatrists with a predominantly psychoanalytic and psychodynamic orientation.

At that time (1948) the development of a significant independent, freestanding department of psychiatry with appropriate hospital and other facilities in a general hospital setting (as opposed to private sanitaria or state hospitals) was unusual, and the enthusiasm and new developments again stimulated my interest. I was accepted for a residency in psychiatry beginning in 1949. The United States Public Health Service was actively supporting the expansion of psychiatric training, both for psychiatrists and for physicians in other medical specialties. The Group for the Advancement of Psychiatry was being organized, and there was an air of expectation and stimulation. Large numbers of medical students and residents were going into psychiatry, and for a variety of reasons related to its role in World War II, psychoanalytic and psychodynamic theory and clinical practice became the dominant paradigm for American psychiatry. The few psychoanalytic institutes around the country were flooded with large numbers of applicants and the best and brightest minds in the young psychiatric expansion were applying for and focused on psychoanalytic thinking, training, and practice. There was a general expectation that those who could get themselves accepted for psychoanalytic training would do so at their earliest possible opportunity.

Early in my residency the psychoanalytic candidates based in Rochester, New York, commuted to Chicago by train every other weekend to attend classes at the Institute for Psychoanalysis in Chicago. Their excitement over the analytic training, the faculty, and the seminars was conveyed to us junior members of the staff, and the department became predominantly psychoanalytically immersed. The pressures on the institute in Chicago became so great, however, that it decided not to continue accepting people from our area, and my fellow residents and I were deeply troubled that we might not be able to obtain this training while working in Rochester.

In spite of this, however, some of us began training analysis with the only training-analyst-at-large in the city in 1952, and by 1955 it became possible to apply for psychoanalytic training at the Psychoanalytic Institute affiliated with the Downstate University Department of Psychiatry in Brooklyn, New York. Beginning in 1955, we commuted by plane every Friday afternoon, arriving in New York in time for an evening seminar, staying over in a local hotel, attending classes from 8:00 A.M. to 1:00 P.M. in Brooklyn, and returning to Rochester by plane late Saturday afternoon. This was an exciting and heady time in which we were exposed to new and stimulating teachers and concepts, and developed significant and long-lasting friendships and contacts in the psychoanalytic world. We conducted our supervised analytic cases in Rochester, and obtained the supervision from faculty at the Institute in New York. The training was expensive in terms of plane fare, hotel, and meals, but we were allowed to augment our full-time academic salaries by private practice in amounts to cover professional and training expenses. Although we were thought of by some of our colleagues in New York as martyrs, in actuality it was significantly easier for us because all of our travel, seminars, and supervision occurred on weekends. Our New York classmates had a lengthy commute back and forth for their analytic sessions, and had to treat their psychoanalytic cases on the grounds of Kings County Hospital. Many of them were away from home three or more nights per week, seldom seeing their spouse or children. However, the spirit of the times made virtually any sacrifices appropriate for obtaining what was then considered to be the ideal form of postgraduate psychiatric and psychoanalytic training.

Our institute was heavily focused on the teachings of Freud and of "classical" analytic theory and technique. Generally speaking, the theoretical framework was of the analyst as the affectively uninvolved and cognitively focused interpreter of the patient's productions and of the patient's transferences, with silence as a significant component of the therapeutic process, and with interpretation primarily directed toward content of the patient's unconscious conflicts and fantasies. Emphasis was focused on maintaining the purity of the patient's transference and avoiding "contamination" of transference responses by interaction or other self-revealing behaviors. The analyst was the observer, and countertransference was seen almost exclusively as an interference in the treatment process, or a reason for returning to or continuing personal analysis. A sense of secrecy about what actually transpired in the therapeutic situation was a common attitude among candidates and teachers alike.

Rigidity of thinking and anxiety at the possibility of being criticized or doing things differently led to an interesting (in retrospect) situation of learning. I had four different supervisors, each of whom insisted on my conducting each case in accordance with their own particular version of psychoanalytic thinking and technique. The result was that my cases were analyzed using the technique of the individual supervisor in question, and things that I might say in one therapeutic situation would never be tolerated in another. I was extremely fortunate to have Jacob Arlow as my fourth supervisor. His emphasis on observing the flow and detail of the process and his integration of the clinical situation with psychoanalytic theory led me to use him as my psychoanalytic ego-ideal. I was thus exposed to a variety of different ways of understanding psychoanalytic process and technique and only afterward developed some type of synthesis of what I was intending to use for myself.

My official graduation from the Institute occurred in 1960, and it was only in the following years that issues such as the importance of defense and resistance, the awareness of one's own interactional processes and experiences vis-à-vis the patient, and the idea of analysis as a two-person interactional experience began to emerge and to play an increasing part in my perception of myself and my analytic technique.

In 1961, for a variety of personal and professional reasons, I left Rochester and came to St. Louis to be part of a new psychoanalytic foundation established with the intention of bringing psychoanalytic education and training to the St. Louis area, where none had previously been available. At that time the St. Louis Psychoanalytic Foundation had arranged to become a geographic training facility with the Institute for Psychoanalysis in Chicago, and I had the opportunity to commute to Chicago, now as a teaching faculty member. There I came in contact with a new group of psychoanalysts and mentors, the most notable of whom (for my own development) were Joan Fleming, Theresa Benedek, and Helen MacLean. From my perspective as a junior faculty member at the Institute, the previous sense of rigidity and intimidation aboout trying new understandings and techniques, and the exposure to still different ways in which psychoanalytic awareness could be applied, led to a considerable loosening within myself and the capacity to begin to synthesize in a more personal and self-selected way between my training, my experience, and the various individuals with whom I identified.

During this time, with the other geographic analytic centers being developed through the auspices of the Chicago Institute, twice yearly there would occur weekend meetings, and the opportunity came to broaden my contacts with analysts from Denver and Cincinnati. We would all meet with Chicago faculty members with the aim of learning more about the function and development of institutes, the teaching of psychoanalytic concepts, the process of supervision, the establishment of psychoanalytic clinics, the selection of candidates, and so on. All this was a very important component of my personal psychoanalytic development and interest in teaching psychoanalysis.

In 1972, anticipating that the Psychoanalytic Foundation would evolve into a provisional psychoanalytic institute in 1973, and recognizing the necessity of having a training analyst as director of the institute, I was elected to replace the (then) director of the Foundation. After eleven years of commuting to Chicago for teaching and the geographic training analysts' meetings, and after serving as a training analyst and supervisor for psychoanalytic candidates commuting from St. Louis to Chicago, we developed plans for an evolving and significantly altered curriculum and wrote the bylaws and constitutional organization for a psychoanalytic institute.

In 1973 St. Louis became a provisional independent psychoanalytic institute affiliated with the American Psychoanalytic Association. As medical director for the next ten years, I found the administrative requirements, the inevitable issues of tension between faculty members, the functioning of the lay board of directors, and the relationship with the community served to occupy much of my time. I continued a full analytic practice as well as participated in the activities of the American Psychoanalytic Association.

Balancing my interests and commitment to psychoanalysis was a characterological predisposition and need to be an active participant in a variety of different enterprises. Upon my arrival in St. Louis I therefore arranged to teach in a variety of different settings—including seminars for residents at the local state hospital as well as with residents in the Washington University and later the St. Louis University medical schools. I continued to apply my psychoanalytic understanding not only to the practice of analysis, but also to the development of my interest in psychotherapy for a broader and more pathologically ill population. One of the benefits of teaching is that to be effective, the teacher must sufficiently understand his or her field so that communication of its essence can be carried out for students. This meant that I had to develop my abilities to synthesize and conceptualize and then present ideas in an understandable form to students who needed clear exposure.

As part of this interest I wrote my first book, *Psychotherapy: A Dynamic Approach,* in which I applied psychoanalytic and psychodynamic concepts to the spectrum of psychotherapy, including the conceptual differentiation between exploratory and supportive forms of treatment. A variety of mental health professionals (psychologists, social workers, psychiatrists, pastoral counselors, etc.) from the general community sought me out for psychotherapy supervision. I might otherwise have had little or no exposure to this form of thinking. I also supervised a number of psychiatric residents, some of whom chose to become psychoanalytic candidates; others elected not to undertake psychoanalytic training but nevertheless were influenced by psychodynamic concepts and principles. Through these efforts my personal needs for impact and expansion of my influence beyond the narrow confines of the psychoanalytic consulting room were satisfied, and directly and indirectly I was able to feel a sense of impact on the psychiatric and psychotherapeutic scene in the St. Louis area, thus fulfilling one of my personal motivational schemes in the application and use of my background and training.

As a further extension of my wish to expand psychoanalytic and psychodynamic thought into the general psychiatric and social community, I served on a number of committees organized by the mental health society as well as the local medical and psychiatric societies. In 1978 the governor of Missouri appointed me a member of the state Mental Health Commission. This commission was charged with the oversight, budgeting, and organization of the public mental health system in Missouri, and my psychoanalytic understanding allowed me a type of observational viewpoint from which to influence the programming and the priorities of the public mental health sector. This was possible even through psychodynamic psychotherapy was relatively rare in the state mental health system, given the limitations of the personnel who provided the service, the pressures on the delivery system, and the limitations inherent in those patients who make use of the public sector psychiatric facilities. At the same time, however, observation of some of the interactional processes and the use of psychodynamic principles in coping with and understanding some of the inevitable conflicts were important skills resulting from my psychoanalytic experience.

The enthusiastic overidealization and overoptimistic evaluation of analytic theory and therapy that held sway in the 1950s and '60s inevitably contributed to a sense of disappointment and some degree of disillusionment as experience led to a more realistic appraisal of the benefits and limitations of psychoanalytic thinking. Simultaneously, the developments of biological psychiatry and the increasing sophistication in psychopharmacology led to a general sense that these areas were the direction of the future, and interest within the medical and mental health communities in what psychoanalysis could offer declined. However, significant, though decreased, numbers of people with problems amenable to psychoanalytic treatment continued to seek psychoanalysis or psychoanalytic psychotherapy, but decreased insurance reimbursement and the rise of managed care programs made provision of such treatment increasingly more difficult and less well reimbursed. The unfortunate possibility that psychoanalysis in its pure form may become available only to a relatively few wealthy individuals or only for the education of mental health professionals and psychoanalytic candidates is discouraging. The need is to find ways by which psychoanalysis can be supported for a broader spectrum of potential patients capable of making use of this specific and highly selective technique. How this will evolve in the future remains an unanswered question.

Returning to a more personal perspective, our Institute implemented a retirement policy for training analysts who were not to begin a new training analysis beyond the age of 68, reflecting the problems of the aging training analyst, but also the uncertainties of how long an analysis will last and life expectancy issues. As more younger colleagues graduated from the Institute and entered psychoanalytic practice, the number of referrals to me for psychoanalysis decreased, and as I approached the mandatory training analyst retirement age, my caseload of psychoanalytic candidates and potential candidates declined. The reduction in full psychoanalytic cases has meant an expansion of patients being seen by me in psychodynamic or psychoanalytically oriented psychotherapy.

My role in the community has become increasingly that of an "elder statesman" in psychiatric and psychoanalytic matters. My sense of responsibility for maintaining an interest in psychodynamic theory and clinical technique, and for recognizing and promulgating the importance of psychoanalytic ideas, has led me to expand my teaching and supervisory roles.

There have been inevitable moments of self-doubt and questioning as to whether or not I had chosen a career that, like the dinosaur, might eventually become extinct. And yet at the present time there is an enthusiastic rethinking and elaboration of psychoanalytic theory from the relatively monolithic structure of earlier thought, which now involves an increased ferment of ideas and conceptual understandings, and research into the analytic process and of the nature of psychopathology.

Although the role of psychoanalysis in American psychiatry has decreased significantly in the 1980s and '90s, younger colleagues manifest an intense interest and appreciation when psychoanalytic and psychodynamic principles are expressed and supported. There is still a significant cadre of psychoanalysts who attend the various local and national meetings. The separation of psychoanalysis from medicine and the struggle to achieve nonmedical psychoanalytic training in the United States has enriched the field with younger enthusiastic colleagues. It has also led some to question whether the years of medical training were necessary or appropriate. From my own perspective I have always felt very pleased to have been a physician, even if not practicing traditional medicine; the years of patient care and the physician's sense of responsibility developed through medical training have always stood me in good stead. Additionally, being a physician has allowed me to make greater use of the new developments in psychopharmacology and to add that component to the armamentarium of my psychotherapeutic efforts. It has allowed me to work with a larger variety of patients without splitting the transference, as often occurs when someone other than the therapist prescribes medication.

In retrospect, I feel increasingly fortunate that I did not enter the type of psychoanalytic world where one focuses all of one's attention upon a relatively small number of analysands, and that throughout my career I maintained the sense of expansion and the importance of applying psychoanalytic and psychodynamic concepts to the general fields of mental health and psychotherapy. My psychoanalytic training was based on the ego-psychological structural model of conflict and compromise formation, including the importance of the patient's transference and the role of abstinence as part of the analyst's maintenance of the psychoanalytic situation. For me, abstinence is not to be mistaken for being cold, aloof, silent, indifferent, or rigid in posture. Instead, it is an analytic attitude that essentially requires that all patterns of interaction and forms of direct support and/or gratification that occur during the course of the analytic process be brought eventually into analytic scrutiny, exposure, and introspective analysis. The analytic situation inherently provides a number of other gratifications to the patient in terms of the analyst's attitude, tolerance, understanding, suspension of moral judgment, relative freedom from anxiety, and manifestations of interest in and dedication to the patient's ultimate well-being. Such things as reliability, respect, empathy, tact, and the helpfulness of the analyst's functions also provide a form of gratification.

However, abstinence involves maintaining the analytic focus and as such may mean analyzing a variety of behaviors, either in the patient or the analyst, that would otherwise be seen as transference–countertransference gratifications. The analyst's relative neutrality and maintenance of the frame limits in the psychoanalytic situation provide a situation of safety for the patient to express and explore the deeper, more threatening, and anxiety-provoking feelings, impulses, transferences, and memories without the risk of being responsible in a behavioral sense for such expression. It is only when the situation is "safe" from action or reaction by the analyst that the patient can feel free enough to express the deepest levels of psychic communication, and that the core of the personality can be reached. Direct gratification without analyzing even derivative transference interactions can make the situation seem threatening to the analysand. If the analyst responds in ways that fulfill the patient's transference wishes at a derivative level (i.e., a pat on the shoulder, extra time, small gifts, critical responses to the patient's provocations, verbal reassurances of caring, unrealistically low fee, direct expressions of positive or negative affect, etc.), this can create in the patient the concern for what the analyst's response might be to deeper, more primitive, or more primary expressed wishes, fantasies, or transference demands or provocations.

The process becomes a continuous interactional one in which the patient expresses or manifests particular positive or negative feelings, wishes, behavior, or fantasies and then observes the analyst's reactions. If these are helpful, or if they provide a situation and framework of safety, then the patient can permit him- or herself a somewhat deeper interactional expression, again followed by subsequent observation and testing of whether the analyst can comfortably tolerate the patient's expression of feelings, reactions, and wishes without undue response or behavioral change.

In that sense a spiraling process takes place in which more primitive and more affectively intense experiences can occur to which the analyst responds in ways that are different from the ways of other people in the patient's life. In that sense the patient's transference reactions represent a reenactment and repetition of earlier wishes, fears, defenses, and adaptations, whereas the analyst's response to these (be it neutrality, silence, understanding, interpretation, acceptance, reflection, containment, comfort, and freedom from anxiety) represents for the patient new and unexpected forms of behavior. This creates dissonance between the patient's transference expectation as compared with the analyst's manifest and observable behavior, leading the patient to experience the analyst as a new and different object from what had been anticipated in the transference expectation. In that sense a continuous and continuing series of "corrective emotional experiences" occur as a result of the analyst's maintaining a state of analytic neutrality, observation, and activity without manipulating the therapeutic framework or situation.

This results in the patient's ultimately recognizing that the transference relationship is emanating primarily from within him- or herself and is based on reenactments of earlier patterns of integration, adaptation, and relationship. The patient's transference response is frequently triggered by observation of some component action or intervention by the analyst that the patient understands or interprets in keeping with his or her prior expectations or affective state. But if the analyst moves out of the neutral, abstinent position and responds behaviorally on the basis of countertransference in a way complementary to the transference reactions of the patient, the analyst may reinforce the prior expectations or fears that the patient had anticipated in the transference reenactment. As such, this would tend to confirm the patient's neurotic expectations and to reinforce former pathological methods of coping.

One of my guiding aphorisms is that "the patient is always right." This means that the patient's productions and sequence of associations or responses or resistances or expressed wishes are always valid in the sense that they reflect the patient's current psychological makeup, organization, and intrapsychic experience. However, patients may not be "right" in terms of their own conscious awareness of the situation or of their motivational state. It is the task of the analyst, in empathic interaction with the patient followed by conscious and secondary-process reflection, to figure out what must be the combination of factors within the patient that would make the experience, association, or affective response appropriate and adaptive for this person at this time. This does not mean that the analyst uncritically accepts the patient's version of some experience, recollection, or transference phenomenon. It does mean, however, that the analyst seeks to appreciate that the behavior or association in question is "valid" from the patient's perspective and that the analyst's role is to help the patient ultimately recognize how the response can be understood as a reflection of what is transpiring internally. This includes the deeply unconscious affects and core fantasies that involve the basic roots of the patient's motivational and compromise formations.

As I understand the analytic process, it involves an intrapsychic elaboration of experience occurring within the mind of the analysand, some of which is reflected and expressed in the form of verbal or nonverbal communication to the analyst, but some of which may be retained privately by the patient. There are always significant components of the patient's psychic experience that are never or only later manifestly expressed in the analytic session. Similarly, intrapsychic processes occuring within the mind of the analyst reflect associations, affective responses, memories, theoretical constructs, technical precepts, and other psychic events related to and stimulated by the patient's productions and manifest behavior. Only a small portion of these psychic events is externally expressed or accessible to the patient through the analyst's verbal and nonverbal behavior.

Each of the participants is acutely sensitive and responsive to the observable input from the other; thus there is an intrapsychic process within the mind of the patient and an intrapsychic process within the mind of the analyst as well as an interpersonal relationship and interaction occurring between them. However, there is a significant "tilt" in the analytic setting in which, by and large, the patient's affects, memories, transference interactions, wishes, fantasies, and defenses are expressed and elaborated in a significantly more intense and sustained form than are the parallel phenomena within the analyst. In my experience, transference components are far more sustained, intense, consciously expressed, and experienced in derivative ways than are countertransference responses occurring within the analyst.

In successful cases the patient will experience major and significantly progressive and continuing psychological change as a result of analysis, and the analyst may from time to time achieve new insights or further working-through regarding his or her psychic experience or organization and may further develop professional skills. But I do not see the analyst as being altered in major ways by virtue of the analytic process with a particular patient. For the analyst to be as intensely altered and reorganized by virtue of the analytic experience with each analysand would involve oscillations within the analyst in response to the various individual patients with whom he or she is working, which would become chaotic and untenable. I agree with those who believe that countertransference is a ubiquitous experience and that such responses can be used diagnostically and therapeutically in terms of the analyst's perception and understanding of the patient's transferences. However, the idea that the analyst is as deeply, affectively involved in a regressive reorganization of personality as the patient is is not in keeping with observations of the experience.

For the patient the analytic procedure should be primarily a therapeutic one, and I make no apology for my consistently therapeutic ambition for the patient and my role in the analysand's development. On the other hand, I keep it clear to myself and to the analysand that although I am hopeful the patient will improve, it is not my responsibility to guarantee the success of the process and that my sense of self-esteem is not determined by the outcome of the specific patient's analysis.

I am also convinced that there is no such thing as a perfect or absolutely complete analysis. There will always be residual elements that have been either ignored or incompletely exposed and analyzed, and the complete elimination of all neurotic tendencies and conflicts is impossible. I therefore do not believe that, purely by virtue of their length, excessively long analyses are better than relatively briefer ones. The issue for evaluation is the degree to which the patient experiences a significant psychoanalytic process and achieves awareness and authenticity concerning his or her intrapsychic core processes, rather than the attempted elimination of all evidence of neurotic behavior. Nor am I surprised or disappointed if former analysands reestablish contact with me at some future time in confronting some upheaval or new distress in their psychic and emotional lives. In such circumstances I find it possible almost immediately to reestablish a deep and intense therapeutic process and relationship, with the option to make significant and direct analytic interpretations, even if a subsequent continuing therapeutic process is not undertaken.

Clinical progress during the course of psychoanalysis is usually not a linear kind of change over time, and frequently there will be long stretches where there seems to be little or no progress. Such long stretches of analytic work must be undertaken and successfully accomplished in order to prepare the groundwork for change, which is then likely to occur in a more rapidly ascending geometric fashion once the crucial preparations have been made.

Much of the early work of an analysis involves the development and strengthening of a psychoanalytic situation and therapeutic alliance in which the patient feels free, increasingly at deeper and more conflicted levels, to expose and express to the analyst experiences, memories, relationships, fantasies, and multiple regressive transference phenomena as they occur. Some of the elements in this preparatory phase include

The patient's increasing capacity to tolerate anxiety without immediate recourse to previously established defensive processes

The capacity to tolerate previously unacceptable or unspeakable impulses, wishes, and fantasies without undue shame, guilt, or fear of rejection by the analyst

The capacity deliberately to set aside reality and to participate in the "as if" quality of transference experience by allowing the affective and fantasied interchanges to be manifestly experienced and expressed without having to assume responsibility in a behavioral sense for the interaction

The capacity to scan one's own inner psychic life and achieve an enhanced degree of recognition of previously inaccessible components

The capacity to experience and tolerate increasingly strong

and at times primitive affective states without immediate resort to defensive avoidance

The capacity to continue introspective and associative processes even in the face of one's own reluctance and resistance and to maintain the analytic procedure in the face of anxiety or other concerns

The ability to tolerate the inevitable transference disappointments and anxieties without withdrawing from the analytic process and relationship

By the time many of these changes have occurred, the analysis is often in the middle phase, and the capacity for synthesis and integration of conscious and unconscious components of current psychic life and experience, as well as the capacity for integration between past and present psychological functioning, has been well established. These achievements permit more definitive and deeper (as well as synthetic) layers and levels of interpretive activity for both the patient and the analyst. As a result, new forms of behavior and understanding are attempted and evaluated.

The neurotic processes continue well into the termination phase of the analysis, however, and it is in the termination phase that the major definitive structural changes take place within the patient's personality. The patient slowly becomes aware of the importance of voluntary renunciation of transference hopes, wishes, and demands upon the analyst and recognizes that the maintenance of these regressive transference repetitions interferes with the fulfillments and satisfactions now possible in the patient's present life, relationships, and contextual experience. The patient now seeks, at least partially, to resolve the intensity of the transference connections. At times during the termination phase, however, some of the most intense experiences of transference hope and expectation occur as well as affective and other responses to their disappointment and frustration. It is as if the patient is giving one last try to achieve the fulfillment that has been sought, and been the source of conflict, since early childhood. With termination as a prospect, there is no longer a need to hold back lest expression of the deepest and most powerful feelings and wishes alienate the analyst since the end is near anyhow.

To the degree that the analytic situation can be maintained in the face of such transference demands and disappointments, and to the degree that the patient voluntarily recognizes (as opposed to pressures from the analyst) the advantages of renunciation of infantile or childhood desires, goals, and relationships, a process of grief and mourning is initiated in anticipation of the loss of the analytic relationship. Inasmuch as the transference repeats and reenacts some of the now age-inappropriate hopes, expectations, and fears of childhood, the degree of resolution of the transference at a voluntary level and the degree of pleasure in the patient's new and expanded capacity for participation and affective investment in current life relationships and situations is enhanced. At least in part, age-inappropriate infantile and early childhood hopes, demands, and relationships (as they once existed in different versions with the original objects) are renounced along with those being reenacted and reexperienced in the analytic transference resolution. Previously during the analysis, separations and temporary losses of the relationship have been dictated mainly by the analyst leaving the patient for vacations, cancelled sessions, meetings, and so on. It has been the patient who has felt left or abandoned. During termination this dynamic is reversed, and it is the patient (by virtue of maturation and relief of difficulties) who leaves the analyst, analogous to the child leaving home.

This does not mean that all traces of infantile and childhood wishes, yearnings, and adaptations are given up, nor does it mean that the resolution of the transference is complete. However, to the degree that the mourning process, which was initiated and maintained as part of the termination phase, is relatively successful, the analysand can free him- or herself of the preexisting and previously intensely cathected childhood and age-inappropriate conflict inducing early traumata, wishes, fantasies, and resulting limitations.

At the time of the final therapeutic session, the transference will not have been fully resolved or mourned, and a significant and continuing mourning process must take place after the last session. As the patient further renounces the continuing cathexis of the analysis and the analyst, both become a once significant but no longer affectively or motivationally predominant memory system of an object relationship that was once of intense emotional importance. This process is never completely achieved, and follow-up studies of successful analyses have shown that transference reactions can be reactivated rapidly in various situations. Usually these newly reactivated transference relationships can be rapidly resolved.

Some of the manifestations of a relatively significant structural modification within the mind of the patient are evaluated by using the patient as his or her own control. This involves comparing the patient's individual as well as overall levels of function at the beginning of analysis with similar observations at the end of the process. Ideally, the comparison might include evaluation at a significantly later period, in order to assess the permanence of the changes. Another type of evaluation involves comparing the patient's degree of change with a composite model assembled out of experience with analytic results in multiple similar cases.

Some of the changes from a successful analytic process are the following:

- Significant (but not necessarily complete) improvement in presenting symptoms and characterological problems
- An increased sense of authenticity and self-cohesion
- The capacity for uninhibited pleasurable fulfillment of physical and emotional needs
- Access to genuine and proportional affective experience, both positive and negative, in response to appropriate stimuli
- Enhanced capacity for interaction and significant meaningful relationships with people outside the analysis
- Enhanced capacity for an empathic awareness, not only of one's self, but also of others in their various emotional and psychological situations
- The capacity to tolerate and to accept the ongoing existence

of previously unacceptable or guilt-inducing wishes and fantasies without undue guilt or anxiety

The capacity to comfortably separate thought, fantasy, and feeling on one hand from action on the other, with the capacity to delay action in favor of reality-appropriate containment

The capacity for pleasure in achievements and fulfillment of one's own potential relatively independent of external reward or recognition

The capacity to experience negative and unpleasurable affect states or desires with the capacity for appropriate action, if realistically warranted, or containment if not possible, from a reality-based perspective

The capacity to achieve an appropriate and fulfilling balance between sacrifice or delay in one's own need fulfillment or gratification in favor of loyalty and willingness to promote gratification and need fulfillment for others when appropriate

The capacity to use and fulfill one's own talents and potentials with pleasurable effectiveness and ability for self expression

The capacity to use analytic self-observation in confronting situations of conflict

As mentioned above, many of these structural changes occur definitively during the termination phase of the analytic process, and not infrequently they are enhanced following the termination of the analysis proper. Follow-up with patients frequently reveals significant further change after the final therapeutic session, and as such indicates the extent of the capacity for the former analysand now to continue the process of self-observation and internal modification initiated by the analysis. In successful cases the analyst feels a sense of pleasure and pride in observing the analysand's growth, maturation, and improved capacity to function and to enjoy life. Neither the analyst nor the patient could bring about such changes without the work and sustained participation of the other. For the analyst the success of the process makes worthwhile all the disciplined self-containment and dedication that the analysis requires.

But many times analysis can achieve only limited structural change or minimal overall benefit, and the process may leave a sense of disappointment in one or both of the participants. Analysis is not a panacea for all people, and the hope that it would be was one of the factors in the backlash against psychoanalysis described earlier.

One of the lessons learned through medical training is the painful realization that in spite of our best and sustained efforts, we frequently fail to cure the patient, and partial or minimal amelioration of distress may be all that can be done. In those situations the caregiver must take comfort in the knowledge that they have done their best to serve the needs of the patient, given the tools at hand.

Psychoanalytic theory and technique continue to evolve, and even today we are able to help patients deemed unanalyzable a generation ago. The hope is that future developments will allow the analyst to work even more effectively and successfully with patients in full psychoanalysis as well as in its applications to psychotherapy.

5

An Analyst at Work

Steven J. Ellman

When I began analytic training the analytic world in the United States was dominated by the classical position. This was in 1972 and psychoanalysis was seemingly defined by the teachings that were present at the New York Psychoanalytic Institute (the institute I was beginning to attend). I previously wrote that I agree with Lipton (1977, 1979) that the classical position is only one possible Freudian position and from my perspective not the closest to the main body of Freud's papers on theory or technique (Ellman 1991, 1995). I remember Winnicott speaking at the New York Psychoanalytic Society in 1968. The audience was so hostile to his talk that he ended by saying that he could see why the Americans were mired in Vietnam. He was obviously upset (there are some revisionist versions of the event) and it was clear that most of the audience who spoke thought that his offerings were not psychoanalytic. This of course was a fatal criticism: not only was Winnicott wrong in his assertions but he was beneath contempt (or at least serious consideration) because his assertions were not psychoanalytic. When Kohut came to New York in 1971 his reception was somewhat different; there was a serious discussion of his paper (on narcissistic rage). This may have been because Eissler was the discussant and it is rare that he was discourteous to anyone, much less a guest or an invited speaker. I remember these two events as marking the beginning of my interest in both Kohut and Winnicott. At about that time I also became interested in other writers as well including Klein, Balint, and Guntrip. It was my intention to integrate these writers with the Freudian opus. I naively saw no difficulty in attempting to accomplish this task.

I realize this group seems like a disparate one, but these were the authors I was intellectually involved with and these were the authors I began to teach in the clinical psychology doctoral program at the City University of New York. It all seemed quite exotic at the time for my training in New York University's clinical psychology doctoral program provided a great deal of intellectual stimulation but most of it was around issues that were framed by analysts who resided in the United States. The center I worked at during graduate school was directed by George Klein and Robert Holt and a number of analysts visited and worked at the center. Fortunately for me, George Klein persuaded me to attend a seminar that David Rapaport gave when he was in New York for a year. During the time I was a graduate student Donald Spence, Leo Goldberger, Hartvig Dahl, Morris Eagle, and Merton Gill were at the research center that Klein and Holt directed. These two wonderful directors developed an intellectual climate that has stayed with me ever since, and one that I hope I pass along to some of the graduate students and analytic candidates who study with me. I feel this way despite the fact that I agree with very few of the assertions that George Klein began to put forth before his untimely death. I believe Klein compounded the confusions in our field when he contrasted metapsychology and clinical theory. This chapter, however, does not deal with this issue but rather addresses how I understand psychoanalytic process.

I should first complete my brief autobiographical statement about the beginnings of my career in clinical psychology and psychoanalysis. After my training at NYU, I interned and did a post-doctoral year at Montefiore Hospital in the Bronx. At that time Morton Reiser was the chief of psychiatry. He had assembled a remarkable group of clinicians and researchers. Edith Jacobson and Leo Spiegel as well as William Grossman were teaching seminars during this period. Most significantly for me, Sheldon Bach was one of my supervisors and supervised me on several different cases. It was through Bach that I began to think about issues I will describe as essential to developing a psychoanalytic process. The questions raised for me during this period involved what I have come to call issues of analytic trust. The patients I was beginning to see found some of the essential aspects of analysis injurious to their fragile sense of well-being.

One woman who was diagnosed with a schizo-affective disorder had already been hospitalized at Montefiore twice in the last year and a half. She had been hospitalized seven times in all. When I began to see her she was 37, had two young children, and a husband who was willing to see her hospitalized on a more permanent basis in one of the state hospitals. In addition, she was alcoholic, and before I had a chance to talk to her in detail she became catatonic and oscillated between mute and agitated catatonic states. This was not surprising to the administrators on the ward because they had viewed this hospitalization as the final staging for her admission to a state hospital, but I saw the situation somewhat differently.

I interviewed her once on a Friday and told her I would see her over the weekend to check on how she was feeling after moving into the hospital. However, on Saturday I was not able to stop by the ward because I was required to do testing on another unit. After that I wanted to go home and reasoned that she was too confused to miss me—I would see her on Monday. Her roommate told me that after inquiring several times on Saturday where I was she became extremely agitated. I became convinced that my disappointing her was the final push on her road to complete collapse. When I guiltily admitted this to my supervisor, he assured me that her collapse was a foregone conclusion and that my missing the session, while hardly a commendable action (I did call to cancel), had nothing to do with the patient's present state. I was overestimating my importance after only one meeting with the patient. I saw this patient over the next twenty years and realized, of course, that the supervisor was both right and wrong. Certainly my one action did not cause the patient's state and no matter what I did she was going to be in a good deal of difficulty for a considerable period of time. However, she was also available to begin a search for someone she could begin to trust, someone who might be a different type of object than had been present for most of her life. I repeated a reality that she had known and was quite familiar with: an indifferent response to her severe desperation. Her retreat continued and I became a familiar object in her confused, delirious state.

How does this example of a woman diagnosed as schizophrenic relate to a psychoanalytic process? It is my view that the first task in analysis (or therapy) is to help the patient begin to create a new reality in the therapeutic situation. This new reality is one in which the patient is understood in a different way than in the past. A necessary condition for this understanding is that the patient must penetrate the analyst's psychological world and the analyst must allow this penetration to be perceptible to the patient. This process has often been described most clearly in treatments with patients not thought of as analytic patients. Winnicott has often stated that the patients he is talking about are not available for classical treatment. I would say that they were not available for interpretative interventions until some conditions had been met in their analytic experience. For many patients their narcissistic vulnerabilities are the main reality they focus on in the beginning of a treatment. How one handles these vulnerabilities often sets the tone of the entire treatment.

The remainder of this chapter employs a theoretical vantage

point I have gradually developed over the years I have been practicing psychoanalysis and psychotherapy. I will briefly attempt to give a condensed view of this position. At the end of the chapter I will try to restate the position more fully.

It is my contention that an analytic treatment can be seen as containing at least several cycles. Each cycle embodies a dominant transference–countertransference theme that when adequately understood and worked through begins the advent of the next cycle. The transition between cycles is where disruptions in the analytic process frequently occur. This is particularly the case with patients who utilize defenses such as splitting or projective identification and who early in the treatment may well see the analyst as quite different in reality as well as in the transference. During the beginning phase of the treatment analytic trust has to be established before there is a space for interpretation to serve a therapeutic function. At the start of each new transference cycle analytic trust to some extent has to be reestablished. Frequently the analyst is bewildered by this since she or he has felt that the treatment has already achieved a type of working rhythm only to have it disrupted by issues that seemingly had been dispensed with earlier in the analysis. Thus I see aspects of analytic trust running through a treatment even to the termination phase of an analysis. In this phase the analysand begins to fully trust the results of the treatment and the analyst begins to trust the analysand to more fully take control of the analytic process. After reaching the termination I will begin to describe the beginning phase of an analysis.

SOME DIFFERENT BEGINNINGS

This topic is one that has received relatively little attention in analytic literature in today's widening scope of psychoanalysis, and yet to my mind it is the crucial phase of therapy. That there is a widening scope today is partly due to the fact that analysts begin treatment in a manner that is different from the one that Freud and classical analysts advocated. Freud's concern involved the patient's ability to comprehend, and associate to, the analyst's interpretative efforts. The patient should

> show compliance enough, to respect the necessary conditions of the analysis, we regularly succeed in giving all the symptoms of the illness a new transference meaning and in replacing his ordinary neurosis by a transference neurosis of which he can be cured by the therapeutic work. [Freud 1914, cited in Ellman 1991, p. 61]

For a patient who criticizes and provokes authority figures, or is not able to talk about certain difficulties, there is an implicit message that Freud sends: either you are able to comply (free-associate) or you have to leave the analysis. Obviously, some patients will be able to comply with this demand for analytic material, but it may be that this type of compliance will lead to a pseudoanalysis at best. Then there are patients who are simply unable to comply with or tolerate the analyst's early interpretative efforts. Are these patients unanalyzable, or are there alternative ways of conceiving the beginning phase of analysis that would allow this type of patient the benefit of an analytic treatment? In what follows I have considered Freud's view of the beginning of the treatment in contrast to my views and those of the authors I am citing. There are analysts who have advocated starting patients in psychotherapy and gradually moving them into analysis. Although these analysts come closer to the views I am considering, I do not refer to them because it would detract from the lines of the discussion.

In Freud and Brenner's (Brenner 1976, 1982) vision of therapeutic change, there is a distinct cleavage between patient and analyst that is closed by the analyst's interpretations. The patient receives new insight through interpretations, which releases the analysand from past conflicts and allows him or her to try activities or access thoughts previously inaccessible. To say this in another way, it is the analyst who puts the patient in touch with an aspect of his or her inner world that was previously unavailable. In Brenner's conceptualization, when the analyst is included in the patient's psychological world, it is as a transference figure. Interpretation aids the patient in understanding that the analyst is "really" outside the analysand's world. In this optimal treatment situation, there is an alliance between analyst and analysand that is mediated by Freud's unobjectionable transference (I think this idea is similar to Greenson's [1965] notion of the therapeutic alliance). The analyst is viewed as a helpful external figure who provides insight into problems that have been previously painful and inexplicable. The insight the analyst provides is the therapeutic agent of change. The analysand transferring onto the analyst should be able to take enough distance to note that his or her reactions are occurring because of some as yet unknown internal, unconscious conflict, not because of something the analyst has done to him. This self-observing capacity is therefore deemed necessary to perform a successful analysis.

Bach (1985) writes that in order to have the conditions that Freud describes, there

> must [be] a working alliance between the two parties and, even more fundamentally, one must have two parties who experience themselves as separately alive and functional. . . . Generally, in the transference regression with the narcissistic disorders, one or both of these conditions is not fully met. [p. xii]

To illustrate Bach's point: a woman I was seeing in treatment would begin a low moaning sound whenever she felt I was beginning an interpretative remark. The moaning increased to a shriek if it turned out she was right and I was oblivious enough to have been making an interpretation.

Sometimes the issues at the beginning of treatment seem simple, almost trivial, but are nevertheless crucial to the patient. When I first began in private practice, a referring analyst told me my new patient had made the rounds and had not been able to "connect" with anyone. After listening to the patient for about thirty minutes, I began to wonder why she had had such difficulty in finding an analyst. I thought I must be missing some important element of her difficulties. Shortly after these thoughts she announced that she would start treatment only if she could address me by my first name. Although taken aback by her request, I was surprised that I was annoyed by her. I stated (with some felt difficulty) that this decision was up to her because in analysis there were no restrictions. She then recounted several encounters with analysts about her concern. One said that he would consider the idea for several weeks, and if he thought it was a good idea he would accede to her wish. I wondered about this response for surely if a patient in treatment starts calling the analyst by his or her first name, how can one stop this behavior? Practically speaking, the patient did not have to ask for permission; she could have just begun to do it and the analyst could then respond as he or she saw fit. In my mind this analyst (as well as others who told her that it was a matter for further "analysis") sensed the extent to which she wanted to create her own environment in analysis and this need of hers created anxiety in them. I suspect that they (and I) were worried she might not let us be analysts but would usurp our function or identity as analysts.

It is not difficult to understand how analysts might be threatened by a patient's demands. Similarly, it is easy to understand that Freud would consider patients who were unable to tolerate interpretative efforts as unanalyzable. If interpretations are the active ingredients in therapeutic change, how is it possible to accomplish change with a patient who shrieks during the interpretation? Given Freud's assumptions (Ellman 1991), the idea of a trial analysis is not only a reasonable practice, it is a humane practice. He is telling a patient quickly and in a straightforward manner whether his procedure can be of benefit. In one of his last papers Freud (1937) suggested that analysts see patients whom they had previously deemed unanalyzable. A number of analysts were doing exactly what Freud had suggested, and many have continued to expand our ideas of analyzability. Certainly Bach and

Kohut tell us that narcissistic patients frequently feel humiliated and shamed by early interpretations. Kohut (1971) indicates that for many people interpretations increase their sense of fragility, and that their experience is one of being intruded upon and assaulted.

Bach has taken this type of observation and painted a compelling picture of the person's subjective world in and out of analysis. In his view narcissistic states are built as an *antiworld,* a way of keeping outside events from impinging on a person's subjective world as well as creating a more satisfying internal world. The term *narcissistic states* can be applied to a wide variety of patients across a wide variety of diagnostic considerations. These antiworlds are constructed for protection and to give the person some stable, continuous sense of self and, hopefully, sense of worth. The experience of being inconsequential and ineffective in the real (consensual or external) world is an overpowering one for people who are compelled to build these internal fortresses. This can happen despite the fact that the person is successful in various aspects of his or her life. The feeling of success is experienced like a nonnutritive filler: tasting good for a moment, but having no lasting experience of satisfaction. It may not be experienced as success in any conventional way, but may be felt as one way of keeping the external (what Bach calls the objective) world outside the person's felt boundaries. Adopting Kohut's concept of selfobject, one can say that narcissistic states do not permit fully developed others from existing in the person's world. Rather, others are either incorporated into the person's world as part of these states (and part of the self) or expelled as alien objects. Narcissistic states are not either/or situations, but continuous functions. They are states that are at times rapidly entered and left. A person may feel narcissistically vulnerable one moment and have little affective memory for this experience at another time. A hypochondriacal patient suffering from insomnia experienced the world as a continuing horror and nightmare that no other person could possibly understand. Her quest to find someone who could understand the torment that continuous fatigue brings had been exasperatingly unsuccessful. This insomnia made the world an alien place in which she was forced to exist. Her *diseased brain* could not shut down and did not allow her to sleep but rather kept her in a fatigued, twilight state in which she felt continuously depersonalized and derealized. Her disbelief that analysis could be of any help to her was matched only by her disillusionment with all medical forms of treatment. Before treatment could begin she had to fill me and the treatment room with the horror of her life.

This woman would not tolerate interpretations of why she felt this way. She needed to completely saturate the treatment room with her pain and suffering. She needed someone to both listen to her and contain her despair. She knew that all active attempts to help her would be futile. It was important for someone to hear all this before she could in any way acknowledge the possibility of her being truly alive, certainly before she could acknowledge the importance she placed in having another separate person in the room with her. It was her view that she was a "walking bag of protoplasm."

In a more extreme example a wealthy, bright businessman had constructed a world that had at its heart his unendurable odor. He was permitted to endure in the objective world only if he performed perfectly in a wide range of tasks, which he believed anyone could perform but they were left to him. Everyone else was laughing at him, even his wife and children. Through their kindness they tolerated him more easily than others (including his partner) could; he felt despised by all around him. Suicide was a constant preoccupation. His fantasies were the obverse of those in Suskind's (1986) novel *Perfume*: his odors were to be eliminated but he wasn't able to do this, and his world was one of putrefying smells that lingered throughout his day and night, wherever he went. The smells remained in his fantasies, in his dreams, and in his interactions with the external world. To tolerate his delusions was the first step in a long therapeutic road working toward his wish to cleanse his psyche.

These brief illustrations are meant to give a sense of what Bach calls other worlds. If the analysis of narcissistic, borderline, or nonclassical patients is to be a real analysis, these other worlds must be brought into the treatment. This may at first glance seem like an odd statement, for if these other worlds are important, what else would a person who enters these states talk about in analysis? Interestingly, they talk about many other things, particularly in an analysis that is pleasant yet implicitly demands compliance. The person might talk about the external world in a manner intended to please the analyst. The businessman might, in an obsessional vein, talk about his life and business, never giving a hint of his inner reality. It may often be too difficult for the patient to bring this stultifying, but nevertheless precious and vulnerable, other world into the "scrutiny" of the analytic situation. It may be that the start of a true analysis takes a long time; that is, it can be a long time before a person can share, or include, the analyst in his or her other worlds.

A patient who was quiet and introverted after four years of treatment began to have dreams about extraterrestrial beings living on earth. These dreams described in detail how difficult it was for these beings to communicate with earthlings. It took a surprising number of these dreams for me to realize that they were about our treatment. I suspect my obtuse stance was a result of his not being able to tolerate me as another being in the room. As important, the patient started to tell me about a fantasy of his being the recorder. I finally found out that the recorder idea was based on a science fiction story that described another planet sending down human-looking organisms to record the activities of the earthlings' society. As a precocious child, this patient saw himself as one of these beings and in this vision found an identity that provided him with a raison d'être for his life. It was one of the few things that made sense to him in his tumultuous childhood. This fantasy was a central component of his sense of self, even as an adult. It took him four years to begin to share these ideas with me and to include me in a complicated world that I had known little about up to that point in treatment.

The patient in this example had difficulty in maintaining a continuous (transference) relationship with me. Some aspects of his conflicts would emerge and would then be submerged when his anxiety about our intimacy disrupted his sense of equilibrium. Unquestionably, homosexual themes were extremely troublesome for him, but the question of intimacy and trust were central to his reluctance to let anyone view his secret, labyrinthine world. It took four years for him to feel he could utilize me as a character in his world. The issue of object utilization is an important theoretical concept in Winnicott's writings. It took a longer time for the patient to allow me to have a separate existence. This occurred while he concomitantly acknowledged and became a part of the consensual world.

Although it took this person four years to allow another into his world, sometimes this fails to happen at all in analytic situations. Bach talks about a woman who attempted suicide a week or two after finishing what her analyst felt was a successful analysis. Bach, her subsequent analyst, found that crucial issues in her life had not come up at all in her previous analysis. She reported that she had never discussed these things with her analyst, because for some reason she never seemed to think about these topics in her previous treatment. We can interpret this to mean that there seemed to be no place in her first analysis for certain types of subjects, even though many of these subjects involved conscious, recurrent fantasies.

ANALYTIC TRUST—A REAL THERAPEUTIC ALLIANCE

How can the treatment situation allow the patient to feel there can be room to bring up these vital but secret and potentially threatening topics? To ask a related question, what are the conditions that have to be met with unclassical patients that will allow them to enter treatment and eventually utilize interpretative efforts? Winnicott (1958) talks about the formation of a false self in which the real world can be experienced in a depersonalized state. It is Winnicott's view that, to some extent, the development of a false self is a normal phenomenon. The false self is designed as a protective shield for the person's inner world, where they can experience, or have the potential to experience, spontaneous, creative impulses (true self). In other terms, it allows these patients to feel they can create a world of their own. Viewing the false self as a metaphor or as a phenomenological statement depends on your reading of Winnicott. My reading is that while at times Winnicott is talking about actual experiences, which he labels *false self experiences,* to make sense of the range of his discussions about the false self, one has to consider this term a theoretical concept. The extent to which the person must protect his or her true self is correlated with the extent to which the world is experienced in a depersonalized and derealized manner. Winnicott conceives of the true self as the focus of the person's spontaneity and sense of creativity in the world. Bach's notions of antiworlds give us a more elaborated version of the extent to which patients must cover their true self, and how they create these worlds to allow some sense of spontaneity in their psychological life. In a variant on Winnicott's terms, we can say that until patients can spontaneously feel they can create their own world in the analytic situation, they will be unable to let aspects of their true feelings or self emerge in the analytic process. They will not be able to create the type of illusion necessary for an interpretable transference relationship. We can conceive of the antiworlds Bach has described as compromise formations in which limited aspects of the true self are expressed while simultaneously providing a defense against the external (consensual) world.

How can the analyst be included in these antiworlds? In less dramatic terms, how does the analyst form a bond with the narcissistically vulnerable patient, such that the analyst is seen as a helpful or facilitating person as opposed to a threat to the patient's sense of self? These are the main questions I have been considering, but a question that is conceptually relevant here is the distinction between the concept of analytic trust and the therapeutic or working alliance (Greenson 1967, Stone 1961, 1967). In my understanding the therapeutic alliance is the modern form of Freud's ideas about the unobjectionable transference. Brenner

(1982) and Stein (1981) have argued against both concepts. While I find Brenner's arguments concerning the difficulties with the concept of the working alliance convincing, I nevertheless think that authors who use these terms are attempting to describe something that has not been adequately articulated in psychoanalysis. Freud implicitly asked how the patient begins to trust the analyst, and answered this question by invoking the concept of the unobjectionable transference. His answer was that we must rely on the patient's trust and respect for authority: his or her conscious, mildly sexualized attraction to the power and knowledge of the physician. Freud assumed that most people would naturally be attracted to and have respect for a person in the position of a therapist or doctor. Stated in this form, it is easy to see why Stein and Brenner argue that the unobjectionable transference should be analyzed as a form of transference. The person should understand their respect for authority as they should understand any other form of transference. Brenner comes to the same conclusion about experiences in treatment that analysts such as Stone (1967), Zetzel (1965, 1966), and Greenson (1967) label as examples of the therapeutic alliance. From Brenner's perspective it is a question of the state of the transference as to whether the patient is willing to "work" as the analyst prescribes in his or her instructions to the patient. Brenner is thus convincing: the clinical examples presented by these analysts are best explained by invoking the concept of transference.

The question I am raising (or raising again, since I have already stated that Freud initially asks this question), is how does the patient come to develop trust in the analyst and in the treatment? Is this simply a matter of the patient's respect for authority (or a form of suggestion), which, I have agreed, is most adequately seen as a form of transference? Or are there some elements of trust that are based on the reality of the analytic situation? To repeat a statement made earlier, I think that in analysis the patient is listened to and understood in a way that is new to their experience. The analyst's consistent empathic attitude is an unexplored and unique element for the patient. It is present in reality, and it is not simply a manifestation of transference. If the analyst can provide a consistent, empathic, facilitating environment, the analysand can begin to realistically trust that analysis will be an environment that is not threatening to the survival of his or her sense of self. To be sure, this trust can be mixed with transference tendencies, but is there an element of trust that is not explained by the concept of transference?

To return to the beginning of therapy, we can say most patients start treatment because of the pain they are suffering. The rational reasons for continuing the treatment depend on the trust that is developed as a result of one's experience in analysis. The mirroring that Kohut describes, the sensitivity to the suppressed and unexpressed that Bach details, and the facilitating environment that Winnicott portrays are all ways of developing what I would call realistic, analytic trust. Some patients enter treatment with a respect for the analyst or analysis (Freud's unobjectionable transference) or simply with a respect for authority. This transference, as I have stated, should be analyzed; however, the feeling of being reliably understood is an achievable concomitant of an analysis. This experience paves the way for the person's willingness to entertain an interpretation. Analytic trust is nothing more than patients' experiencing the analyst as being consistently understanding of their world in a way that promises to (and hopefully eventually does) help them to comprehend and gain control of their lives. The crucial element to establishing trust initially is the analyst's consistent provision of a framework of empathy. This involves the consistent ability to reflect and to synthesize the person's experiences (this is particularly the case early in the treatment). If the patient's reaction to the analyst is merely transference, then the analyst has not provided in reality what is necessary in the beginning phase of analytic treatment. What I mean here is that some patients may trust their analyst despite the fact that adequate conditions for the analysis have not been established. Thus they find that they cannot talk about certain crucial experiences but nevertheless trust their analyst. From my point of view this is an example of transference rather than analytic trust. From Freud's point of view it may be an instance of the unobjectionable transference, but, from my perspective, this transference may be quite objectionable. I should add that substantial analytic trust is not easily achieved and is not fully achieved, in my view, until the end of the treatment. This again is an interesting topic that I cannot fully explore here.

The analyst must also maintain an atmosphere that is conducive to the expression of difficult and indeed destructive material. To use Bion's (1962) term, it is important that the analyst be a willing container for the patient's feelings. At times this is extremely difficult with patients who seem to fill the room with their anger, accusations, and sense of betrayal. However, the atmosphere of freedom to express negative as well as positive affect is quite important. The analyst should neither suppress nor return these negative states to the patient. Vulnerable patients often experience interpretations about their negativity as retaliation by the analyst. This is one way that negative feelings may be experienced as being returned to the patient. There are a variety of implicit ways to return feelings to the patient; at times, of course, the analyst may simply get annoyed and return the feelings more directly. This freedom to express anger, aggression, and doubts about the analyst as well as about themselves is an important facet of analytic trust. In my view it is this aspect of analytic treatment that Freud found most difficult to tolerate. It seems to me that the handling of the negative affect and negative transference is the most difficult part of analytic treatment. I agree with Bird (1972) when he says that it is the negative (or *destructive* to use his term) transference that is most frequently not dealt with in psychoanalytic treatments. I also agree with recent commentators that "borderline" patients are frequently inflamed unnecessarily by analysts who attempt to enforce analytic rules early in the treatment. A rule may be simply the tendency to provide interpretations when the patient is neither ready for nor wants to hear the analyst's interpretations. This is frequently accentuated in the early parts of treatment with the unclassical patient. I must repeat here that if the analyst is not able to provide an environment that contains the patient's affective world, then the trust that the patient experiences may be an example of transference. The analyst in this instance would have provided inadequate conditions for the patient to begin the treatment.

In my experience most unclassical patients will not display extensive negative transference if they feel appropriately understood. Usually they will give the treatment some chance to progress before displaying continuous negative affect. We may then conclude that in the beginning of the treatment the analyst must be understanding enough to know that the analysand does not want to hear the analyst's conception of the patient's unconscious fantasies. This is especially true of narcissistically vulnerable patients. Interpretative efforts may puncture the person's (defensive) grandiosity and may lead to acting out and even premature termination. We can now ask when is the unclassical patient able to tolerate interpretative efforts? How does one determine whether analytic trust is established? This discussion is a chapter in itself, but briefly I would state that when the analyst feels the need to interpret, it is crucial to help the patient understand the adaptive aspect of his or her present self-destructive or hostile behavior, not merely focus on the patient's destructive wishes. When the focus in the beginning of the treatment is only on the patient's destructive wishes, there is a strong moralizing tone in the analytic interpretation. In my view it is impossible for patients not to take this type of interpretation as a criticism of themselves. Therefore it is crucial to show patients why they felt that this type of response was the only one available to them. If the analyst cannot do this, in my opinion it is best not to interpret and attempt another type of intervention.

Although I have stated that most nonclassical patients will usually give treatment some chance to progress before displaying continuous negative affect, I wish to expand on this point. I said earlier that it is extremely important for both the patient and the analyst to state boundaries and to understand the meaning of boundaries. At times it is necessary to state the boundaries emphatically, particularly if the analyst finds him- or herself consistently getting irritated. A supervisee related that a patient would not pay on time and would frequently bounce a check when actually paying. This preyed on the therapist's mind and he offered constant interpretations to deal with this issue. When he dealt with the problem as a boundary issue instead, he was able to conduct the treatment without nearly as much conflict. (He put forth that as a condition of treatment the patient had to pay on time, and if checks were bounced, then he had to pay with a money order.) It seems to me that these issues come up most frequently with patients who use projective identification as a main or primary defense.

When the patient gives some indication that the analyst is included in his or her subjective world (i.e., the analyst is accepted in a way that does not *only* repeat the patient's past), the interpretative aspects of the analysis can begin. It is important to recognize that this acceptance is a fragile commodity. A patient in a mid-analysis retrospective commented that she knew the analysis had begun when she could refer to me as being the same as her father and a variety of other sadistic men in her life, without really believing it to be completely true. She and I would set the date of the beginning at a somewhat different point in time. From my perspective she had already begun to develop an observing ego when she made this comment. I believe that the analysis began when she allowed me to represent some fantastic elements of her father and relate this to me. That was when she began to include me (and to relate this to me) in her subjective world in the analysis. "I feel that you hurt me, but I know that you don't want to." She trusted that the aggression she expressed and feared would not come back at her from the analytic chair. She got to that point after her repeated attempts at provocation were contained in the treatment and her frequent regressions "were not looked down upon." She needed to establish an analytic world in which she could roam from provocateur to victim and back again without being stopped or hurt. In some occasional spaces it was possible to communicate to her the pain that this flurry of sadomasochistic activity either obscured or mechanized. The past relationships, components of the pain, were concealed by her creation of a stereotypical picture of the world as a frightening, horrible montage of brutal, self-centered people. In a simplified version of what she went through, we can say that first this woman was able to create her vision of me, without my protesting my innocence, by pointing out that I was the product of her creations. We were gradually able to concentrate on the pain that was present outside the stereotypical sadomasochistic behavior that she exhibited. It was then that she slowly began to accept me as someone who could focus with her on the conscious experiences that she had some difficulty in acknowledging. It was important to allow these experiences to flow from her, and to put into words those experiences that she found difficult to state. Eventually she could acknowledge the inexplicable nature of the experiences. Simply stating the inexplicable often provided her with some relief and gradually paved the way for her trust in my understanding of what she was going through. It also led to her beginning to accept a formulation that did not stay within the boundaries she had established in the treatment.

SELF, DRIVE, EGO, AND OBJECT

I conclude this chapter by answering a series of questions that Fred Pine (1988, 1991) has put forth in his work. Pine describes how he uses different models at different points in the clinical situation. He has distinctly eschewed offering a theoretical rationale for his use of these models. Rather, he has tried to describe his clinical practice. The four models that he postulates might really be called four perspectives: self, drive, ego, and object. If we take the self as the first perspective (and it usually is what is presented to us in initial meetings), one might say that the analyst concentrates on issues surrounding the synthesis of experience (self-cohesion) as well as those that involve embarrassment and shame. This occurs during the period when analytic trust is initially being established. Moreover, we try to feel the intensity of the person's feelings and reflect back how they are at times disrupting the person's sense of self or how the person needs to expel these feelings from his or her experience of him- or herself. In terms of the intensity of affect in my theoretical model, we are encountering a drive derivative but we are focusing on this derivative more in terms of the person's experience of self than in terms of the deeper meaning of drive, which, of course, demonstrates some of the artificiality of the division in these four models. In one way or another we are attempting to titrate the intensity of the person's feelings so that the experience of treatment is not overly aversive. In this vein some patients may need to regulate the temperature of the room or the lighting, and our focus in this aspect of the treatment is to see how the boundaries of the treatment situation can accommodate the way the person experiences this new analytic world. Clearly I am dwelling on this in terms of how some narcissistic and borderline patients experience the analytic situation, but I would say that while some patients may go through this phase of the treatment more quickly than others, it is an inevitable part of all treatments.

When patients begin to include me in their object worlds, then the possibility opens up to include aspects of the other within the final part of the initial phase of analytic trust. A hypochondrical patient who has focused exclusively on her body and the sensations attendant to certain experiences (which for her denote a fatal illness) begins to recognize aspects of my waiting room or reading material or a tie. Along with that development she talks about the impact she has on others; she is now not exclusively focusing on the toxins that her family and colleagues are pouring into her literally and symbolically. When this interplay begins (between self-experience and some consideration of the other), the analyst naturally sits further back in his or her chair and elements of unconscious fantasy begin to drift into his or her consciousness and are retained. At that point I begin to think that drive elements can now be integrated into the person's self-object world. Thus the question of how pleasurable experiences have turned unpleasant becomes a leading focus of the transference. With narcissistic patients it is my experience that there usually are two or three transference cycles before one is able to put drive (pleasure–unpleasure) experiences into their self and object relationships. For most patients, of course, drive derivatives are always present and at the very least color the intensity of affectual experiences in the treatment. In other cases drive derivatives determine how quickly the patient has to evacuate the affectual experience from their psychological world. But I would say that before one can interpret drive experience (in the transference) one first has to show how one understands how self-experiences are disrupted by the intensity of affect (or drive). Also, it is frequently important to picture how the other is experienced as an impingement, and then, as the treatment progresses, how the other is actually another and may be affected by the patient's actions. All of this comes before endogenously generated experiences or unconscious fantasy can be interpreted. The ego (or various cognitive functions) is usually brought into play at every stage of the treatment. When analytic trust is being established, the patient frequently complains about not being able to think; if possible, it is useful to at least describe how the patient often feels disrupted, upset by the internal buzz. (A patient of mine would make whirring sounds to describe the internal clamor that he was experiencing.) More and more through transference cycles the patient is helped, to paraphrase Winnicott, to experience the drives (with respect to some object in the transference) as part of the self (not as a clap of external thunder, which if experienced in this way usually is projected into some other object).

In summary, the self is in the forefront as analytic trust is being established and the patient begins to feel free to utilize the analytic situation. The object makes an appearance first as part of the self after the analyst has been able to reflect and synthesize and gauge the intensity of the patient's experience. Drives make their appearance only when they can be experienced as part of the self and the self–object sequence. If possible, the patient should be allowed the freedom to create the transference so that the drives can be experienced as an active component of the self. Ego (or cognitive functioning) is always a component of what is being disrupted by the drives; thus, depending on the stage of treatment, the ego is either part of the description of what is being disrupted or part of the interpretative effort. In my version of contemporary Freudian analysis, as the treatment progresses more and more destructive aspects of conflicts emerge, and envy and the destructive consequences of envy dominate the treatment situation. As opposed to Kernberg's (1975, 1984) view, my view is that certain splits must be endured for several transference sequences before they can be interpreted.

Certain patients fill the room and the analyst with destructive impulses, and frequently the analyst feels the need to interpret in self-defense. If the analyst in these situations is unable to contain the patient's destructiveness, then it is important to help the patient understand why and how he or she sees this response to the world (the world as an impingement) as the only adaptive alternative. In early interpretations it is important to include an adaptive aspect in the interpretative material.

Because I am a Freudian who is not a classical analyst, the last question that I will pose slightly more formally is how my views fit in with a Freudian position. During what I (1995) have labeled his object relations phase of theorizing (the period 1905–1915), Freud (1915) attempted to explain the ontogenetic development of love within what he called the three polarities of the mind: ego (self)-object, active-passive, pleasure-unpleasure. He tells us that the instincts do not love or hate, but that loving or hating is a relationship of the self to the object. During this period Freud is both attempting to explain the development of object love and he is writing his papers on psychoanalytic technique (Ellman 1991). I maintain that Freud is close to a comprehensive theory of technique if we are to take his ideas on transference, object relations, and the polarities of the mind seriously. I will state this view in an overly condensed manner. Insofar as we are conducting an analysis, we must explore the polarities of the mind and allow analysands to process conflictual material so that the capacity for object love and work is widened. Analysands must first develop the capacity of experiencing things in terms of the self as well as the other (selfobject). They must then come to understand the pleasure–unpleasure series and how and why they have defended against something that once was pleasurable and is now greeted as unpleasurable. They must also be able to tolerate passivity (and learn receptivity) and not be inhibited in terms of their own activity.

In this context then, the analyst should make interpretations only when "a well-developed *rapport*, is established in the patient. The first aim of the treatment is attaching him to the treatment and to the person of the physician" (Freud 1913, cited in Ellman 1991, p. 171).

After that the transference should be a consistent focus in the treatment and has to be dealt with bit by bit and allowed to enter the treatment situation. It is only by allowing the transference to enter the treatment that conflicts and compulsions can be rendered "harmless" if "[w]e admit [conflicts] as transference into the treatment—it is admitted as into a playground in which it is allowed to expand in almost complete freedom" (my translation) (Freud 1914, cited in Ellman 1991, p. 61).

While Freud did not have a completed theory of technique, his most developed ideas about technique occurred when he was writing about narcissism and the pathways to object love. I believe his ideas formulated at that time lead to the type of concepts I have tried to formulate. In any case, this is my rendition of a contemporary version of the Freudian onion.

REFERENCES

Bach, S. (1985). *Narcissistic States and the Therapeutic Process.* New York: Jason Aronson.

Bion, W. R. (1962). *Learning from Experience.* London: Heinemann.

Bird, B. (1972). Notes on transference: universal phenomenon and hardest part of analysis. *Journal of the American Psychoanalytic Association* 20:267–301.

Brenner, C. (1976). *Psychoanalytic Technique and Psychic Conflict.* New York: International Universities Press.

——— (1982). *The Mind in Conflict.* New York: International Universities Press.

Ellman, S. J. (1991). *Freud's Technique Papers: A Contemporary Perspective.* Northvale, NJ: Jason Aronson.

——— (1995). *Freud's four theories and contemporary psychoanalysis.* Paper presented at the Edmund Weil Memorial Lecture, New York Academy of Medicine, May.

Freud, S. (1913). Further recommendations in the technique of psychoanalysis: on beginning the treatment. *Collected Papers.* Vol 2. New York: Basic Books, 1959.

——— (1914). Further recommendations in the technique of psychoanalysis: recollection, repetition and working through. *Collected Papers.* Vol. 2. New York: Basic Books, 1959.

——— (1915). Instincts and their vicissitudes. *Standard Edition* 14.

——— (1937). Constructions in analysis. *Standard Edition* 23:255–269.

Greenson, R. R. (1965). The working alliance and the transference neurosis. *Psychoanalytic Quarterly* 34:155–181.

——— (1967). *The Technique and Practice of Psychoanalysis: Vol. 1.* New York: International Universities Press.

Kernberg, O. (1975). *Borderline Conditions and Pathological Narcissism.* New York: Jason Aronson.

——— (1984). *Severe Personality Disorders: Psychotherapeutic Strategies.* New Haven, CT: Yale University Press.

Kohut, H. (1971). *The Analysis of the Self.* New York: International Universities Press.

Lipton, S. (1977). The advantages of Freud's technique as shown in his analysis of the Rat Man. *International Journal of Psycho-Analysis* 58:255–273.

——— (1979). An addendum to "The advantages of Freud's technique as shown in his analysis of the Rat Man." *International Journal of Psycho-Analysis* 60:215–216.

Pine, F. (1988). The four psychologies of psychoanalysis and their place in clinical work. *Journal of the American Psychoanalytic Association* 36:571–596.

——— (1991). *Drive, Ego, Object and Self.* New York: Basic Books.

Stein, M. H. (1981). The unobjectionable part of the transference. *Journal of the American Psychoanalytic Association* 29:869–892.

Stone, L. (1961). *The Psychoanalytic Situation: An Examination of Its Development and Essential Nature.* New York: International Universities Press.

——— (1967). The psychoanalytic situation and transference: Postscript to an earlier communication. *Journal of the American Psychoanalytic Association* 15:358.

Suskind, P. (1986). *Perfume,* trans. J. E. Woods. New York: Knopf.

Winnicott, D. W. (1958). *Collected Papers: Through Pediatrics to Psychoanalysis.* New York: Basic Books.

Zetzel, E. R. (1965). The theory of therapy in relation to a developmental model of the psychic apparatus. *International Journal of Psycho-Analysis* 46:39–52.

——— (1966). The analytic situation. In *Psychoanalysis in the Americas,* ed. R. E. Litman, pp. 86–106. New York: International Universities Press.

6

Growing Up Orthodox

Arnold D. Richards

My aim in this chapter is to locate myself and my work in relation to the current state of psychoanalysis. Specifically, I want to consider my relationship to orthodoxy and deviance, pluralism and uniformity, free exploration and dogmatism. Let me acknowledge at the outset that each of us who practices psychoanalysis is a product of his or her training, institute traditions, and the values and approaches of analytic teachers, supervisors, and training analyst or analysts. The influence of these factors varies with the individual. Some analysts are very much bound by tradition and influenced by authority and reluctant to question received wisdom. Other analysts are more freewheeling, free-spirited, and antiestablishment. Openly questioning, they are committed to an attitude of "show me." One would hope that in matters of science such personal differences would eventually succumb to the corrective of verifiable experience, logical demonstration, and rational proof. To be sure, even in some "hard" scientific endeavors ideology may determine differences in theory and preferred explanatory systems. Yet there probably isn't a single scientific or intellectual discipline as value-laden and colored by emotionality as psychoanalysis.

I think I can show this most vividly by relating a little bit about my own personal route to psychoanalysis. I believe that my earliest lexical memory is of seeing an article in the Yiddish *Forward* about the death of Sigmund Freud when I was 5 years old. I remember the picture of the bearded man and the announcement, which I read or which was read to me by a grandfatherly figure, also bearded, who taught me to read Yiddish and Hebrew. This may well be a screen memory, but I am certain that Sigmund Freud and psychoanalysis were subjects I knew about and was interested in during my latency years.

I know I read about him in the encyclopedia and pursued some of the subjects described as part of my broader prepubertal search for sexual knowledge. In retrospect, it is difficult to determine whether my interest in sexuality fueled my interest in literature or the other way around. But I do remember reading novels for both their literary and their titillating value, selecting from a wide range of books that included Pearl Buck's *The Good Earth* and Aldous Huxley's *Point Counter Point.* My second great childhood passion was politics, and I was exposed by a succession of leftist elementary school teachers to writers such as Lincoln Steffens, John Dos Passos, Upton Sinclair, and John Steinbeck. Theirs was the literature of rebellion, revolution, and social justice.

The first important nonfiction book that I read was Flanders Dunbar's work *Emotions and Bodily Health.* I was about 12 ½, and my interest in the book was fueled by my yearly bouts with hay fever when I felt as if I were drowning in a sea of secretions. Dunbar's book made the case that allergies, asthma, and hay fever were psychosomatic, somehow connected to the poisons of my child's mind. Conflict, sexuality, and the unconscious were concepts that offered me the hope of mastery, a power over my membranes that came from understanding how the mind worked and how the mind in its workings affected the workings of the body. I found these explications about the mental and bodily machinery as interesting and exciting as the drawings of the mechanisms of the cars in the pages of *Popular Mechanics* or the steam engines and cotton gins in the *Encyclopaedia Britannica* and the *World Book of Knowledge.* About four years after reading Dunbar I read *New Introductory Lectures of Psychoanalysis,* the yellow Permaback edition of Sigmund Freud (1933).

Freud's interlocutory style in those lectures was for me absolutely convincing. The concepts of psychic determinism, unconscious mental processes, and infantile sexuality offered a way to order the mysterious world of mind and human interaction—mind at work and mind at play, mind during the day and mind at night—that simply brooked no competition. The "Introductory Lectures" and the "Dream Book," in A. A. Brill's translation, formed a foundational pair; they represented a solid psychology that could be applied to everyday functioning and to the world of pathology. Starting from that point, psychoanalysis became a lens through which I observed a whole host of intellectual, literary, and scientific experience. It served a role similar to that of Marxism for others of my generation. Whether I was reading T. S. Eliot, e. e. cummings, Homer, Aeschylus, or Euripides in high school, Aristotle, Plato, or Kant at the University of Chicago, or works on neurophysiology and brain functioning in medical school, psychoanalysis offered relevant organizing principles. Through it, I could understand a broad range of intellectual movements that I read about during the day; it likewise helped me parse the dreams I had at night.

I relate the circumstances in which I first became exposed to psychoanalytic ideas to show how their compelling nature stems from their ability to help the individual make sense of experiences that are personally meaningful. Similarly, of course, physics appeals to us because it orders the world of physical things; literature draws its power from its relevance to the real-life personal and interpersonal dramas to which we are always exposed. And so with psychoanalysis. A person who never gives much thought to dreams, never makes slips of the tongue, and never puzzles other symptoms, inhibitions, or delusional thoughts will not be drawn to psychoanalytic explanation. But inasmuch as most everyone does, psychoanalysis continues to hold its own in the intellectual marketplace along with other powerful explanatory systems that account for important aspects of human experience.

Thirteen years elapsed from the time I began college until I started my analytic training at age 30. During that period my early wish to become a psychoanalyst was both at risk—subject to dissuasion, disenchantment, and disillusionment—and open to reinforcement. The period in question—the fifties and sixties—was, it turns out, the heyday of psychoanalysis.

Psychoanalysis enjoyed a boom right after World War II when a cohort of psychiatrists returned from the service and sought analytic training. The American Psychoanalytic Association grew rapidly, training institutes had many applicants, and treatment centers had large backlogs. Psychoanalysis seemed to be a profession that provided for the intellectual, therapeutic, and socioeconomic needs of a group of physicians who were perhaps ambivalent about the choice of medicine as a profession because of its trade-school aspects and its seeming lack of intellectual and humanistic excitement.

During this time my interest in psychoanalysis was challenged by the attraction of other sciences: mathematics in college, medicine and pathology in medical school, and forensic psychiatry and criminology during my psychiatric residency. But their allure was more than offset by the support and reinforcement I received from both peers and mentors during my college and professional education. Between my third and fourth years of medical school I spent a summer as an extern at the Marine Hospital in Staten Island, assigned to a medical and a psychiatric service. The doctor in charge of the psychiatric service was in analytic training, and his own rather well-known analyst, who specialized in psychosomatic illness, practiced her calling with almost religious conviction.

During my internship in Baltimore I serendipitously had as a neighbor a first-year psychiatric resident at the University of Maryland who was just starting his analytic training and had entered into the program with enthusiasm and gusto. It was then that I almost succumbed to the lure of a New York psychiatric residency program that was almost totally identified with psychoanalysis in general and the New York Psychoanalytic Institute in particular. I don't know whether there was some adaptive or self-preservative mechanism at work that made me opt for a residency in Topeka, Kansas, that, while analytically oriented, was much broader in overall outlook. There certainly was a difference between Karl Menninger's view of psychoanalysis and that of Milton Rosenbaum, Herb Weiner, and the other Cincinnati transplants in the Bronx. And I think that I benefited greatly from exposure in Topeka to some of the great minds of the twentieth-century—Konrad Lorenz, Aldous Huxley, S. I. Hayakawa, Margaret Mead, and Ludwig von Bertalanffy, among others. In Topeka, as in Chicago during my college days, my emphasis was on trying to place psychoanalysis within the wider context of Western humanistic and scientific thought. I like to tell myself that when I began analytic training at the New York Psychoanalytic Institute in 1964 I brought to that rarefied and perhaps somewhat stultifying atmosphere a sense of the larger scientific landscape. At the same time I had the personal sense that psychoanalysis, as an investigative and explanatory tool, accounted for human behavior and human motivation in a way no other discipline or approach did. Psychoanalysis contained a set of explanatory constructs—the Oedipus complex, infantile sexuality, the dynamic unconscious—that seemed to me to be of awesome power.

My analytic class began as a group of thirteen: twelve men and one woman, twelve psychiatrists and one psychologist. Graduates of elite colleges and medical schools, we were convinced that we were the best and the brightest and that our training was going to bring us to the top of the psychiatric profession and provide us with the most effective tools for relieving psychological suffering. We were awed by our instructors, who were indeed recognized as among the greats in contemporary psychoanalysis. Several, transplanted from Vienna not so long before, could claim a direct lineage from Freud and had written the definitive works in the field. I refer of course to Heinz Hartmann, Rudolph Loewenstein, Edith Jacobson, Annie Reich, Kurt and Ruth Eissler, and George Gero. There was a group of American psychoanalysts, somewhat younger but also giants in the field: Phyllis Greenacre, Jacob Arlow, Charles Brenner, and David Beres.

With so distinguished a faculty, the institute was conductive to idealization, identification, and acceptance of theory and ideology. It was hardly a place that promoted skepticism, questioning, and argument, although several members of my class developed a sufficiently disbelieving posture that they left the program. Of course, much depends on whether the candidate's own experience in analytic treatment is positive—whether the analysis provides the sense that all the hypothetical and theoretical constructs about the way the mind works ring personally true. After all, what is taught always stands or falls not on its strength as a hypothesis or theory but on the extent to which the constructs can be personally validated. This is not to say that one can pursue a course of training in a totally objective fashion. The fact is, a training analysis can never be purely for oneself, uncontaminated by the pressure for advancement, success, and graduation; it is inevitably influenced by strong pushes toward conformity and acceptance. I think it is remarkable how well candidates generally come through this experience. And I have a hunch that the candidates who didn't finish training were those who tended toward total acceptance rather than toward a more questioning attitude.

Analytic training at that time mostly involved reading Freud, in depth and in detail. Since completing training, I have read all of Freud twice as part of a private seminar exercise; reading him the second and third times gave me a sense of how little I had understood in the classroom setting. Yet I am convinced that analytic training provided me with understanding and conviction about what I consider the basic principles of psychoanalysis. The fundamental tenets of my training had to do with (1) the basic principle of psychic determinism; (2) the centrality of unconscious mental functioning and its implications for the theories of motivation, symptom formation, and personality disorder and personality development; (3) the ambivalence and conflicts of childhood and the centrality of experiences with parents and siblings and of the bodily processes; and (4) the role of transference. Finally there was the overarching idea of the centrality of affect—that psychoanalysis is a psychology of emotionality and not just an intellectual discipline.

I trained during the era of the psychoanalysis of plenty: there were plenty of candidates, plenty of patients, and lots of prestige for psychoanalysis and psychoanalysts. This had an effect, I think, on the kinds of patients who were treated and on the nature of their treatments. Training analysts had full analytic practices with candidates who were patient, docile, and compliant. It was the kind of situation in which analytic neutrality, abstinence, and inflexible methodological rules were accepted without question. The candidates understood that there was always someone waiting in the wings to take their place if they did not go along with the program. Perhaps that was an exaggerated view, but I think it fostered changes on both the national and the local level. It was at this same time that people began to write about widening the scope of psychoanalysis and to look at the ways in which psychoanalysis could or could not be adapted to the treatment of the sicker patient. My own experience and that of my fellow candidates suggested that the scope had already widened and that the so-called ideal analytic patient—cooperative, neurotic, without serious psychopathology—was becoming the exception.

At meetings of the affiliated staff some of the training analysts would respond to case presentations of sicker patients by readily diagnosing schizophrenia, psychosis, or worse and by dismissing such patients as unanalyzable. Others seemed to take a different approach and, operating from a continuum point of view, espoused a wider tolerance for severe illness. In New York the European group, the older analysts closer to Freud, were most willing to diagnose serious illness and take this exclusionary approach. The younger, American-trained analysts, such as Arlow, Brenner, and Beres, seemed to have a much more tolerant approach.

The debate in the International Psychoanalytical Association (IPA) Congress in 1969 among Arlow and Brenner and Freeman (1970) and Greenson and Wexler (1970) revealed these different points of view. This all influenced me because my first patient presented severe psychopathology. David Beres, my supervisor, kept my focus on analyzing and understanding, to the ultimate clinical benefit of the patient and to the benefit of my training experience. My own style has developed out of the fact that I trained at a classical institute, yet early in my career had the experience of analyzing patients with severe psychopathology. I reported on one of these patients (Richards 1984), a woman who was a self-mutilator. I saw her in analysis four or five times a week, which resulted in a very positive therapeutic outcome. The case was dramatic because it turned out that her psychopathology was in part a response to the severe trauma of father–daughter incest. Memories of these experiences were recovered through the analysis of dreams and transference–countertransference constellations and enactments.

And so I had the interesting experience of undergoing orthodox analytic training with a group of instructors and colleagues who were committed to the analytic cause, while at the same time I honed an attitude of philosophical and intellectual questioning about theory and practice. Very early on I was drawn to alternate schools of psychoanalytic thought. I remember, sometime during my training, reading Edward Glover's (1950) *Freud or Jung.* I know I did this on my own; it was not assigned in any of my courses. The message of that book was very simple: the difference between Freud and Jung was that Freud believed in the unconscious while Jung did not. This may sound like something of an oversimplification, but I think it is one of those simple ideas that is profound in import. Even today, there is a tendency in discussions of psychoanalytic theoretical diversity to accept the position that everyone believes in the unconscious, that it is, indeed, an operative assumption across the spectrum of psychoanalytic perspectives. But my sense is that this is not the case, and I have argued as much in publications critical of popular theories put forward by Mitchell, Greenberg, Stolorow, and others (Bachant and Richards 1993).

Recent stress on the "here and now" of the therapeutic interaction often shifts the focus away from unconscious fantasy determined by childhood experiences and revolving around libidinal and aggressive themes with the primary objects. An interactive approach to the patient in the analytic situation may also muddy the waters at times, and make it difficult to see the contribution of the unconscious to the patient's symptomatology, experience, behavior, and character. It is a foundational idea that the unconscious reveals itself in an environment of quiet contemplation and observation—a situation closer to dreaming than to waking. Of course, the unconscious also becomes evident in the noise of interaction and in the noise of a patient's life. But it seems to me that one is on much more solid ground when symptomatic acts and maladaptive behaviors can be understood through inferences about the material of dreams and free associations.

Although such an approach perhaps sounds fashioned, it remains for me the heart of the analysis, with its unique interpretive mode. The issue may be one of background versus foreground: for analysts trained in my tradition the relationship is a given, in the background; insight occupies the foreground. Insights are received by the patient in the context of a positive therapeutic relationship, which is fueled in turn by the insight and understanding that the analyst offers the patient.

One misconception is that the centrality of insight in this approach emphasizes intellectual understanding and downplays the affective component of the treatment. Nothing could be further from the case. Affect remains central. Intellectual insight without its emotional concomitants is pallid and hardly therapeutic. I think a crucial aspect of psychoanalytic training is developing a *feel* for what is analytic. This doesn't necessarily involve a rigid adherence to rules of analytic conversation. It does involve learning to eschew interactions that are primarily of a counseling nature: advice giving, reassurance, approval, and so forth. The idea is that, even though patients may want to be counseled, at some level they understand that such interventions are not really what they need.

The trick in conducting this kind of analysis is to be able to maintain this posture without being experienced as cruel, withholding, or self-serving. There is no doubt that the approach can be carried to an extreme, and it is often caricatured by critics of traditional analytic technique. It cannot be stressed enough that classical technique does not preclude common sense. At no point does the analyst deny the legitimacy of the patient's needs and wishes, which are recognized by the analyst as understandable in content and pressing in nature. The emphasis is on helping the patient assume a stance in which short-term benefits are given up for the sake of long-term, lasting change.

The major controversy when I completed my analytic training in 1969 involved psychoanalytic metapsychology. No major alternative points of view had yet been advanced, and the main theoretical issue was the concept of identity developed by Erik Erikson and Heinz Lichtenstein. But a group of psychoanalysts, primarily students of David Rappaport, were questioning Freud's metapsychology, in particular its energic assumptions. George Klein's (1973) "Psychoanalysis: One Theory or Two?," an influential statement of the antimetapsychological position, argued that psychoanalysis was a clinical theory and that its metapsychology was at best superfluous, at worst confusing and irrelevant. The antimetapsychology movement continued until the present time and has drawn into its orbit theoreticians as different in their orientation as Roy Schafer and Charles Brenner.

The issues raised in the debate tended not to have important clinical consequences. The language of energy, libido, cathexis, and decathexis and Hartmann's language of neutralization and deneutralization were not readily translatable into strategies germane to the analytic situation. The most cogent response to the antimetapsychologists came earlier, from Robert Waelder (1936), who conceptualized the levels of psychoanalytic theory from the most clinical to the most metapsychological. His idea that people were arguing from different levels of abstraction had for me a compelling logic. But then, I have always been drawn to approaches that are dialectic rather than dichotomous.

Heinz Kohut's *The Analysis of the Self* (1971) and *The Restoration of the Self* (1977) represented the first serious challenge to classical psychoanalysis from both a theoretical and a clinical or technical point of view. His psychology of the self offered a new theory of pathogenesis and of treatment and cure. Kohut was not alone in offering the self as the rubric for a psychoanalytic paradigm. His work was in certain ways anticipated by George Klein, for whom the concept of the self was also important. John Gedo (1979), who collaborated with Kohut and then broke away, offered a concept of a superordinate self in the theoretical and clinical system that he began propounding in the 1970s.

Neither Klein nor Gedo achieved the same prominence and following as Kohut. Kohut's rhetoric was engaging, and his two books represented a serious challenge, a well-thought-out alternative to received psychoanalytic wisdom. He offered the appealing dichotomy of "guilty man," whose problems originate in interpsychic conflict, and "tragic man," whose problems result primarily from developmental arrest and disturbance in the self. According to Kohut, tragic man has to be treated according to the principles of self psychology, whereas guilty man can be treated according to the older precepts of Freud's psychoanalysis.

Beginning in the late 1970s and carrying over into the 1980s, self psychology developed into a new psychoanalytic movement with its own publications, conferences, and so forth. Nevertheless, it remained within the organizational framework of the American and International Psychoanalytic Associations. Kohut did not suffer the same fate as Jung, Adler, Horney, and Clara Thompson before him. He came out of an orthodox Freudian tradition, trained in Vienna, was analyzed there by Aichorn and in Chicago by Ruth Eissler. He taught at the Chicago Institute, where he was one of the outstanding presenters of psychoanalytic theory for successive classes. He was known as a brilliant theoretical synthesizer and systematizer who had the entire Freudian corpus at his fingertips. The response to self psychology by many of my mentors at the New York Psychoanalytic Institute, and by some of my colleagues and peers as well, was generally dismissive. It was disturbing to me that the rejection of Kohut's point of view was not always based on a careful study of his work. Exceptions at that time were two reviews by members of the institute, Martin Stein (1979) and Lester Schwartz (1978): the first critical, the second more appreciative. In discussions with colleagues and teachers, I had the sense that I was being given the task of studying self psychology and reporting back to them as to whether there was anything in Kohut worth considering seriously. The resulting study and critiques of self psychology (1981, 1982) enhanced my career and my standing with the powers that be in the orthodox New York psychoanalytic establishment.

The challenge of self psychology as an alternate theoretical, clinical, and therapeutic system is still with us today. Kohut's dichotomy of tragic man and guilty man remains a cogent alternative guide to the practice of psychoanalysis. And many of the controversies, both theoretical and therapeutic, that have become part of the psychoanalytic debate over the decades come down to this distinction. The role of insight and interpretation as opposed to the role of the therapeutic relationship has to do with whether the patient's primary psychopathology is a function of a childhood environmental failure and developmental deficit. This raises questions as to the best mode of therapeutic intervention. John Gedo's (1979) ideas about working through and the needs to address consciously the cognitive deficits that are part of the patient's difficulty represent a more recent contribution to this fundamental debate.

During the past decade, self psychology has been on the wane as the flash point of psychoanalytic controversy. It has been supplanted by the relational, intersubjective, and interpersonal schools. The prime movers of these approaches are not members of the psychoanalytic establishment; indeed, like other non-M.D.'s, they were not eligible for training and membership in the American Psychoanalytic Association until 1989. This fact may partly account for certain skewed views of contemporary Freudian psychoanalysis that appear again and again in their papers and books. Unsurprisingly, my own writing during the past ten years has involved discussions and critiques of these points of view. I have followed the same route as I did with self psychology in the 1970s, and my position within my group remains that of a contemporary Freudian analyst who interprets and critiques new approaches.

In pursuing this course I am fortunate to have had the advantage of greater opportunities for interaction with nonmedical analysts than many of my colleagues have. In part this is a result of my own interests, my training in Topeka (where there has always been a very strong nonmedical presence), and my marriage to a psychologist/psychoanalyst. My career and my approach belie the claim that the American Freudian establishment is an orthodox monolith. This position fails to recognize the revisionist trends within the ranks of the Freudian orthodox. Melanie Klein's approach exemplifies one such trend abroad, and the Arlow-Brenner group within the New York Psychoanalytic Institute exemplifies it today in this country. Arlow and Brenner have been quite outspoken in their criticism of various aspects of classical Freudian theory. Their own approaches, particularly that of Brenner, are theoretically very close to that of the antimetapsychologists. Brenner's eschewal of reification and his rejection of concepts of psychic agency and mental structures are consonant with the assumptions that underlie Roy Schafer's action language. My own commitment to Arlow and Brenner's emphasis on conflict, compromise formation, and unconscious fantasy works well for me as a personal compromise formation, enabling me to be part of the establishment while espousing what I see as an evolutionary, though not revolutionary, Freudian point of view.

What does all the foregoing have to do with how I work? I think I have come to listen with a fourth ear. The third ear, as Theodor Reik observes, listens to the patient's unconscious. The fourth ear, I believe, tries to listen from the various vantage points of competing theoretical schools. I practice this kind of listening because it holds the promise of validating clinically competing hypotheses about how the mind works. But I also do so because a receptivity to new ideas, a willingness to consider them on their own merits, follows from the therapeutic nature of the analytic situation, which requires a pragmatic commitment to what works best for one's patients. I distinguish this kind of pluralism from an indiscriminate eclecticism. Pluralism involves a willingness to consider new points of view, but not an acceptance of all points of view as equally valid and clinically helpful.

My espousal of pluralism does not lead me to endorse extreme versions of the doctrine of narrative truth, in which anything goes and any story is as good as any other. I think there are more or less consensually validated facts: some things really happen to our patients, and although the ultimate truth may not be knowable, patients and analysts are involved in a quest to come as close as possible to some veridical understanding of the past. Einstein maintained that an extreme relativist position and a belief in uncertainty were antithetical to the proper motivational stance of the scientist. Only some belief in truth, he held, can motivate the scientist to expend great energy studying the laws of nature that govern the universe. I think that the same can be said of the psychoanalyst and the analysand.

REFERENCES

Bachant, J. L., and Richards, A.D. (1993). Review of *Relational Concepts in Psychoanalysis: An Integration*, by S. Mitchell. *Psychoanalytic Dialogues* 31:431–460.

Freeman, T. (1970). The psychopathology of the psychoses: a reply to Arlow and Brenner. *International Journal of Psycho-Analysis* 51:407–415.

Freud, S. (1933). *New Introductory Lectures on Psychoanalysis*, trans. W. J. H. Sprott. New York: Norton.

——— (1950). *The Interpretation of Dreams*, trans. A. A. Brill. New York: Modern Library.

Gedo, J. (1979). *Beyond Interpretation: Toward a Revised Theory for Psychoanalysis*. New York: International Universities Press.

Glover, E. (1950). *Freud or Jung.* London: Allen & Unwin.

Greenson, R. R., and Wexler, M. (1970). Discussion of "the non-transference relationship in the psychoanalytic situation." *International Journal of Psycho-Analysis* 51:143–166.

Klein, G. (1973). Psychoanalysis: One theory or two? *Bulletin of the Menninger Clinic* 37:102–132.

Kohut, H. (1971). *The Analysis of the Self.* New York: International Universities Press.

——— (1977). *The Restoration of the Self.* New York: International Universities Press.

Richards, A. D. (1981). Self theory, conflict theory and the problem of hypochondriasis. In *Psychoanalytic Study of the Child* 36:319–337. New Haven, CT: Yale University Press.

——— (1982). The superordinate self in psychoanalytic theories and the self psychologies. *Journal of the American Psychoanalytic Association* 30:717–736.

——— (1984). Self-mutilation and father/daughter incest. In *Fantasy, Myth and Reality: Essays in Honor of Jacob Arlow,* ed. H. P. Blum, Y. Kramer, A. K. Richards, and A. D. Richards. Madison, CT: International Universities Press.

Schwartz, L. (1978). Review of *The Restoration of the Self,* by H. Kohut. *Psychoanalytic Quarterly* 47:436–443.

Stein, M. (1979). Review of *The Restoration of the Self,* by H. Kohut. *Journal of the American Psychoanalytic Association* 27:665–680.

Waelder, R. (1936). The principle of multiple function: observations on over-determination. *Psychoanalytic Quarterly* 5:45–62.

7

Listening to and Interpreting a Psychotic Patient

David Rosenfeld

I hope to demonstrate, through a detailed clinical description, the usefulness of psychoanalytic technique for the treatment of psychotic or severely regressed patients, and also to communicate my own experience in detecting subtle transference clues.

I will discuss only a very limited period in the treatment of a patient: the first interviews and the first months of treatment. I will describe moments of psychotic transference and then the psychoanalytic work during the psychotic episode. Thus I hope to stimulate theoretical discussion on the basis of clinical data and in this way suggest a number of themes to be discussed, in particular the relationship between models or theories and their influence on the interpretative technique.

I would first like to enlarge the concept of psychosis and the psychotic part of the personality. Freud's (1940a) description of the splitting of the ego in the psychoses into a normal part and another that detaches the ego from reality is of fundamental importance for the understanding of the psychoses.

In the course of treatment the analyst avails himself of the patient's neurotic part, with its minimum capacity for verbalization, in order to establish a transference relationship. In other words, if on the basis of some of Freud's writings we may infer that in every psychotic there is a neurotic part, this part could be the basis for the establishment of a transference relationship in accordance with Freud's (1912) own definition. Abraham (1908, 1911, 1916) began to suggest, perceive, and state that there is transference in schizophrenia. As Freud (1940b) points out, "Even in a state so far removed from the reality of the external world as one of hallucinatory confusion . . . that at one time in some corner of their mind . . . there was a normal person hidden" (pp. 201–202). He adds, "Two psychical attitudes have been formed instead of a single one—one, the normal one, which takes account of reality, and another which under the influence of the instincts detaches the ego from reality. The two exist alongside of each other" (1940b, p. 202). I insist, then, that a healthy part is necessary in order to work with a psychotic patient. As Shakespeare puts it: "Nothing can be made out of nothing" (*King Lear*, Act I, Scene iv).

Herbert Rosenfeld (1979) has defined the term *psychotic transference*: "psychotic patients project their feelings because they are too frightened to cope with them or to think them themselves. The analyst, however, like the parents in more normal development, has the potential both to face the feelings and to think about them, and it is this capacity which he gradually offers the patient to develop for himself" (p. 488).

Kernberg (1979, 1992) also discusses short, transient psychotic episodes in borderline patients. In the more recent book he has developed the theoretical and clinical concepts of sadism, aggression, and violence. I agree with Kernberg's technical suggestion, namely, not to interpret projective identification at the moments of psychotic transference. H. Rosenfeld (1987) says something similar in his book, *Impasse and Interpretation.*

The patient, whom I shall call Charles, was referred to me for consultation six months after he had a psychotic episode. The picture was first perceived by his family when the patient returned from his holidays and it became more acute and exuberant while he was spending a couple of days at a weekend cottage. By then he and his girlfriend had decided to put an end to their relationship. At present I have good reason to believe there was a previous episode approximately a year before of which his family seemed to have been unaware and which, according to the description, was of a confusional nature.

The psychotic episode that led to my being consulted had, I was told, an exuberant and delusional onset with disorganized speech. The patient began to call himself by the names of some of the great current tennis players and, holding a tennis racquet in his hand, at one moment said he was Borg, or Connors, or Vilas. Then he assumed their identity. According to his family, he spoke in an incoherent and unintelligible way.

The patient, 21 years old, lived with his parents and a sister. His relatives told me that the patient's psychotic episode had taken them by surprise: "It was a complete surprise to us because he was a very quiet, orderly, peaceful boy. It was a shock, a scandal, to see him talking and running, or speaking in a delusional way at the weekend cottage where there were other friends too." They mentioned almost in passing that the patient found it hard to study and spent endless hours trying to get organized to prepare for his exams.

We agreed upon a contract according to which treatment would be started on a five-hour-a-week basis. In addition, I suggested that family interviews with a well-known psychoanalyst be started later on. Medication was left in the hands of my team of collaborators and the patient was to end his previous treatment with a wild psychotherapist.

INTERVIEW AND FIRST DREAM

Charles impressed me as unexpressive and uncommunicative, nor did his gestures convey affective states. He never looked me in the face. He was undemonstrative and seemed to be armored and/or blocked. His father accompanied him to his first interview. At the time of the consultation, Charles had finished high school and was trying to enter a school of fine arts as he is a painter and musician.

In his first interview the patient seemed frightened. During several months of psychoanalytic treatment (one of the members of the family usually accompanied him to my consulting room), Charles used an obsessive language that included the repetition of phrases, concepts, and grammatical structures of an idiosyncratic type, which were difficult or impossible to understand. He wanted to show that his logic and his thinking really worked; I was able to show him that he used the logistics of thinking as a defense against the fear of a new psychotic disorganization.

During the first months this happened quite often and always generated strong countertransference feelings in me as his therapist. (The question of countertransference in these moments of obsessive doubt—or of psychotic disorganization, despair, or suicidal threats—is perhaps the central axis on which the future of research on regressed and psychotic patients will turn.) Sometimes he brought written descriptions of feelings he had experienced during a psychotic episode, feelings that he found incomprehensible.

Charles's father had been orphaned at 9 and his maternal grandfather, who lived with them, had died painfully of cancer. The grandfather, of whom he was very fond, slept in the room next to his and spent many months there in agony before his death.

Sometimes the patient got mixed up about the time of his sessions. One day he looked at his agenda and said something that surprised me: "My mother writes things down in my agenda and has a look at it every morning, and she has been doing this for many years. She writes everything down in my agenda and fixes my schedule every morning."

After the fifth month he brought his first dream, from which he woke up quite shaken. He entered the consulting room surprised at having had a dream.

Charles dreamed that he was crossing a parking place; his father was behind him and his mother was behind his father. They went into a big building through the front door. At that moment he did not know where he was going. They walked along a corridor and took the elevator to the top floor: the patient, his parents, the elevator operator, and the grandfather standing by Charles. As the elevator was going up the patient underwent a transformation: he was no longer made of flesh and bone but was like a doll made of transparent glass. When they reached the top floor, Charles was worried about his fragility. When they left the elevator the grandfather had disappeared, but a nurse led them to a ward and said the grandfather was there. At that moment Charles was no longer made of glass and felt he was going to be very sad. When he got to his grandfather's bed, his mother was behind him and he thought his sister was coming along the corridor.

I asked him for clarification and more details about the dream. The patient cooperated and I interpreted, "The fact that you can dream is proof that you have more confidence in the treatment, for now you have somebody to tell your dream to." In addition, I told him, it was the first time he had brought a dream where he was trying to elaborate the death of someone he had loved dearly in his childhood. The dream also showed an important part of the patient's personality. Actually, Charles (as represented in the dream) was showing that he was a fragile person who, faced with such a traumatic event as the death of his grandfather, had became aware of his fragility.

I said that he was showing a part of himself in the dream: a fragile person, made of glass, who could tolerate, without fragmenting or breaking, being near his sick grandparent's bed. While he was in the elevator with his grandfather standing beside him, his body, his mind, and his self were fragile yet not fragmented and seemed to be contained by the characters in the elevator—those of his childhood—as if they were some kind of skin or container.

The other part of the dream—when he entered the hospital ward and saw his grandfather in bed—implied bringing to the consulting room all his pain at his grandfather's illness. I then said that the most important aspect of the dream was that he was going to visit his grandfather and say good-bye to him for the first time in his life. The patient replied, "I never attached any importance to my grandfather's death, and I always thought I hadn't cared at all. I never thought I had felt anything."

Later on I told him that perhaps he had never been able to say good-bye to his grandfather because no one had helped him to cope with his sorrow and pain. We mentioned the fact that his mother suffered a severe depression and that his father became quite depressed and isolated after the grandfather's death. Then I told him, "Here you seem to have found a place from which you can start to work through this painful childhood mourning." I added that the dream seemed to reflect his belief that he was a fragile being made of crystal, who could become fragmented any moment.

In later sessions Charles returned to this dream and thus I could realize and interpret to him that the parking place also meant he had found in his treatment (his father always drove him to my consulting room) a place where he could park his mind; he could get into a building and make a long trip in his inner world, which was represented by the elevator space where he made an analytic trip accompanied by all his inner objects (Ogden 1986).

Some time afterward I was able to get a full and more detailed picture of his mother. The patient described her as a domineering, demanding woman who could not tolerate untidiness and was intrusive but also affectionate as well as basically depressive. At one time he described his father as a man who made a very sad face if he was contradicted and, above all, when another child was in the house, someone who had to be taken care of.

TWO DREAMS ABOUT IDENTITY AND TRANSFERENCE

On a Monday that same month Charles brought a very important dream, which condensed the transference and his life history, particularly as regards the loss of personal identity. He entered the room disheveled. He had not shaved and wore an expression of astonishment. He said he had had a nightmare from which he woke up screaming with anxiety. This was the dream:

"You were in front of me, but you were some kind of demon, and with different features. Your hair was stiff, long, and standing out of your forehead . . . your eyes were strange. Then we spoke about something that frightened me. And here is the most terrifying part: my face began to change, to transform, it was gradually changing and started being another face. My face was changing, my cheeks, my mouth, my nose, very slowly, and the feeling was so vivid, this feeling of becoming transformed, that I woke up screaming and sweating and I woke up my whole family. They all ran into my room and stayed with me." Then he added something quite significant: "But that person didn't do anything to me; I realized he hadn't done anything to me."

After asking him about some details of the dream, I interpreted that the dream condensed in a plastic way everything that was taking place in his relationship with me. He felt that receiving an interpretation designed to make him think meant I was going to change his identity, represented in the dream by his face; he believed I could model his face, as if I were a monster. "Besides, it accounts for the transference crisis you are going through and the psychotic episode last year, when you thought people brought things by means of the dream, your fear of my wanting to change your identity."

I emphasized his final remark, for I saw it as a sign of hope. The end, which he added on waking, was really quite hopeful. After all, in the dream he expressed his terror of receiving something from me, but he also said "[he] didn't do anything to me."

The dream was analyzed in the course of several sessions, partly because it was a key dream showing his history and his identity crisis and partly, too, because after several days the patient was still under the impact of the nightmare. I pointed out that bringing the dream was a way of showing greater confidence in me; more precisely, it was proof of his confidence in me as an analyst capable of containing him with his nightmares and fears.

A week later Charles narrated a new dream. He had written a piece of music and taken it to his music teacher. He felt happy at having composed it, but his teacher made so many corrections that the composition was transformed into something quite different. In the end, only the corrections made by the music teacher were left. He was unhappy, for his own musical composition had disappeared. I asked him for clarification and more details of each of the different parts of the dream.

I interpreted the dream to be a continuation of the previous one about my transforming or changing his face. Here I was the teacher to whom he brought his thoughts and personal ideas. But he was afraid I was actually changing his ideas, probably mistaking an interpretation, which I gave him to stimulate his thinking, for corrections that would modify or do away with his way of thinking or, more important, modify his identity. This was the most urgent or important aspect of what was taking place in his transference relationship with me. He brought something that formed part of his own thinking or personal identity and thought that I corrected it or modified it, or that I ultimately turned him into a piece of me. He feared that when he left my consulting room he would not have his own thinking but the corrections—the personality and identity of Rosenfeld, his music teacher. The patient's associations confirmed the adequacy of this interpretive line.

For many weeks he fell back on the monotonous, repetitive obsessive language, devoid of emotion and abounding in empty, hollow words. In my notes at that time I wrote that, apart from conveying boredom and monotony, it included new elements: complaints and reproaches. This went on for several weeks until one day in the sixth month of treatment he brought a dream.

The dream seems to announce the return of a split or psychotic part. This is how the patient told it:

> I saw flying saucers coming closer from afar, from space. Extraterrestrial beings like those in the movie *E. T.* came down. I felt terrified when I saw the flying saucers coming closer from outer space and even more terrified when the extraterrestrial beings began to come near.

After asking him for clarification and associations, I interpreted the flying saucers and extraterrestrial beings to be an unknown part of himself that had been previously dissociated, projected far from him, into another galaxy or space far removed from his mind. I suggested it was a disturbed or crazy part that he could not recognize as his own.

The dream shows the mental functioning of his most regressed or disturbed part. This dream about extraterrestrial beings reappeared in treatment, but with a significant difference: as the extraterrestrial beings came closer, they were no longer terrifying and not so hostile. But this corresponded to the second version of the dream, not the first. The patient's mental dynamics seem to be as follows: Charles made massive splittings and projected those contents outside (Klein 1930, Segal 1988). The dream led to my feeling worried about the possible renewed invasion of the patient's mental apparatus by the psychotic part.

CLINICAL CONSIDERATIONS ABOUT THESE DREAMS

In the dream of the flying saucers, I chose to interpret the dynamics of the patient's inner world (the return of the parts of the self that had been projected). In the two other dreams I chose instead the transference dynamics. We might say that the fact that the patient can bring dreams to the session may be conceptualized as his first attempt at differentiating between inner world and outer world.

As regards the first dream (in which Charles is with his grandfather), we may assume that the patient thus brought his libidinal bond with his grandfather; perhaps he was looking for an affectionate, infantile bond.

We might try to compare the dream of the transformation of the face and the dream of the musical composition. In the former the patient expressed modification through his body; in the latter there was a more symbolic intermediary element. There, the musical score involves primitive verbal language (Avenburg 1992). The patient seemed to distance himself from his body, that is, he shifted to another level of representation. The first dream corresponded instead to a narcissistic or hypochondriacal level (Ahumada 1990, López 1985). In the dream of the body made of glass (when he visited his grandfather) there was a more obvious bodily fantasy, which may be a hypochondriacal fantasy.

EMBRACING THE FATHER

This stage was followed by many weeks during which Charles made detailed, obsessive remarks. On several occasions he brought copybooks in which he had written down his ideas—obsessive ruminations about a question, an idea, or a problem. On other occasions he read what he had written in the course of the psychotic episode. The patient came regularly to his sessions, often accompanied by one or another member of his family, but sometimes alone.

I interpreted his obsessive narrations as logical defenses against disorganization. One day, after a session in which he had managed to communicate well with me, Charles introduced some changes into his obsessive language or system. He told me he had felt weak while walking along the street and so he held on to his father's shoulder. "That frightened me a lot," he said. "After I had embraced Dad I felt paralyzed. My left foot became paralyzed." I interpreted, "You wanted to hold on to your Dad's shoulder, as a child would. The boy inside you wished to embrace Dad." I added,

"Perhaps you were so frightened because you thought that was something a boy would not do that you paralyzed a part of you that you regard as a female part." Later on in that session I interpreted, "It's as if inside you a boy had said, 'I want to be helped by Dad, that's all.' But you got frightened and so you paralyzed the female part that frightens you every time you come close to Dad or to a man. I, Rosenfeld, am a man, and perhaps what happened to you has to do with the fear of your coming close to me." It seemed to be clear that intense homosexual fantasies were expressed through bodily sensations. Another theoretical subject for discussion has to do with the analytic technique to interpret the emergence of sexual and hysterical levels that may coincide with pregenital levels in many patients. Yet another subject for theoretical discussion is the analyst's choice of the patient's developmental level he will interpret at that moment.

The rest of the session was devoted to showing Charles that his expression of affection toward his father was also a way of communicating with me, that he wanted to embrace me, to show me his affection, but this frightened him. I said that perhaps even thinking of me and remembering me with fondness outside the session might be experienced as frightening.

PSYCHOTIC EPISODE

During the week in which the patient became disorganized, his communication with me was characterized by greater emotion and affection. A few days before we had seen that he could embrace his father, an unusual show of affection that had shaken him.

One day the patient wondered out loud, "I asked my family therapist to kill me, then take my neck strongly." I told him again that what he actually wanted was to have someone kill the crazy part he had inside that was controlling him, but that he should take into account that he was asking a psychoanalyst to do it, both the previous night and at that moment. "Besides, what you want to kill is a part that believes it is a woman if it gets close to me, like when it got close to Dad and embraced him." Then I added, "But I will try to cure you with words. There's no need to kill the crazy and female parts."

In the last minutes of the session the patient recovered a new infantile memory. "Do you know something, Doctor? When I was a child they made me wear a tuxedo when the school kids had their birthday parties and sometimes I wore white gloves to go to the party so I wouldn't get dirty." Then he added, "I feel as if I were far from here, I feel stiff." I said to him, "It's as if every time you tell me something, you get frightened and end up drawing away, feeling that you're far away. It's as if you were repeating with me your own history with your Dad."

THE CRISIS

In the following sessions, the patient was connected to me. He seemed to be far more relaxed, his body less rigid, and he told me he had had sexual intercourse with his girlfriend. Then he said something strange had happened to him, bodily sensations he had never had before, and he had been frightened, "as if they were frightening sensations or coming from outside." He added, "It happened while I was having an orgasm during intercourse." (I want to clarify that the patient had never mentioned sexual feelings or intercourse up to that moment.) "The bodily sensations you have now," I told him, "are similar to the dream with the flying saucers and the extraterrestrial beings."

The following day Charles's parents phoned me to say the patient had become disorganized and was very "excited." Charles arrived at my consulting room that morning terrified and rigid, and said, "I'm delusional, I'm psychotic." *"I am being telepathically controlled."* "I have funny sensations and I'm crazy." "Out there in the street there are men who are half men and half women. . . . I'm delusional, I'm being telepathically controlled from outside and I feel funny things all over my body, they are making me feel funny things. . . ."

I told him to calm down, that over the previous days and in the last few sessions he had had good, affective communication with me, as perhaps he had never had before. "Perhaps that frightened you," I said. "You have a fantasy about me, a kind of delusion of what's happening to you with me here, and then you project that onto the street and you see what happens to you here in the others. What is happening is something that originates exclusively in your own emotions toward me and what you feel here with me. You've never had such intense affects because you've never allowed that to happen . . . or else you were a boy forced to disguise himself in a tuxedo, rigid all over and having to repress his affects. You think that when you show affection here that implies loss of mental control or some kind of madness. In addition, you imagine, you suppose, that you will turn into a woman if you are affectionate."

In the same session the patient moved the chair and placed his legs (he had his shoes on) on top of my desk, almost in front of my face. Then he put his feet down, walked round the consulting room, quite angry, took some earthenware dishes on which the flowerpots stood, and broke them violently against the floor.

Later on, after having broken some saucers, the patient said, "You are controlling me." And I interpreted, "You believe that this happens just when you remember or think about my interpretations after a session." I emphasized, "You believe that to receive my words is the same as to receive orders. That's why you feel that I'm telepathically controlling you from a distance. You think I am directing you telepathically and perhaps this is because there was a real story with your mother: she directed everything you did and you ended up thinking I would do the same with you." The patient answered, "If I receive an interpretation, then I become the interpretation."

In the evening his parents and the psychiatrist and psychoanalyst in charge of the family therapy got in touch with me and told me about what had happened that day in the course of the family therapy session. Charles was violent: he grabbed his neck and then tried to grab the psychiatrist by the neck. It was the first time he had attacked the psychiatrist physically. Faced with this violent reaction, the psychiatrist gave him an injection to tranquilize him, to which the patient did not object.

I was also told that in the course of that session the patient kept talking about "penises, phalluses, having sexual intercourse with his parents," and insistently repeated that he was "psychotic." In the conversation I had with his mother, she remarked that Charles saw "penises and men everywhere," as if he were having hallucinations. However, he appeared to be calm at that moment, thanks to the tranquilizer.

In his session with me early the following morning, Charles stated again that he was being influenced and that he was convinced that he was being telepathically directed and that outside, "in the street, men are half men and half women."

My interventions continued along the interpretative line adopted in the previous sessions. Then he spoke again about "penises and phalluses" and read to me from a book dealing with those subjects. He gave verbal expression to suicidal ideas, which led me to decide upon his immediate hospitalization. When the session was over, I explained to his parents in his presence that the repeated emergence of a suicidal idea led me to decide to hospitalize him.

HOSPITALIZATION

In the clinic I spent several hours with the patient to contain his anxiety and disorganization, but I also interpreted his fantasies as an analyst.

While we were walking to his room, Charles started expressing a delusional fantasy. He repeated again and again, "All this is a lie. You are not doctors and those people down there in the dining room are neither doctors nor patients."

When we got to his room, I sat down and Charles sat on the bed as if he were trying it. When he seemed to be feeling more relaxed, he opened the closet to put his clothes there; that reassured me because it meant that he had accepted staying at the clinic and his hospitalization. Suddenly something unexpected happened, something that shook me and the staff deeply.

When the patient opened the closet to put his clothes there, he took the hangers out and shouted: "You have lied to me. . . . I know that all the people down there are actors. This is the unquestionable evidence: this is the Ritz Hotel."

Deeply shaken, I jumped up. At the same time the doctor at the door came in because he had heard the shouting. The patient was beside himself but triumphant, for he had corroborated his delusional ideas and the omnipotence characteristic of psychosis. He took the hangers out and showed them to me, one by one. As a matter of fact, the hangers really belonged to the Ritz Hotel: the words "Ritz Hotel—Buenos Aires" were written on all of them.

It is hard for me to describe what took place between the moment when the patient saw the hangers and shouted his belief that he had seen his delusion of omnipotence confirmed by external evidence and the moment when the doctor came in and explained to Charles that a foreign patient had been in that room, someone who before his hospitalization had stayed at the Ritz Hotel and must have brought those hangers with him. The doctor repeated this explanation for approximately half an hour while Charles listened attentively. Later on, when he had calmed down a bit, we went through all the rooms in the clinic to show him the hangers in all the closets. Fortunately, the name of the clinic was written on all of them.

But the search for corroboration continued and at one moment he said that the woman he had seen in the dining room was not a patient and asked us to show us the rooms where the women were staying. The head nurse asked the female patients permission to show him the rooms and then told Charles he could see them. The patient became somewhat calmer.

I told him he needed to know that the female area, that is, his own female parts, was far away, not mixed with his own male part. I insisted he needed to corroborate that he would sleep with his male part, that is, in the men's area.

This was the shocking episode in which the patient thought he had found external evidence corroborating his psychotic omnipotence. We went back to his room and I stayed there to accompany him in accepting and elaborating his hospitalization. When I left, after a mutual "See you tomorrow," Charles asked me not to close the door between his room and the room of one of the clinic doctors.

THEORETICAL AND TECHNICAL REMARKS

My purpose in this chapter has been to show how I interpret and how I use theoretical models in psychoanalytic practice, that is, in the technique with a psychotic patient, and to describe my intense countertransference feelings in connection with him. In this particular case one important technical requisite had to be taken into account: the need to avoid being intrusive or invasive like the patient's mother.

With a patient who has had a delusional episode (my patient thought I was telepathically directing him) interpretations should not be rigidly stated but suggested in the interrogative, because he can take interpretative statements to be orders he has to carry out. For instance: "Do you think these flying saucers coming from outside could be a part of you? What do you think? Could it be something like that?"

Another technical aspect to be taken into account: the analyst has to be cautious and must avoid the early use of words the patient can distort and interpretations about the oedipal and sexual levels.

I suggest avoiding words that the patient may take as definitions of identity, accusations, or seductions. The use of the word "homosexual" may be risky when precociously made. At the beginning the therapist should say that the patient feels "weak or not very strong if he trusts the therapist," "he feels fragile" or "feminine" and so "less manly." Only after many months do I use the word homosexual, and only if the patient brings the obvious kind of material in a dream, a fantasy, or a delusion. The same applies to aggressive or murderous fantasies directed to the therapist or to the internal objects, paternal or maternal.

It is true that these elements (homosexuality and aggression) are there from the beginning of treatment, but I suggest that we must be very careful when interpreting them. I waited a long time before I made a direct interpretation of this patient's aggression and I did so only on the basis of a dream in which the patient crashed and damaged his mother's car. By the way, at that moment I learned that the car was in his mother's name. In the dream the patient was accompanied by a man.

It is important to note that throughout my analytic work with this patient I tried to bring together the fragmented, disperse, and projected aspects of the self, an extremely difficult task indeed.

The analyst makes a great effort to integrate his countertransference feelings with his thoughts and his theoretical background. As Schafer (1993) points out, we can very seldom leave behind all the theories in which we have been trained; we have our own internal map and we use it in the course of the analysis. I could add that we accept and use theories on the basis of our affects and our own life histories, and our infantile histories are probably as important as what we have learned from books and teachers. I accept theories and use them as an internal map, but I accept them on the basis of my affective and emotional background. Perhaps I have not learned from theories more than from my grandmother in order to construct a model and be able to listen to, understand, and think about a human being who is talking of his life and his feelings. I think my personal history determines the way in which I make use of my internal theoretical map.

I have tried to show how we can apply some of the theories we employ in the psychoanalytic treatment of patients whose transference shows regressed characteristics, also described as psychotic or delusional.

I believe theories do not change patients. They are valuable to explain psychopathology more or less richly or broadly. What theories do change is the explanation, but not the patient's actual pathology or his clinical picture.

I do believe that a valuable aspect of this chapter is the detailed clinical account and the way in which it shows the practical and technical use of theoretical models. Searles (1979) says that theories are useful or not depending on the moment the patient is going through. Green (1986) is another important author in the field of psychoanalytic theory and a clinician who has dealt with this question.

A true master in the investigation of severely disturbed or psychotic patients, Boyer (1982) says something very interesting about impasse situations and countertransference:

> The type of psychoanalytic impasse described above is due to a combination of factors which result in a specific kind of interaction between the patient's psychopathology and the analyst's ego ideal and self-representation. In each of the cited instances, the impasse was transient because the analysts were able to resolve the countertransference reactions which had created the impasses. The impasse arose in each instance because the analyst sought to remove his own discomfort by expecting the patient to change the manifestations of this psychopathology.
>
> The question can be raised whether it is inevitable that the analyst feel disturbed. Because of particular character adaptations, it may be necessary for the patient to seek to provoke certain reactions in the analyst as the transference relationship develops. But should the patient be allowed to succeed? If one were familiar with such situations and could anticipate them, perhaps it would be possible to simply analyze them without feeling personal upheaval. [p. 83]

In his contribution to *Master Clinicians*, Boyer (1990) deals with the developments of psychoanalytic technique in connection with countertransference. His view coincides with mine when he stresses the importance of using countertransference in the psychoanalytic treatment of severely regressed patients. I would like to stress once more that, in my view, the future of the investigation on psychotic or severely disturbed patients depends on two factors. The first is the therapist's personal ability to contain the intense affects and emotions aroused by this type of patient. The second is the detection and decoding of the messages the patient sends us through verbal means, nonverbal means, and communications systems of which we know very little as yet. These patients force us to experience intense emotions that they cannot feel or express with words. Our task as therapists is to decode them, in the course of supervision analysis or personal analysis, in order to be able to adequately discriminate the personal aspects from what is projected or communicated by the patients through different means.

I believe this hypothesis changes the theory of insight and mental space. In the treatment of psychotic patients insight sometimes takes place first in the therapist's mind and not in the patient's, because the patient's mental space may be projected onto the therapist's mind. This is part of a broader theory with which I try to account for the violence of schizophrenic patients. Sometimes these patients attack the therapist, hitting him or her violently and mercilessly because their perceptual apparatuses have been projected into the therapist's mind. What they attack, or actually try to murder, therefore, is their own perceptual apparatus placed in another space, in someone else's head, when they detect painful experiences they cannot tolerate.

The following quotation from Freud (1910) helps us to reflect nowadays, especially as regards the treatment of severely disturbed patients: "We have noticed that no psychoanalyst goes further than his own complexes and internal resistances permit . . ." (p. 145).

In this chapter countertransference is used in the sense of certain feelings, certain affects, that the therapist experiences when confronting facts specific to the transference field and to his or her emotional relationship with the patient. It is therefore a signal—just a signal—that needs to be decoded, reflected upon, and finally evaluated by the therapist to be better understood, and not projected. The therapist must try to translate into words the feelings evoked by the patient through preverbal language, or through the phonology or music of his or her voice. Above all, he or she must differentiate these feelings from personal neurotic problems.

Countertransference is a phenomenon that can shed light on certain elements of clinical psychoanalysis if it is kept in mind during all investigations. In my opinion it is an indispensable tool, especially for very perturbed or psychotic patients.

> Occasionally it may fail to express itself overtly as a fact or a phenomenon, and stems from an a priori methodological definition of our objectives. If we take black-and-white pictures, we might say that colour does not exist; but, of course, colour pictures also exist. The same happens with the greater richness provided by the proper use of countertransference. [Rosenfeld 1992, p. 83]

REFERENCES

Abraham, K. (1908). The psycho-sexual differences between hysteria and dementia praecox. In *Selected Papers of Karl Abraham,* trans. D. Bryan and A. Strachey, pp. 64–79. London: Hogarth.

——— (1911). Notes on the psycho-analytical investigation and treatment of manic-depressive insanity and allied conditions. In *Selected Papers of Karl Abraham,* trans. D. Bryan and A. Strachey, pp. 137–156. London: Hogarth.

——— (1916). The first pregenital stage of the libido. In *Selected Papers of Karl Abraham,* trans. D. Bryan and A. Strachey, pp. 248–279. London: Hogarth.

Ahumada, J. (1990). On narcissistic identification and the shadow of the object. *International Review of Psycho-Analysis* 17:177–187.

Avenburg, R. (1992). Personal communication.

Boyer, L. B. (1982). Analytic experiences in work with regressed patients. In *Technical Factors in the Treatment of the Severely Disturbed Patient,* ed. P. L. Giovacchini and L. B. Boyer, pp. 65–106. New York: Jason Aronson.

——— (1990). Countertransference and technique. In *Master Clinicians:*

On Treating the Regressed Patient, ed. L. B. Boyer and P. L. Giovacchini, pp. 303–324. Northvale, NJ: Jason Aronson.

Freud, S. (1910). Future prospects in psycho-analytic therapy. *Standard Edition* 11:139–151.

——— (1912). The dynamics of the transference. *Standard Edition* 12:97–108.

——— (1940a). Splitting of the ego in the process of defense. *Standard Edition* 23:271–278.

——— (1940b). An outline of psycho-analysis. *Standard Edition* 23:141–207.

Green, A. (1986). *On Private Madness*. New York: International Universities Press.

Kernberg, O. (1979). Technical considerations in the treatment of borderline personality organization. In *Advances in Psychotherapy of the Borderline Patient*, ed. J. Le Boit and A. Capponi, pp. 269–305. New York: Jason Aronson.

——— (1992). *Aggression in Personality Disorders and Perversions*. New Haven, CT: Yale University Press.

Klein, M. (1930). The psychotherapy of the psychoses. In *Love, Guilt and Reparation and Other Works 1921–1945*, pp. 233–235. London: Karnac, 1975.

López, B. (1985). Una distorsión semántico pragmática: El paciente del discurso ininterrumpido. *Revista de Psicoanálisis (APdeBA)* 7:279–300.

Ogden, T. (1986). *The Matrix of the Mind: Object Relations and the Psychoanalytic Dialogue*. Northvale, NJ: Jason Aronson.

Rosenfeld, D. (1992). *The Psychotic Aspects of the Personality*. London: Karnac Books.

Rosenfeld, H. (1979). Transference psychosis in the borderline. In *Advances in Psychotherapy of the Borderline Patient*, ed. J. Le Boit and A. Capponi, pp.485–510. New York: Jason Aronson.

——— (1987). *Impasse and Interpretation*. London: Tavistock.

Schafer, R. (1993). Personal communication.

Searles, H. (1979). *Countertransference and Related Subjects*. New York: International Universities Press.

Segal, H. (1988). *Introduction to the Work of Melanie Klein*. London: Karnac.

8

The Political Psyche: A Challenge to Therapists and Clients to Politicize What They Do

Andrew Samuels

WHAT SHALL WE DO ABOUT POLITICS?

This chapter explores how the practice of psychotherapy might be politicized so that therapists and analysts who seek to work with the whole person, including the social and political dimensions of the experiences of their clients, may do so with greater confidence and clarity. I do not focus much on the political dynamics of the therapy encounter itself, and hardly at all on the politics of the profession, though both remain concerns of mine. Rather, I intend to present some ideas about the relationship between therapy practice and politics as one small step to realizing the century-old project of depth psychology to shed light on what Freud referred to as "the riddles of the world."

By "politics" I mean the concerted arrangements and struggles within an institution, or in a single society, or between countries, for the organization and distribution of power, especially economic power. On a more personal level, there is a second kind of politics. Here, political power reflects struggles over agency, meaning the ability a person has to choose freely whether to act and what action to take in a given situation. This is often feeling-level politics, a politics of subjectivity, a politics to which feminism introduced us.

But politics also refers to a crucial interplay between the public and the personal dimensions of power. There are connections between economic power and power as expressed on the domestic, private level. Power is a process or network as much as a stable factor. This version of political power is experienced psychologically in family organization, in gender and race relations, and in religious and artistic assumptions as they affect the lives of individuals.

Where the public and the private, the political and the personal, intersect, I think there is a special role for analysis and psychotherapy in relation to political change and transformation. But there would be little point in working on the orientation of psychotherapy to the world of politics if its own basic theories and practices remained completely unaltered. I support the continuing practice of therapy and analysis with individuals and small group because I do not agree that analysis and therapy inevitably syphon off rage that might more constructively be deployed in relation to social injustices. In fact, I think that it is the reverse that often happens: experiences in therapy act to fine down generalized rage into a more constructive form, hence rendering emotion more accessible for social action. Even when this does not happen, the potential remains for a move from private therapy to public action.

The idea is to develop a portrayal of the clinical setting as a bridge between psychology or psychotherapy and politics rather than as the source of isolation from politics. Critics of the clinical project of depth psychology (e.g., Hillman and Ventura 1992) have noted the isolation—and this is not a totally wrong observation.

But I want us also to see the potential links and to create a truly radical revisioning of clinical work and not a simplistic huffing and puffing aimed at its elimination.

One of the most potent criticisms of therapy and analysis is that the client is encouraged or even required to turn away from external concerns—for example, political commitments—and focus exclusively on the "inner world." This, it is argued, makes any statement about therapy engaging the whole person an absolute nonsense. Textbooks of therapy and analysis accentuate the introspection by making it clear that exploration of outer-world issues is simply not done in "proper" therapy and analysis.

Over a period of time, I sensed that this professional consensus was collapsing and that therapists and analysts were indeed beginning to pay more attention to what could be called the political development of their clients (see below). In my own practice I noticed that many clients seemed to be introducing political themes more often than they had before. Talking to colleagues confirmed this was also going on in their work. We tended to put it down to the fact that since the mid-1980s the pace of political change in the world appeared to have quickened. At times I still felt that the usual formulation—that such material needs to be understood as symbolic of what is going on in the client—worked pretty well. At other times it turned out that clients had a need to talk about some public issue, maybe to work out what their true feelings and opinions were. But they might also have learned that you're not supposed to do that in therapy or analysis. For example, during the Gulf War there were certainly some clients who used war imagery to tell me something abut their inner state. Yet others hid a profound need to talk abut the Gulf War behind the flow of regular, ordinary clinical material.

I decided that what was needed was a large-scale investigation, by means of a questionnaire, to see if analysts and therapists were experiencing something similar in significant numbers. I therefore obtained the cooperation of fourteen professional organizations with differing theoretical orientations in seven different countries and sent out 2000 survey forms. I got a return rate of almost exactly one-third (quite high for a cold-calling survey on which the respondents had to spend some time and write fairly lengthy and thoughtful answers). The American psychoanalytic organizations involved were the National Psychological Association for Psychoanalysis and the San Francisco Psychoanalytic Institute.

Among many other questions, I asked the participants how they reacted to, handled, or interpreted the material. Seventy-eight percent of the respondents mentioned that they understood the material as referring in some sense to reality. For many, this was in conjunction with a symbolic interpretation or an exploration of why the client was interested in that particular theme at that particular moment. The replies, thoughtful and extensive, showed the respondents' considerable struggle as they endeavored to mark out their positions.

I went on to ask if the respondent "discussed" politics with his or her clients. Of course I realized the explosive nature of the question and deliberately did not define what might be covered by the word "discuss." Worldwide, 56 percent said they did discuss politics and 44 percent said they did not. American Jungian analysts do the most discussing (72 percent) and British psychoanalysts the least (33 percent). However, it is interesting to note that one-third of the British psychoanalysts admit to discussing politics with clients.

I asked the respondents the obvious question: Have you ever been/are you politically active? Sixty-seven percent said they had been politically active at some time—a figure that, unsurprisingly, has dropped to 33 percent at the present time. My intuitive impression, just from talking to colleagues, that a good deal of them had been politically active at some time was borne out. The stereotype of a profession composed of introspective, introverted, self-indulgent types was challenged.

So what might it all mean? It could mean that the profession is divided about politics in the session. Even if everyone who did not return the survey forms were absolutely purist, there would still be a significant minority of practitioners who are not. This other, hitherto unknown, group of clinicians sees that involvement in and concern for the world is part of growing up, of individuation, and maybe even part of mental health. The split in the therapy profession is probably at its most destructive when it is between the public, apolitical, hyperclinical face of the profession—which has quite rightly been criticized—and a much more politically aware private face of the profession. Many therapists and analysts seem all too conscious that they are citizens too, that they have political histories themselves, that they too struggle to find the balance between inner-looking and outer-looking attitudes.

The survey on political material brought to the clinical setting was not a scientific instrument, and not even a conventional social scientific instrument. Nevertheless, several eminent social scientists have kindly commented that my methodology not only resembles certain cutting-edge practices in social science ("naturalistic research") but was appropriate to my project. The survey has been published in a leading sociology journal (Samuels 1994). Hence, I hope that discussion of the survey will not focus only on issues of methodology and detract from its utility as background material for what follows (see Samuels 1993 for a fuller account of the research).

POLITICIZING THERAPY PRACTICE

When attempting to link psychoanalysis or psychotherapy with political and social issues, we need to establish a two-way street. In one direction travel men and women of the psyche, bringing what they know of human psychology to bear on the crucial political and social issues of the day, such as leadership, the market economy, nationalism, racial prejudice, and environmentalism. Going the other way down this street, we try to get at the hidden politics of personal life broadly conceived and understood: the politics of early experience in the family, gender politics, and the politics of internal imagery, usually regarded as private. The dynamic that feminism worked upon between the personal and the political is also a dynamic between the psychological and the social. It is so complicated that to reduce it in either one direction (all psyche) or the other direction (all sociopolitical), or to assert a banal, holistic synthesis that denies difference between these realms, is massively unsatisfactory. There is a very complicated interplay, and this chapter trades off the energy in that interplay. One hope is to develop a new, hybrid language of psychology and politics that will help us to contest conventional notions of what "politics" is and what the "political" might be. The aspirations of so many disparate groups of people worldwide—environmentalists, human rights activists, liberation theologians, feminists, pacifists and peacemakers, ethnopoliticians—for a reinvented and resacralized politics would gain the support of the psychological and psychotherapy communities.

It is worthwhile to focus on therapy and clinical work for two main reasons. First, the results of the survey show that this is a hot issue for practitioners just now. Second, exploring the politicization of practice might help to answer an awkward question: Why has the political world not shown up for its first session with the therapists who are so keen to treat it? Freud, Jung, and the great humanistic pioneers like Maslow and Rogers truly wanted to engage with the institutions and problems of society. But they, and even more so their followers, did this in such an on-high, experience-distant, mechanical fashion, with the secret agenda of proving their own theories correct, that the world has been, quite rightly, suspicious. Objecting to psychological reductionism in relation to politics and society is reasonable—not resistance. But what if clinical experience were factored in? At the very least there would be a rhetorical utility. For, without their connection to the clinic, to therapy, why should anyone in the world of politics listen to the psychotherapeutic people at all? What do we have to offer if it doesn't include something from our therapy work? Therapy is certainly not all we have to offer, but it is the base.

The professional stakes are very high. In certain sectors of humanistic and transpersonal psychology, clinical work is becoming more overtly politicized so that the whole client may be worked with. But this is still very much a minority view in the psychodynamic and psychoanalytic sectors of psychotherapy. Politically speaking, most clinical practice constitutes virgin territory. The stakes are so high because people like me are trying to change the nature of the field, change the nature of the profession—what we profess, believe, and do. As the survey showed, this attempt is part of a worldwide movement in which the general tendency is to extend the nature of the psychotherapy field so as to embrace the social and political dimensions of experience.

If we want to treat the whole person, as some of us do, then we have to find detailed ways of making sure that the social and political dimensions of experience are included in the therapy process regularly, reliably, and as a matter of course. We must try to achieve a situation in which the work is political always—not unusually, not exceptionally, not only when it is done by mavericks, but when it is done in an everyday way by Everytherapist.

The detailed work is not easy to do. About seven years ago a remarkable book appeared, entitled *Psychoanalysis and the Nuclear Threat: Clinical and Theoretical Studies* (Levine et al. 1988). All the editors and all the contributors were the most *echt*, kosher psychoanalysts one could find—in fact they were all members of the American Psychoanalytic Association. In the editorial introduction it is argued that the destructive potential of nuclear weapons means that politics must enter the analytic space and that a "politically neutral analytic setting may be a fantasy, one that embodies the wish that the outside can be ignored, denied, or wished away" (p. x).

In a basically favorable review of this book, psychoanalyst and social critic Alexander Gralnick (1990) stated:

> Unfortunately, few of the contributors to the theoretical part of the book deal with the many important assumptions and unsettled issues in psychoanalytic thought and clinical practice that the editors hoped consideration of the nuclear threat would prompt them to discuss. . . . Though bound by traditional concepts, some authors seemed to recognize that psychoanalysts may not be as neutral as they believe them-

> selves to be. . . . These psychoanalysts are plagued by their own resistances and anxieties about the further changes they face and how creative they dare be; they are naturally limited by being at *the earliest stages* of changes we all face, and, like the rest of us, are *handicapped by lack of a needed new language.* [pp.72–73, emphasis added]

I too am at the earliest stages of this, and I too am handicapped by the lack of a much-needed new language. These thoughts and speculations are my best shot.

I will discuss and propose the politicization of therapy practice under the following headings: (1) the therapeutic value of political discussion in the session; (2) exploring the political myth of the person in therapy; (3) the hidden politics of internal, private imagery; and (4) working out a socialized, transpersonal psychology of community.

However, as this project has developed, I have found it useful at the outset to attempt to deal with or at least discuss the objections to what is being proposed. In this way readers are alerted to my own awareness of the radical and often risky nature of these ideas. Moreover, dealing first with the objections resembles good psychoanalytic technique whereby resistance is analyzed before content. Of course, the objections are not only resistances, and I am convinced that an ongoing engagement with objections (and objectors) to the politicization of therapy practice is beneficial for all sides in the debate.

The first objection is that removing the focus of the clinical enterprise away from the internal world and onto the political world constitutes bad clinical practice. The reply to this objection can be equally assertive. Foreclosure on politics, the privileging and valorizing of the internal over the external, may, as we stagger toward the end of the century, constitute bad clinical practice. From today's perspective, maybe I want or need to do some bad practice as I change my practice. Those who do not or cannot change their practices may, from tomorrow's point of view, be the ones guilty of bad practice. What is or is not "in" in clinical technique has evolved strikingly over the psychoanalytic century. These matters are *not* definitively settled.

The second objection concerns the problem of suggestion and undue influence on the part of the therapist. This is a sensitive issue these days, given the moral panic surrounding psychotherapy stemming from the notion of false memory syndrome. Is there a risk that a politicized therapy practitioner will foist his or her own political ideas, principles, and values onto the vulnerable, open-to-suggestion client? Would not that be a shattering objection to the politicization of therapy? In reply, I would ask if we are really supposed to believe that a practitioner who sticks to the way he or she was trained and keeps the political out of the consulting room is thereby devoid of the sin of ever suggesting anything to the patient or client. Many studies show that an enormous amount of influencing by the therapist of the client goes on and in fact may be essential for some kind of psychological movement to happen. At times even Freud equates transference and suggestion, making a defensive point that also serves me well: you cannot suggest something into somebody unless they are ready for it, unless it "tallies" with what is already alive in them. I would use Freud against the objection. Suggestion is going on already. There is no reason to suppose that a politicized practitioner would necessarily be intruding his or her own values more than somebody whose interest was in object relations, sexuality, aggression, spirituality, or the soul.

Of course, there is always a risk of discipleship in the analytical situation, as those who have had training analyses know. But I feel confident in saying that there is a huge amount of uncritically accepted suggestion in analytical practice today and that, from a certain point of view, the more "bounded," "contained," and "disciplined" the behavior of the practitioner, the more suggestion is taking place in his or her practice. I think this is inevitable. The technical rules of analysis are not politically or culturally neutral; they do more than "facilitate" the unfolding of the self. They have cultured depth psychology in a permanent way and have done it to a certain extent by suggestion. Based on the replies received to the questionnaire on political material that is brought to the consulting room, it is clear that a good deal of rule breaking goes on in ordinary therapy and analysis—probably much more than is revealed in supervision, wherein words like "discussion" are dirty words. If psychotherapists and analysts are already discussing politics with the client, then it is clear that the hygienic sealing of the consulting room from politics is a virginal fantasy on the part of practitioners.

The third objection concerns what is to be done when the therapist is confronted with somebody with political views he or she finds repulsive. Discussing my ideas at a meeting of the British Association of Psychotherapists, I was once asked: "What would happen if Hitler came into your consulting room?" Well, psychodynamically speaking, I think I have seen quite a few Hitler-types in my consulting room already. Although this point cannot settle the very real worries that working with somebody whose views you find repulsive creates, surely as we agree that, from time to time, every practitioner will meet a version of this problem. Moreover, politics is not the only source of repulsion.

A fourth objection concerns the alleged elitism of what I am proposing. Do I have some kind of fantasy that we are going to send a well-analyzed vanguard of the psychopolitical revolution out into the world? Of course I have had that fantasy from time to time but, in a more moderate vein, and in terms of developing an argument about changing the field, I do not for one minute think that a person who has had psychological analysis or therapy is in some kind of elite vanguard. However, as indicated, I do recognize that there is some strength in this objection, and I try to stay conscious of the problem.

The fifth objection is extremely subtle and hence difficult to deal with. This objector claims that he or she is carrying out a political therapy practice already. Sometimes I feel this is undoubtedly the case. At other times, when I am told that the mere practice of therapy, or even just the making of interpretations, are political acts, I must demur. Similarly, when it is blandly observed that all of inner life obviously involves the outer world, including politics, and there's no point in going on about it, I feel I need to know about the fate of the outer world in therapy done by the objector. I think it is a sign of the times that many practitioners do not want to admit to working oblivious to the world of politics. The rules of the game are changing. And, as the survey shows, it is clear that many people are trying to work in a more politically attuned way. But the mere recognition that inner and outer are connected cannot constitute a politicization of practice. This is a difficult objection to engage with, being told that politicizing practice is all old hat and that everyone is doing it. It injures the narcissism of the pioneer!

A sixth objection concerns the scope and timing of political work in therapy. I am often asked if these ideas are applicable to every client. Of course, they are not. There is a further question in connection with timing, and it is certainly important to wait and see where the client is headed. This is easy to say but I think there may be a smear in the way this objection is sometimes posed in that the not-so-secret intent is to characterize political work as inappropriate and likely to be done in a clumsy way. Sometimes a politicized therapist will mistime or misplace his or her interventions. But therapists often take ideas derived from object relations or archetypal theory or psychosexuality and make use of them in situations where these ideas turn out to be woefully inappropriate and irrelevant. It happens all the time and it is not meant as damaging to the client. Somehow "politics" is singled out as more likely to lead to such an abuse of the client.

While there is little doubt that a client's political action outside therapy can be defensive or resistant, this is surely not always the case. Sometimes, when working with politically active clients, there has come a move from within the client to withdraw from politics for a while—and this is, of course, respected. Nevertheless, we might perhaps question the psychoanalytic (or maybe the bourgeois) depreciation of action in general and political action in particular. Political action is psychologically valid, positive and creative. Not to act would sometimes constitute a special form of repression—one supported by the institutions of therapy and analysis themselves.

These six objections need to be taken seriously and I think I have taken them seriously. I have tried to suggest where there is some mileage in them, and where I think a firm reply can be made.

THE THERAPEUTIC VALUE OF POLITICAL DISCUSSION

For the first of my positive proposals, concerning the therapeutic value of political discussion in the session, I will bring in the experiences of important practitioners who sought to politicize the practices of their own fields.

The German dramatist Bertolt Brecht conceived of the idea of a politicized theater and developed a whole body of practices to go with that notion. Some of his practices, which constitute a sort of Brechtian clinical theory, are relevant to psychotherapy. For example, consider his well-known idea of the alienation effect, or distanciation effect. Via certain technical theatrical devices, the audience is encouraged to step back and to distance itself from the drama on stage to apperceive more clearly what the social, political, and economic dynamics of the drama are. The intention is that the audience should not only *identify* emotionally with the characters in the play but should also try to understand and analyze what those characters are doing. Brecht replaces involvement in theater with what I would call *ex*volvement. In psychotherapy it is possible to conceive of a therapeutic situation in which therapist and client get *ex*volved, without worrying that this could be a transgression of the principle that requires maximum emotional involvement and identification with the issues being processed in the therapy. Brechtian exvolvement serves, in very general terms, as a helpful model for the introduction of political discussion in the session as a therapeutic tool.

Another parallel is even more pertinent, and it concerns certain developments in feminist art practice, in particular what could be described as the framing of the everyday. For example, in

1976 the feminist conceptual artist Mary Kelly produced a work, which became notorious, called "Post Partum Document." This was a record of her evolving relationship with her son over the first few years of his life. The part that everybody remembers, and on which I will concentrate, was the first room of "Post Partum Document" in which the only works on show were the feces- and urine-stained diaper liners of this little boy, backed by white vellum, well-framed, and hung on the walls of the Hayward Gallery in London. The condition of the diaper liner showed how ill or healthy the baby (or his bowels) was at any one moment. Kelly could thereby track and comment upon her "success" as a mother. The irony and political pointedness were deliberate.

A similar art work created by Cate Elwes in 1979 was called "Menstruation." Seated on a clear Perspex stool in a clear Perspex booth in a white, diaphanous dress with no underwear or sanitary towels during the time of her period, she would allow the menstrual blood to flow, to stain the garment, all the while dialoguing with an audience that surrounded this booth about what the wider implications of her female bodily processes were, what they meant to her, and about what the audience thought was going on.

Mentioning these art works is not intended to start a discussion about conceptual and feminist art. But these works worked because the ordinary was framed, whether in the traditional frame of a picture, in which the artist puts a stained diaper liner, or by the frame of the Perspex booth, in which a bleeding woman stains her garments before spectators and discusses it with them. My argument is that political discussion within the therapy frame will be different from ordinary political discussion in a bar, livingroom, or workplace. Just as menstruation, framed in the way I described, ceases to be menstruation and becomes conceptual art with an impact in the cultural sphere, so, too, a discussion of politics in a therapy situation, which if transcribed would look ordinary, takes on a wholly other significance. Contained within the therapy vessel or frame (itself a therapy term), the ordinary becomes something other and enters the psychological processes of therapist and client in a way that may be profoundly unsettling, possibly clarifying, and occasionally transformative. If we seek to explore the meaning and relevance of the political for ourselves and our clients, then an espousal of political discussion, in which the therapist has to make all the usual therapist decisions about his or her degree of involvement, openness, and the timing, is one way to proceed. Perhaps it is necessary to try it to see what happens. For a practitioner reading this who already discusses politics with clients, maybe these thoughts will help to theorize what is currently being done on an intuitive or ethical basis. There are simply no books or articles about the matter.

THE POLITICAL MYTH OF THE PERSON

The next proposal concerns what I call the political myth of the person. Is there such a thing as a person's political development? Just as we refer to psychological development generally, or people talk about how they have or have not developed over a lifetime, there might be a way of approaching politics on the personal level that can make use of the idea of development without getting hooked up on linear, normative, and mechanistic notions of development.

How does the political person grow and develop? An individual person lives not only his or her life but also the life of the times. Jung told his students that when you treat the individual you treat the culture. Persons cannot be seen in isolation from the society and culture that has played a part in forming them—as much feminist thinking has demonstrated.

Once we see that there is a political person who has developed over time, we can start to track the political history of that person—the way the political events of his or her lifetime have impacted on the forming of their personality. So we have to consider the politics a person has inherited, so to speak, from their family, class, ethnicity, religion, and nationality—not forgetting the crucial elements of their sex and sexual orientation. Sometimes people take on their parents' politics; equally often, people reject what their parents stood for. Social class often functions within the unconscious and sometimes I have found that it is the social-class issues of the socially mobile client's parents that are truly significant.

But all this is a bit too rational. If there is something inherently political about humans—and most people think there is—then maybe the politics a person has cannot be explained only by social inheritance. Maybe there is an accidental, constitutional, fateful, and inexplicable element to think about. Maybe people are just born with different amounts and kinds of political energy in them.

If that is so, then there would be implications both for individuals and for our approach to politics. What will happen if a person with a high level of political energy is born to parents with a low level of it (or vice versa)? What if the two parents have vastly different levels from each other? What is the fate of a person with a high level of political energy born into an age and a culture that does not value such a high level, preferring to reward lower levels of political energy? The answers to such questions not only shape a person's political myth but affect the shape and flavor of the political scene in his or her times.

The questions can get much more intimate. Did your parents foster or hinder the flowering of your political energy and your political potential? How did you develop the politics you have at this moment? In which direction are your politics moving, and why? I do not think these questions are currently on either a mainstream or an alternative political agenda. Nor are they on the agenda of many therapists or analysts.

My interest is not in what might be called political maturity. No such universal exists, as evidenced by different commentators evaluating the same group as "terrorists" or "freedom fighters." My interest is in how people got where they are politically and, above all, in how they think, feel, explain, and communicate about how they got to where they are politically—hence my reference to the political myth of the person. From a psychological angle, it often turns out that people are not actually where they thought they were politically, or that they got there by a route they did not know about.

In therapy we can explore how the client got to where he or she is politically and, above all, how *the clients think, feel, explain, and communicate about how they got to where they are politically*—a subjective narrative of political development. We ask how a person *became* a Manhattan liberal, not whether being a Manhattan liberal is a good thing in itself—while not denying that we have a viewpoint about Manhattan liberals. Moreover, not all Manhattan liberals became Manhattan liberals in the same way. We want to know how Manhattan liberals have experienced their becoming Manhattan liberals.

When a client describes his or her political experiences, in the sense of formative or crucial political experiences, an analyst or therapist would listen with the same mix of literal and metaphorical understanding with which he or she would listen to any kind of clinical material—but with the ideas of political myth and political development in mind as permanent heuristic presences. Sometimes the most productive path to follow would be to accept the client's account of his or her political history. At other times what the client says may be understood as image, symbol, and metaphor; at still other times, as defensive and/or distorted. Sometimes it will be a mélange of these ways of understanding; sometimes a tension or competition may exist between them. In a sense, all of this moves us toward a conception of what could be called the "psychological citizen."

The implications for depth psychology of taking in these ideas about political development could be profound. In 1984 I suggested to my fellow members of the training committee of a psychotherapy organization that we should start to explore with candidates something about their political development—its history, roots, antecedents, patterns, vicissitudes, and current situation—just as we looked into sexuality, aggression, and spiritual or moral development. At that time the idea was regarded as a bit way-out, but more recently it has evoked a favorable response.

Similarly, if political and social factors are part of personality and psychological development, should not analysts and therapists explore those areas in initial interviews with prospective clients?

Incidentally, here, as so often, I have found that what looks like new theory is really only a necessary theorization of cutting-edge practice. In the survey, when I asked the respondents to say something abut their own political histories and what had influenced their own political development, they tended to cover the same ground I have covered in this section of the chapter, though with very wide linguistic, conceptual, and hermeneutic variations.

Why do I refer to political "development"? Might this not be rather conservative from an intellectual standpoint? There are now numerous books on "moral development," "spiritual development," "religious development." "The development of personality" is a well-researched and much argued-over field. So the general idea of development seems to be in the Zeitgeist. The idea of development is obviously intended to be applied as nonnormatively, nonjudgmentally, and nonpositivistically as possible, though it will be as well for me to admit immediately that my own personal political beliefs and values will enter the picture and help to bring a kind of hierarchy into play. This is absolutely unavoidable, but I do not believe that my having beliefs and values of my own makes me any less neutral than or different from theorists in the fields of moral, spiritual, religious, and personality development who undoubtedly have moral, spiritual, religious, and psychological positions of their own to defend and privilege.

THE HIDDEN POLITICS OF PRIVATE, INTERNAL IMAGERY

The Image of the Parents in Bed

My first proposal about the hidden politics of private, internal imagery concerns the primal scene—the image of the intimate relationship between father and mother, whether in bed or not. I have suggested on several occasions that primal scene imagery functions as a kind of psychic fingerprint or trademark. Now I want to extend that idea in a political direction, to argue that the kind of image held of the parents' relationship demonstrates, on the intrapsychic level, a person's capacity to sustain conflict constructively in the outer world—a crucial aspect of the person's political capacity. In the image of mother and father in one frame, the scene can be harmonious or disharmonious; one side may dominate the other side; one parent could be damaging the other parent. There will be patterns of exclusion, triumph, defeat, curiosity, or total denial. These great and well-known primal scene themes are markedly political. How they work out in the patient tells us something about that patient's involvement and investment in political culture and his or her capacity to survive therein.

I see the primal scene as *a self-generated diagnostic monitoring of the person's psychopolitical state at any moment.* The level of political development is encapsulated in the primal scene image. This is why images and assessments of the parental marriage change so much in the course of an analysis. The parental marriage is not what changes in the majority of instances; nor is it merely an increase in consciousness on the part of the patient that makes the image change. The image changes because the patient's inner and outer political styles and attitudes are changing. The specificity of the image communicates what the new styles might be. The parents stand for a *process* as well as for particular attributes and capacities.

The experience of primal scene imagery may be additionally understood as an individual's attempt to function politically, coupling together into a unified whole his or her diverse psychic elements and agencies *without* losing their special tone and functioning—a sort of universalism versus multiculturalism on an individual level. What does the image of the copulating parents tell us about the political here-and-now of the client? The image of the parents in bed refers to an unconscious, pluralistic engagement by the client with all manner of sociopolitical phenomena and characteristics, many of which appear to him or her as so unlikely to belong together (to be bedfellows) that they are opposites, just as mother and father, female and male, passive and active sexual partners, are said to be opposites, or whites and blacks, Israelis and Palestinians, Catholics and Protestants, or rich and poor are regarded as irreconcilable political opposites.

Thus the question of the image of the parents in bed as a harmonious coming together of conflicting opposites can be worked on in more detail, according to the degree and quality of differentiation a person makes between the images of mother and father. A primal scene only becomes fertile when the elements are distinguishable. In plain language, it's not a *stuck* image of parental togetherness that we see in a fertile primal scene, but something divided and unstuck, hence vital, or as well as linked, hence politically imaginable. The psyche (society) is trying to express its multifarious and variegated nature (multiculturalism) and also its oneness and integration (universalism). Primal scene images can perform this pluralistic job perfectly and the message they carry concerns how well the job is going. Via primal scene imagery, the psyche is expressing the patient's pluralistic capacity to cope with the unity *and* the diversity of the political situation he or she is in. As Aristotle said, "Similars do not a state make."

I do not think that the reproductive heterosexuality of the primal scene should be taken as excluding people of homosexual orientation. Far from it: I am convinced that the fruitfulness signified in the primal scene, and the problems therein, are completely congruent with homosexual experience. I also think that there is a set of cultural and intellectual assumptions that need to be explicated. Why is it that psychological fecundity, variety, and liveliness do not yet get theorized in homosexual terms? Why is psychological maturity still envisaged in a form of complementary wholeness that requires heterosexual imagery for it to work at all? Why do we not refer to a conjunction of *similars*? One could easily defend the thesis that heterosexual primal scene imagery works quite happily for persons of a homosexual orientation by recourse to metaphor, saying that primal scene heterosexuality refers not to the fact of reproduction but to the symbol of diversity, otherness, conflict, potential. Similarly, one could also point out that, since everyone is the result of a heterosexual union, heterosexual symbolism is simply inevitable and not excluding of a homosexual orientation. But I am dubious about these liberal maneuvers because they still leave a question mark in my mind concerning the absence of texts replete with *homosexual imagery that would perform the psychological and political functions of primal scene imagery.* We might begin a search for the homosexual primal scene. Though this idea may sound controversial, it merely involves a recognition that the primal scene is about processes and functions and not about the actual parents. Hence the proposition that there could be a primal scene couched in gay or lesbian imagery will only cause problems to homophobic members of the psychotherapy world. We know by now how much psychoanalytic theory about homosexuality is little more than dressed-up prejudice, marching in step with the moral majority.

Personal narratives of primal scene imagery, and their working through, demonstrates to a considerable extent a person's capacity to sustain political conflict constructively. This general point about politics becomes more pertinent when applied to the professional politics of the field of depth psychology. Stuck parental imagery fits the field's symptoms of intolerance, fantasies of superiority, and difficulties with hearing the views of others. If depth psychology's primal scene imagery could be prodded into vigorous motion, perhaps by active ideological dialogue, I would feel more optimistic about its future.

The example I will give of these ideas concerning political readings of primal scene imagery is the well-known general problem of *not being able to imagine the parents' sexual life at all*, or of having a bland and nonerotic image of it. Clearly, denial and repression play important parts in this, but my argument will be that to restrict our understanding to these personal ego–defense mechanisms is to cut ourselves off from the plenitude of collective and public meanings in primal scene imagery.

Before discussing the "nonprimal scene," I want to say something further about why the primal scene is so important for politics. One particular reason for choosing to focus on the primal scene is that we are then invited to address the conventional twinning of man with active and woman with passive sexual behavior. This twinning both reflects and, I think, inspires many gender divisions. When individuals access and work on their primal scene imagery, often in fantasy or via the transference in analysis, it is remarkable that the conventional male-active/female-passive divide does *not* invariably appear. In fact, it often seems as if the unconscious "intention" of the sexual imagery associated with the primal scene is to challenge that particular definition of the differences between men and women. The challenge to the sexual status quo symbolizes a kind of secret challenge to the political status quo.

From the standpoint of gender politics, this discussion of the political relevance of a primal scene enables us to introduce the mother in a transmogrified and politicized form: as an active player in the sexual game, and hence, potentially, an active player in the political game.

Here I am reminded of the Midrashic story of Lilith. She was, as readers will recall, the first consort of Adam, and was created from the earth at the same time as Adam. She was unwilling to give up her equality and argued with Adam over the position in which they should have intercourse—Lilith insisting on being on top. "Why should I lie beneath you," she argued, "when I am your equal since both of us were created from dust?" But when Lilith saw that Adam was determined to be on top, she called out the magic name of God, rose into the air, and flew away. Eve was then created. Lilith's later career as an evil she-demon who comes secretly to men in the night (hence being responsible for nocturnal emissions) and as a murderer of newborns culminated, after the destruction of the temple, in a relationship with God as a sort of mistress. Lilith's stories are well documented by scholars of mythology. The importance for us is that the woman who demands equality with the man is forced to leave the Garden and gets stigmatized as the personification of evil.

What of the missing primal scene, the inability to imagine the parents' sexual life that I referred to earlier? I regard this nonprimal scene as deriving in the first instance from a colossal fear of the consequences of conflict. (Again, sexual conflict symbolizes political conflict.) For, if the bodies of the parents are not in motion, then psychological and sociopolitical differences between them, including asymmetries and inequalities, need not enter consciousness. Over time, consciousness of political problems impacts on individuals' internal processes: their capacity to experience different parts of the self in their own particularly and diversity while at the same time sensing that they participate in the whole in a more or less coherent sense of identity. The denied primal scene signifies a loss of faith in the political nature of the human organism and of society itself. Conversely, images of vigorous, mutually satisfying parental intercourse, including, perhaps, some kind of struggle for power, reveal a private engagement with the conflictual dynamics of the public sphere.

Dream Imagery

An Italian client dreamed of a beautiful lake with clear, deep water. He said this represented his soul and then immediately associated to the pollution on the Italian Adriatic coast. The image of the lake and the association to coastal pollution suggested, in the form of one symbol, the client's unconscious capacity for depth and his present state, of which he was all too conscious—being clogged up by "algae," like the coastal waters of the Adriatic. When disparate psychological themes are thrown together like this, the symbolic image makes a powerful impact on the individual, who cannot ignore it. In this particular instance, the notion that was possibly a solution for the clogging up of his lake–soul potential, and the idea that being clogged was a state he had gradually gotten into over time and was not a witch's curse, together with the vision that depth and clarity and beauty were options open to him, were powerful and liberating thoughts for the client to entertain. He made a choice to return to Italy, to tell his father that he was homosexual and, in his words, to "get more involved"—perhaps in environmental politics.

Returning to the dream of the lake, I would like to suggest an alternative reading, couched in more political terms. I think that this rereading constitutes a further statement about the political properties of private, internal imagery. The images of the dream can be approached via their individual presence, via their political presence, or via the movement and tension between the two. In the dream of the lake, the tension between the individual and the political presences of the image was prominent and insistent; after all, the client was Italian. What, the client and I asked together, is the role of pollution in the soul, or even in the world? What is the role of pollution in the achievement of psychological depth? Can the soul remain deep and clear while there is pollution in the world, in one's home waters? Did the lake, with intimations of mystery and isolation, clash with the popular, extroverted tourism of the Adriatic? Eventually, the patient's concern moved onto the social level: Who owned the lake? Who should have access to such a scarce resource? Who would protect the lake from pollution? These were his associations. From wholly personal issues, such as the way his problems interfered with the flowering of his potential, we moved to political issues, such as the pollution of natural beauty, not only by industry but also by the mass extroversion of tourism. And we also moved back again from the political level to the personal level, including transference analysis. I do not mean to foreclose on other interpretations, but rather to add in a more "political" one so that the client's unconsciously adopted political commitments can become clearer.

I think much imagery can be understood in therapy as performing this particular kind of transcendent or bridging function: transcending and bridging the gap between the apparently individual, private, and subjective and the apparently collective, social, and political. Much of this chapter argues for the general thesis that there is a constant relationship and articulation between the personal/subjective and the public/political dimensions of life. Can we discriminate these separate dimensions in such a way that eventually we can, on a more conscious level, better bring them together? I think we find that private, internal imagery carries a public and political charge. Moreover, we need to be better placed to make practical, clinical use of the by now conventional observation that the external world, particularly its social and power relations, has an effect on our subjective experience.

Applying this approach to imagery to a psychological analysis of the politics of the client, we would try to discriminate the individual and the social aspects of an image and see whether they can be brought to an equal level of consciousness. This process would increase the range of choices available to the client, rather than collapsing them into a solution. In the example, the question of ownership of the lake at first seemed a distant "political" concern. But gradually the client's social sensitivity came to the fore: he asserted that the lake, like his soul, was not a commodity to be owned by anyone. Then a celebration of his social conscience came to the fore. He addressed the fate of his "Italian-ness" on a personal, individual level. Finally, as the hidden politics of his imagery continued to pulse, he discovered more collective, cultural, and political associations to pollution on the Adriatic. I hope it is clear that the public/political and private/subjective dimensions were both thoroughly alive.

This interpretive reworking of the imagery onto a sociopolitical level provides the beginnings of a model for tracking in therapy moves between individual and social realms and a means of studying conflicts and harmonies between culture and individual as these appear in the session. Individual and culture are not the crude opposites that many, including Freud, have taken them to be. Both terms enjoy the complex interaction produced by their dynamic relationship; the relationship changes the nature of the original "opposites." The more deep and personal the experience, the more political and public it may turn out to be.

The politics of imagery now operates, in the external world, at a pace that often precludes rational debate. If we are to avoid being permanently after-the-event—an unending social deferred action or *Nachträglichkeit*—then we have to try to engage with the political dimensions of psychological imagery.

A SOCIALIZED TRANSPERSONAL PSYCHOLOGY OF COMMUNITY

In contemporary Western politics the buzz word is "community." Aside from the politicians, many clients also speak in therapy of a sense of pulling together that used to exist and is now lost. They feel the loss keenly. For other clients the idea of community is more proactive, referring to their belief in a new kind of egalitarian politics based on what is shared, held in common, and faced together. Communitarian thinking will (hopefully) refresh our ideas both of the state and, for many among this group of clients, of the power dynamics of the therapeutic relationship.

It is extraordinary that in the many lucid discussions about community that are taking place, there has been little space for a psychological contribution. Communication politics requires an overtly socialized psychology, and when we try to create one we find that it will have, at some level, to be a transpersonal psychology. Politics is also a transpersonal activity and, like most transpersonal activities, politics points in what can only be described as a spiritual direction. Psychotherapy is not a religion, though it may be the heir to some aspects of conventional religion. The project of factoring the psychological into the political seems to want to be done in quasi-religious language. Perhaps this is because psychotherapy, politics, and religion all share, at some level, in the fantasy of providing therapy for the world. The very word "fantasy" must, I am sure, make problems for some readers. Fantasy is not in itself pathological and there is a necessarily utopic role of fantasy in political discourse.

Sometimes I see psychotherapy as a new monasticism, meaning that just as the monks and nuns kept culture in Europe alive during the so-called Dark Ages, so too in their often equally rigorous way the therapists and analysts are keeping something alive in our own age. However, the values that psychotherapy keep alive are difficult to classify. They do not always have the ring of absolute truth (though such a possibility is not ruled out), nor are they based on a fixed account of human nature (though that is what is invariably being attempted, time and again). In its discovery of values and value in that which other disciplines might reject, psychotherapy helps to keep something alive in the face of threats ranging from state hegemony to vicious market forces to nostalgic longings for a return to a past in which it is assumed that the old certitudes of nation, gender, and race would still hold.

We sometimes hear calls for a global ethic or a global sense of responsibility to be placed at the heart of political theory and the political process. My question is: How can this be done without some kind of psychological sensitivity and awareness? Such sensitivity and awareness may not be easily measurable by the sturdy tools of empiricism but reveal themselves in dream, in parental and primal scene imagery, in an understanding of a person's own political history, development, and myth. Hence, clinical work on oneself coexists with political work in one's society.

My working out of a "clinical" model with which to engage political problems is intended to make every citizen a potential therapist of the world. An active role for the citizen-as-therapist is highlighted and nowhere will this be more apparent than in relation to experts (myself included). People's active, generative, inventive, compassionate potential is not being tapped and as I see it, in order to tap into that kind of energy, we need a reinvention of politics inside and outside the therapy session.

REFERENCES

Gralnick, A. (1990). Review of *Psychoanalysis and the Nuclear Threat: Clinical and Theoretical Studies*, ed. H. B. Levine, D. Jacobs, and L. J. Rubin. *International Journal of Mental Health* 20:71–73.

Hillman, J., and Ventura, M. (1992). *We've had a Hundred Years of Psychotherapy and the World Is Getting Worse.* San Francisco: Harper.

Levine, H. B., Jacobs, D., and Rubin, L. J., eds. (1988). *Psychoanalysis and the Nuclear Threat: Clinical and Theoretical Studies.* Hillsdale, NJ: Analytic Press.

Samuels, A. (1993). *The Political Psyche.* London and New York: Routledge.

——— (1994). Replies to an international questionnaire on political material brought into the clinical setting by clients of psychotherapists and analysts. *International Review of Sociology* 3:7–60.

9

Staying Afloat in the Paradigmatic Flux

Joseph W. Slap

For a semester during my second year of residency, I had the good fortune to spend one afternoon per week with Jacob Arlow. For the first hour, Arlow lectured on psychopathology to the entire group of twelve second-year residents then at Hillside Hospital. He spent the rest of the afternoon, three hours, with a subgroup of four of us. We each presented a case to him for an hour and a half every other week. In other words, he ran four continuous case conferences, and we had the opportunity to hear him discuss and supervise a variety of patients. Although Arlow has been consistently impressive to sophisticated audiences, he seemed absolutely magical to us at that stage of our professional development. When presenting to him, we often had the experience of his making a comment on how the patient must feel, only to look down at our notes to find that he had anticipated the patient's next remarks practically verbatim.

He stressed the threads or motifs that ran through the clinical material and taught us to listen to our patients in such a manner as to recognize the fantasies that underlay their mental life and repetitive patterns of behavior. His lectures on psychopathology, however, were a much different matter. He was deeply involved with psychic energy concepts and discussed such topics as libido, cathexes, and neutralization. Sometimes there was a spillover of his abstract theoretical concepts into his discussion of the cases we were presenting. At one point in the discussion of a case, he asked a question that telegraphed the answer he was looking for. I have forgotten the question, but the answer I gave was ". . . because it was no longer neutralized." He walked halfway around the conference table—he was standing with a piece of chalk at the blackboard—and clapped me on the back, exclaiming, "That's the way to say it!"

While I was flattered by this accolade, I was left with an uneasy feeling. At the break I said to him that of the several ways in which patients had been discussed, he made the most sense to me when he spoke of patients' feelings and fantasies but that I got little out of discussions of psychic energy and other concepts, which seemed abstract and hypothetical. He explained that there were five metapsychological points of view: dynamic, genetic, structural, economic, and adaptive. During the case discussion he approached the material from the dynamic point of view, but when lecturing on psychopathology, he stressed the economic and structural points of view.

I was unconvinced. The dynamic and, I add, genetic points of view represented the essence of what attracted me to dynamic psychiatry. They provided a perspective that treated the patient as a human being with ambitions, hopes, frustrations, and guilt and made understandable his dynamic configurations and repetitive patterns of behavior. The dynamic and genetic points of view, taken together, helped bring order out of chaos and made the task of understanding the patient an activity much like solving puzzles, an activity that has a particular appeal to me. The economic, and certain aspects of the structural, points of view seemed much different. They did not help you understand the patient. Rather, once you understood the patient you might try to fit the material to these points of view. Or if you did not understand the patient, it was often easy enough to come up with an explanation based on the abstract concepts associated with these points of view. Waelder (1936) once said of the economic point of view that first you translate the clinical data into economic terms and then when you wish to apply this understanding to the patient, you must translate them back. What is gained by this? he wondered.

As I have said, I had trouble with certain aspects of the structural model. These were the concepts added to the structural model by Hartmann (Hartmann 1964, Hartmann, Kris, and Loewenstein 1946, 1949): for example, the ideas that the ego is the sum of its functions and that the superego functions with aggressive energy. Because I never found such concepts useful, I paid them little attention and based my understanding of the structural model on "The Ego and the Id" (Freud 1923), more particularly on Freud's diagram of the psychic apparatus. The dynamic unconscious was a piece of the ego that had been repressed and was now lodged in the id. It could not become conscious directly and could find expression only through derivatives rising through the preconscious. This version retained the topographic model fairly intact. My thinking that this was a useful way to organize the data found support in a remark by Waelder to the effect that, with the addition of the idea that defenses were unconscious, he could get along perfectly well with the topographic model. Later Waelder (1962) was to write that some of the best analysts he had ever known knew next to nothing about metapsychology.

In time a new problem troubled me. Much of the theory had to do with somatic drives giving rise to drive derivatives that were shaped or defended against by ego defenses acting at the behest of the superego. Such a model stressed and focused on the seeking out of drive–defense couplings. My patients, however, had issues involving parents, siblings, other relatives, self-esteem, gender determination, medical traumata, and so forth; in other words, their dynamics were so rich and complicated that they could not possibly be encompassed by the drive–defense model.

Sometime in the early 1970s I met Joe Lichtenberg at a conference in Washington. Joe had a stack of unfinished manuscripts and asked my help in getting them into shape for publication. He supplied most of the ideas, and I acted largely as critic and editor. We published a number of papers dealing with aspects of defense; one of them, (Lichtenberg and Slap 1973) on splitting, is occasionally cited to this day. Joe used to say that psychoanalytic theory is "atomized," meaning so much attention is paid to instincts, defenses, affects, energies, and the like that one loses sight of the forest for the trees. He wished to study larger blocks of material, which he called suborganizations. I was reminded that Schafer (1968) had written of discrepant suborganizations of the mind, by which he meant mental organizations that contained elements which, based on their function, could be assigned to the ego, superego, or id. We settled on the term intersystemic suborganizations.

His ideas about the atomization of psychoanalytic theory and about thinking in terms of blocks of intersystemic material were extremely useful. Moreover, in the course of working with Joe, I became aware that my private version of the structural model was at significant variance with what Sandler (1983) has called the "official theory." It was during this period that I began to think of constructing a model that contained these larger blocks of data and that was free of the many problems I felt were inherent in the structural model. Also at about this time I was serving on the dissertation committee of a graduate student at Hahnemann whose topic was a comparison of the concepts and developmental timetable of Freud, Mahler, Kernberg, and Piaget. As this student, Andrew Saykin, seemed to have an excellent grasp of these matters, I suggested to him that we try to come up with an internally consistent model of the mind based on the dynamic and genetic points of view. In one of our discussions I brought up the concept of the schema, which I had come across in a paper by Paul

(1967) in an early volume of *Psychological Issues.* Saykin responded by speaking of Piaget's usage of the term and the corollary concepts of assimilation and accommodation. I, in turn, was reminded that George Klein (1976) had made much of these Piagetian concepts in his well-reviewed but soon forgotten book *Psychoanalytic Theory: An Exploration of Essentials.*

Turning back to Klein, I was taken with his idea that the dynamic unconscious could be viewed as a nonaccommodating schema, that is, as an organization of the mind that assimilates the data of the external world into its own templates and ignores the differences between the current situation and the past. This concept provided the foundation for a model that Saykin and I felt had the following advantages: it was experience near; it was able to reconcile or explain such analytic concepts as trauma, repetition phenomena, dream formation, sublimation, transference, developmental lines, and working through; it was based squarely on the dynamic and genetic points of view; and it allowed one to think in terms of organizations at whose core lay traumata and reactive fantasies to these traumata that did not ignore, but rather encompassed, drive–defense interfaces.

Although we were convinced of the superiority of this model, which I employed in my work with patients and in supervision, we soon found that the psychoanalytic community was not receptive. In an attempt to discover the reason for this unpleasant development, I turned to Thomas Kuhn's (1970) *The Structure of Scientific Revolutions*; there I learned that it had taken four centuries for the Copernican discovery that the sun is the center of the solar system to replace the Ptolemaic geocentric model. Sooner or later a good idea will catch on.

Papers about the schema model were turned down by the major journals but were accepted by second-line ones. When the ideas were presented at meetings, there was generally some support and the criticisms tended to be varied. I soon realized that part of the difficulty was that, while almost everyone claimed allegiance to the structural model, this apparent unanimity was a pseudoconsensus; actually, many different versions of the structural model exist. I arranged to cochair a discussion group on the current status of the structural model at the meetings of the American Psychoanalytic Association; these sessions amply confirmed that there is no clear, internally consistent, widely held understanding of what the structural model is.

Recalling that early on I had been happy with a particular version of the structural model, I returned to that model to see if I could show that the schema model was a derivative of Freud's (as opposed to Hartmann's) structural model and not a competing model. I pointed out that Freud (1915, 1923) made two questionable assumptions about perception in his construction of the structural model; first, whatever his model, he made perception the province of a particular agency through which stimuli must pass before reaching other parts of the psychic apparatus; second, he treated perception as a true and exact copy of external reality. In general psychology this has been called the theory of immaculate perception. When I made the logical changes in Freud's (1923) model, the structural model became roughly congruent with the schema model. *The Journal of the American Psychoanalytic Association* published a paper based on these arguments (Slap 1987).

Thus the structural model, as it has evolved under the aegis of the ego psychologists, is in a theoretical cul-de-sac and does not serve as a guide to clinical work; that is, we have a handed-down theory that is not relevant to our practice. Among the consequences of this situation are the following: our institutes teach two virtually separate curricula. Candidates are asked to study the theory in some courses, but they learn to ignore it in clinical seminars and in supervision. Our literature has become repetitious, and analysts pay scant attention to it, perhaps, as Kernberg (1983, personal communication) once commented, because they feel, "Why bother? It has all been said." And lacking a shared working theory, we cannot adequately communicate with one another, a circumstance that has restricted progress in our field.

Undoubtedly there will be readers who feel they work more or less as I do and that, in my attempt to compare thinking and therapeutic approach as guided by the structural model with that guided by the schema model, the characterization of the former has been distorted. I believe that this perception is bound to occur, because it has occurred in the past and for very good and logical reasons. As I stated earlier, psychoanalysts and analytically oriented therapists have two sets of theory. One set is the official theory of Freud, Hartmann, Kris, and Loewenstein. The other body of theory has to do with what therapists use to guide their clinical work. The model presented here is different from the official theory but often is quite close to how many people work. For many who tolerate this dichotomy in their theory, the ideas presented there will be nothing new; and when I characterize how some therapists work and how many more would work if they took the structural model seriously, they are apt to cry, "I don't do that! That's a straw man."

The lines you have just read were originally written as a contribution to a panel on how the thinking of senior analysts has changed over three decades held at the Philadelphia Association for Psychoanalysis in 1988 and constituted the preface of *The Schema in Clinical Psychoanalysis,* a monograph I published with my daughter, Laura Slap-Shelton, Psy.D., in 1991. This material depicts my struggle with psychoanalytic theory as accurately as I can imagine and therefore I employ it one more time.

Three sections follow: a description of the model, clinical examples, and my experiences following publication of the monograph.

THE MODEL

According to this model, the mind is understood as a unitary schema—an organization of memories, appetites, moral values, factual knowledge, affects, and cognitive skills—which, in the ideal condition is generally interconnected. In neurosis, situations or events that cannot be mastered become the nidus for an organization of these traumatic experiences and reactive fantasies with their associated affects, which is also a schema but one that is sequestered from the general or unitary schema. The unitary schema is conceptually analogous to the ego of prestructural theory and the sequestered schema to the repressed or dynamic unconscious. The sequestered schema may be latent; when it is active and disruptive the term *pathogenic schema* is appropriate.

In Piagetian terms, the unitary schema, which will be referred to as the ego, assimilates and accommodates; that is, such a schema is able to interpret fresh data (perceptions) in terms of past experience (assimilation) and is able to adapt to or accommodate fresh data that differs from past experience (accommodation). The sequestered schema assimilates but does not accommodate; that is, it functions throughout life, interpreting current events in terms of templates of past experience. Thus the neurotic goes through life remaking the same film or play with people from current life cast into roles originally created by parents and other important figures of childhood. Transference is the consequence of the assimilation of persons from current life into these roles and is a misperception and not a projection or displacement as it is usually conceptualized. The phenomena that led Freud to conceptualize the repetition compulsion are accounted for by the ongoing activity of the pathogenic schema. Analogous to the principle of multiple function (Waelder 1936) is the understanding that everything one experiences is parallel-processed (Horowitz 1977); that is, mental experience and behavior are the resultant of forces of the activity of the unitary and pathogenic schemas.

The mode of cognition of the pathogenic schema is consistent with what Piaget called "ego-centric" thought (Piaget 1926). Ego-centric thought is intuitive and syncretic, by which is meant that diverse elements are intimately associated on the basis of concurrence or juxtaposition; primitive modes of reasoning control current reasoning without recognition of their influence. Thus idiosyncratic schemas of analogy and visual schemas prevail over logical reasoning and deduction, and assimilation prevails over accommodation. As this is the kind of reasoning that characterizes the child during the years in which infantile neuroses are established, one would expect this type of reasoning to characterize the organized residues of those neuroses.

This is a simple model. Essentially all that is claimed is that the painful impressions and situations of childhood, those not mastered by the immature mind, become nidi for the formation of separate organizations of the mind, here called pathogenic schemas. The pathogenic schema is a freeze-frame of the mind during the painful period of its formation and encompasses traumatic impressions, reactive fantasies, associated affects, and infantile cognition; over time this organization accretes to itself later experiences that have been perceived egocentrically.

According to the schema model there are two conceptually distinct kinds of conflictual interface. One arises in the original childhood situation. The other is formed when the childhood situation—traumatic core, impulses, defenses, reactive fantasies, and associated affects—is sequestered or repressed en bloc. This is an important theoretical point, as I shall attempt to demonstrate.

It is not at all unusual for patients to oscillate over time between untenable positions. Thus a patient may take an aggressive attitude in dealing with an authority at work or in an academic situation only to worry that he is pushing things too far and may suffer unpleasant consequences. In response to this anxiety he adopts a meek, conciliatory posture in the hope of appeasing the now dreaded authority and escaping retribution. In time feeling that such self-castrating behavior is unbearable, he reacts by once again taking an aggressive stance. Analysts local to the structural model may understand such seesaw situations as instinctual conflicts between activity and passivity or between heterosexuality and homosexuality. Arlow (1963), for example, wrote:

> Where there appears to be a conflict between opposing drives, the ego takes sides with the expression of one set of drives, i.e., permits the discharge of the cathexis of one drive, in order to fend off the expression of the other, the more objectionable drive representation. Conflicts of this type . . . in actuality represent a conflict between the ego and the id, with the

> superego apparently in accord with the defensive position taken by the ego. [p. 16]

Such a view of how neurosis is structured is not apt to be helpful because there is no escape. If the patient adopts a passive-submission attitude out of fear of the consequences of his aggressiveness, one might say the ego is taking sides with the passive drive derivatives; and if the passivity becomes intolerable, one might say the ego is taking sides with the aggressive drives in order to defend against the passivity.

The analyst guided by the schema model will view the situation differently. He will understand that the aggressive and passive fantasies and behavior and the reasons for oscillating between them are within the pathogenic schema. He will work with the patient's ego to understand what elements of this organization are being manifested in these oscillations. Thus he may discover that as a child the patient had reacted to his father's absences with fantasies of his father's death and taking his position with the mother, only to become terrified when the father returned. Given this perspective, the patient will no longer be trapped into alternating between aggression and submission but will have the new alternative of seeing both positions, the reasons for shifting from one to the other, and the associated affects as elements of an anachronistic, pathogenic residue. He will then have the newly appreciated option of striving to deal with the situation from the perspective of mature reason and judgment.

Before turning to clinical examples, consider some observations on how perception is treated by the structural model as compared to the schema model.

According to the topographic model, perceptions enter the psychic apparatus via the unconscious (Freud 1915).

> Normally all the paths from perception to the *Ucs.* remain open, and only those leading on from the *Ucs.* are subject to blocking by repression. It is a very remarkable thing that the

> *Ucs.* of one human being can react upon that of another, without passing through the *Cs.* [p. 194]

The passage of perceptions from *Ucs.* to *Pcs.* and *Cs.* is not a free and simple process, as there are repressive barriers between the systems. It is necessary for a presentation in the *Ucs.* to acquire a word presentation to become preconscious.

> The system *Ucs.* contains the thing-cathexes of the objects, the first and true object-cathexes; the system *Pcs.* comes about by this thing-presentation being hypercathected through being linked with the word-presentations corresponding to it. [pp. 201–202]

When one turns to *The Ego and the Id* (Freud 1923), however, one reads: "All perceptions which are received from without (sense-perceptions) . . . are *Cs.* from the start" (p. 19). Freud's diagram of the psychic apparatus (p. 24) makes clear that perception is a function of the ego and is linked to consciousness in that the perceptual system (*Pcpt.*) is joined with the *Cs.* to form *Pcpt.-Cs.*, which forms the ego's surface, that is, its interface with the external world. The repressed unconscious is now part of the id which is "cut off from the external world" (Freud 1940, p. 198).

Thus we see that according to the topographic model the perception of external stimuli takes place in the unconscious layers of the mind and rises to preconscious and conscious layers by attaching word presentations. The structural model turns things around in that perception takes place at the most conscious level, the *Pcpt.-Cs.*, and is sharply cut off from the unconscious layers.

There are problems with the theory of perception within the frame of the topographic model; for example, the distinction between thing-presentations and word-presentations has not proven useful and has dropped out of theoretical discourse. Since the topographic model has been superseded by the structural model, however, it is the latter that commands attention. There are difficulties with the understanding that perception is a function of the conscious ego (*Pcpt.-Cs.*) and that there is no direct perceptual pathway to the unconscious layers of the mind. It is an everyday observation in analytic practice that individuals react to seductive, hostile, and other behaviors on the part of others without recognizing these behaviors consciously. Registration of tachistoscopic and other subliminal stimuli are demonstrable under experimental conditions. More troublesome for this theory is the problem of accounting for the stimulation of unconscious drive derivatives, guilt, and other elements of intrapsychic conflict by the events of the external world. If the ego stands between the external world and the repressed, why does it not function to block these percepts from the repressed? If the ego is unable to function in this way and percepts have an easy path to the repressed, what is gained by maintaining that the id is cut off from the external world? Arlow (1969) has tried to deal with this issue as follows:

> There is a mutual and reciprocal effect of the pressure of unconscious fantasy formations and sensory stimuli, especially stimuli emanating from the external world. Unconscious fantasy activity provides the "mental set" in which sensory stimuli are perceived and integrated. External events, on the other hand, stimulate and organize the re-emergence of unconscious fantasies. In keeping with its primitive nature, the basic fantasy is cathected with a highly mobile energy, and presses for gratification of the sort which Freud characterized as tending toward an identity of perception. The pressure may affect many functions of the ego. Derivatives of fantasies may influence ego functions, interfering, for example, with the neutral processes of registering, apperceiving and checking the raw data of perception. Under the pressure of these influences, the ego is oriented to scan the data of perception and to select discriminatively . . . those elements that demonstrate some consonance or correspondence with the latent preformed fantasies. [p. 8]

A complicated sequence is described here. Arlow states that "External events . . . stimulate and organize the re-emergence of unconscious fantasies"; he thus seems to concede a perceptual capacity to the unconscious fantasy organizations in contradiction to the notion that perception is exclusively an ego function. The fantasies thus stimulated press for gratification and influence the ego "to select discriminatively from the data of perception those elements that demonstrate some consonance or correspondence with the latent, preformed fantasies." Some questions are raised by this sequence; for example, if the fantasy formations perceive, that is, if they are stimulated by external events that have significance for them, why must they influence the ego to search ("scan the data of perception") for elements that demonstrate consonance or correspondence with the fantasy formations themselves?

Given those clinical and theoretical difficulties for the current theory of the locus and flow of perception in the structural model, it seems more reasonable to attribute a perceptual capacity to both psychic organizations, that is, to the ego and to the repressed. It is true that this alteration in theory entails the surrender of the idea consistently held by Freud that perceptions enter the psychic apparatus via a particular part, a notion that possibly has its origin in Freud's early concept of neurosis arising from interference in a reflux arc between stimulation and discharge (Breuer and Freud 1893–1895). The psychic apparatus, however, is a model of the mind, not an anatomical entity; whether sensory data, mediated by the brain, become available only to one or to more than one psychic organization is a matter to be decided by clinical considerations.

Nonetheless, it should be noted that the schema model finds some support in modern understandings of brain function. According to the schema model, events are simultaneously perceived and processed by both the ego and the sequestered (or pathogenic) schema; further, the model contends that there is a difference in the mode of cognition of the two organizations. This understanding is isomorphic with certain established understandings of neuroscientists concerned with information processing. Moscovitch (1979), in a review article on information processing and the cerebral hemispheres, states that information processing at an early peripheral level is similar in both hemispheres and that hemispheric asymmetries emerge at a higher level of analysis in which relational or categorical features are represented. He writes, "If to these assumptions we add another that states that the reflection of hemispheric asymmetries in behavior is determined as much by the cognitive demands of the task as by the stimulus material per se, then this set of assumptions will account for a great deal of the evidence on hemispheric specialization" (p. 412).

CLINICAL EXAMPLES

A young attorney was extremely sensitive to any situation that could be perceived as his being displaced by a younger rival. When he was 2 years old, the patient's mother required hospitalization for several months. He reacted poorly to his separation and was unfriendly to his mother when she returned. She soon became pregnant and delivered a brother, whom the patient despised. Another brother, born a few years later, was better tolerated by the patient.

After the birth of the first brother, the child was trapped in a painful situation for which he could not find a resolution. His brother was there to stay, and his rage at this sibling and at his parents for having him was not acceptable to his parents and engendered guilt and fears of punishment. The configuration of traumatic distress, fantasies of murder and punishment, and associated affects of anger, fear, and remorse remained as a separate organization within the patient's psyche and constituted a freeze-frame of this period of his life. The activity of this organization in processing events and relationships in his adult life was abundantly clear.

When given the files of several law students who were applying for summer positions in the firm for which he worked, the patient left them in the locker room of his squash club. He had been impressed with the background and achievements of these prospects and felt that he would be overshadowed were they to join the firm. When he was asked if he would mind if a space he intended to move into were given instead to two paralegals who worked closely with a partner in an adjacent office, he created a storm that hurt his standing in the firm. When a junior associate complained about what would otherwise have been a long holiday weekend, the patient called him, among other things, a spoiled brat. When the entire city was excited about the local team playing in and winning the World Series, the patient secretly rooted against them; they were, after all, everyone's darlings. When his wife became pregnant, he dreamed of encountering a stranger in his favorite childhood play spot and fighting with him.

In another instance, a little girl strove to win her father's love, attention, and respect while feeling despair at his exclusive interest in her younger brother, whom the father seemed determined to mold into a perfect male. She harbored resentment toward her brother but defended against it, fearing that her father would despise her if she were mean to the boy. Years later, now an art history doctoral candidate, she was attracted to a homosexual male professor. She strove to win his attention, love, and respect while recognizing that his preference was for males. Indeed, it was known that he had provided several thousand dollars of personal funds to enable a favored male student to do research in Italy. She was teaching a course on women artists and, to meet the requirement that one's teaching be evaluated, invited this professor (she could have chosen any faculty member) to observe her class. She wished desperately that the class would go well. At a point late in the class, the patient called upon the only male student taking the course, as he had not contributed to the discussion up to that point. The student was not able to answer the question he was asked, and the patient was horrified by the thought that she had embarrassed him and that the professor would be enraged at her for doing so. The class ended, leaving the patient shaken in spite of the professor's smiling and making a thumbs-up gesture as he left.

The parallels with the childhood situation are clear. She was making a presentation to her professor who, like her father, preferred boys. The content of the course, as the patient pointed out, was designed to show that women and men alike were valuable. She thought that she had hurt the male student qua brother and that the professor would punish her. As it turned out, the professor rated her highly, sought to arrange a teaching award for her, and was particularly complimentary about the tactful way she had handled the male student.

Now a case described in more detail:

A woman of 50 years came for treatment because of depression manifested by a difficulty in concentration and a profound sense of despair over what she had accomplished in her life. She complained of difficulties in her marriage to a surgical subspecialist who had little regard for her career as a painter and begrudged her the time and money, insignificant in relation to their assets and his income, she wished to devote to her art.

The patient was born in a small town to a family of modest means. She had two brothers, a year and a half and three years younger. She recalled that when she was 3 ½ years old she overheard a conversation between her parents in which her father said that he could not stand the financial strain imposed by the children. The patient felt responsible for her parents' difficulties and this feeling was compounded when the father left the home not long after the conversation. Under the terms of the divorce the father had no financial responsibility for his children but was barred from having contact with them. The patient was told by an aunt that her father continued to love her, was interested in any news of her, and would unobtrusively observe her at play in the schoolyard. The mother was soon married again, this time to a man of violent temper who had undergone harrowing wartime experiences. He would beat the boys, although he did not physically molest the patient. The patient slept in a room off the parental bedroom that had no door separating the chambers.

She was regularly exposed to the noises of their arguments and sexual activity, which she interpreted as an assault consistent with her stepfather's usual behavior and personality. He was given to imposing arbitrary, seemingly senseless restrictions. For example, the patient was allowed to go out for an evening activity only one of the weekend nights; no reason was given for this rule. He was hostile to her drawing and coloring, regarding it as a waste of time. The patient detested her home life and longed to escape. Her parents expected her to become a teacher or nurse and to settle in the area. Although greatly conflicted, the patient enrolled in a nursing program in a local hospital where her grades fluctuated widely as she was intermittently depressed and unable to concentrate on her studies. After two years she noticed an advertisement for flight attendants, applied, and was accepted. At last she made a break for freedom.

While flying within the country and on international routes the patient took along art supplies and would spend much of the time she had to stay in hotels drawing and painting; her apartment in her base city served as a studio. She established a relationship with the man she later married early in her flying career; they had difficulties, broke up, but after a while began seeing each other again. The patient was wary of marriage as she feared she would lose her hard-won freedom. After going with him a number of years, pressures from both families mounted and they married. She continued to fly and her income supported him while he was training in his subspeciality; as they were together only a few days each week she did not feel her freedom compromised. In time he went into a successful practice and she began to fly less and less. Finally, when she was in her early forties, she gave up flying altogether with the intention of devoting herself to painting.

Her husband took no interest in her art and resented any expenditure devoted to this activity; he expected her painting to be self-supporting, that is, that sales of paintings would cover the expenses of studio rental and art supplies, a position she considered manifestly unfair, particularly because she had supported him during his training. He objected to any disorder created by supplies and canvases brought into the home. He inhibited her from going to art openings and other art-related affairs. She deeply resented these attitudes and restrictions but was unable to stand up to him. Finally she was offered an all-expense-paid weeklong visit to London as part of an exchange program organized by the British government. Her husband objected to her going as it would be an inconvenience for him; the patient acceded to his demand that she not go. Her unexpressed rage over this incident brought her into treatment, although it was not reported until she had been in treatment ten months.

The patient had perceived and processed the marriage as she had her childhood. She accepted her husband's authority while resenting him and allowed herself to be restricted in her social and artistic activities. Thus she did not go to openings and other art functions in spite of her desire to become part of the art community; she offered to go to just some, the important events, a compromise reminiscent of the one-night-per-weekend rule. Her husband, like her stepfather, had little regard for her work, refused to hang it in his office, and disparaged the activity among their acquaintances. When she showed signs of making a financial success he was intrusive with advice.

Derivatives of her primal scene experiences were manifest in her paintings. When she came into treatment her canvases were largely a dark gray with small, bright, poorly defined figures discerned in the background; these were reminiscent of the later Turners, which had exciting events seen through a murky foreground, for example, his paintings of the burning of the House of Parliament, and of Greenacre's (1973) discussion of the relationship of Mondrian's art to primal scene experience. As time went on her painting changed, and although abstract, depictions of the primal scene appeared. Thus one tall painting was dark in its upper part with phallic shapes looming in several areas. In the middle right there was an irregular figure walled off from the rest of the painting by a thick Roualt-like boundary; it was a flat white and the patient was definite that this area represented herself. Below there was a mix of reds suggestive of mucous membrane and blood; overlying this red area were smears of white that seemed to represent semen. It was the discussion of this painting, treated much like a dream, that elicited the history of long-repeated primal scene exposure. The flat-white, walled-off representation of herself was an apt depiction of her childhood attempts to blank out while being subjected to the noise of her parents' sexual activity; it was also a reflection of her sexual experience in her current life during stormy periods in her relationship with her husband.

She was inhibited in her efforts to display her work and win appreciation. She delayed endlessly getting slides of her work to gallery owners and curators. When established artists showed interest in helping to promote her, she missed cues and opportunities. Consistent with this behavior, images appeared in her work of phallic forms being contained as they came up against barriers. The patient was invited to participate in a workshop in New England and, uncharacteristically, decided to accept without first discussing the matter with her husband; she anticipated that he would object. There had been severe friction and talk of separation as she was beginning to assert independence; he raised no difficulty. After she had been away a few days he called her at the workshop sounding depressed and complaining about problems in his practice and at home. Up to this point she had been active and productive. Her mood abruptly changed; she felt she could do nothing well, became embarrassed about her work, and left early. She wondered if her work had any value.

In subsequent weeks it developed that she had started on a few pieces that were turning out well, there had been movement in an evolving trend in her painting, and she had been admired by other participants. Her perception of herself as a failure was not realistic but precipitated by her husband's call and determined by the pathogenic schema, which might be summarized as follows:

She perceived the relationship between her mother and stepfather as one in which the mother was abused and mutilated by his phallus. Frightened and horrified, she rejected this role for herself; she could either surrender and accept a fate like her mother's or she could exact revenge by castrating her stepfather (and later her husband) by defying and surpassing him. Thus success was tantamount to destroying him. The contamination of her efforts to advance her career by the fantasy of destroying her stepfather/husband accounted for the inhibition of her efforts at any sign of displeasure from her husband. Men were stereotypically seen as angry, castrating brutes like her stepfather or benign, well-meaning, but peripheral figures, like her natural father.

AFTER THE PUBLICATION OF THE MONOGRAPH

My relationship to our analytic institute had undergone several phases prior to publication of the book. When I first began to publish articles on the schema model there was little reaction from my fellow training analysts. In time this changed. I had supervised many candidates who found the model useful. Some of these individuals had graduated and had become junior faculty members. One evening I presented the model at a regular scientific session of our institute. Several training analysts, some of whom rarely came to meetings, occupied the first row of the small auditorium in the institute building. My presentation was met with great hostility, including ad hominem remarks. The candidates and younger members who came prepared to speak in favor of the model were intimidated and did not speak. It was a sad day for our institute. Evidently the powers that be sensed that matters had gone too far and I was later invited to give a presentation of the model at a meeting of the training analysts where the ideas were treated with interest and objectivity. Other conciliatory gestures were made and a state of peaceful coexistence prevailed.

Meanwhile, I found that I had fewer candidate analysands. One candidate, who had seen me twice in the process of selecting an analyst, told me he had decided against entering analysis with me as he thought it would make sense to see an analyst whose theoretical position was more consistent with that of the institute. I suspect that I lost the opportunity to analyze other candidates and to supervise still others because of my advocacy of the schema model.

My daughter and I awaited the reviews with wishful fantasies of rave notices but also with the sober realization that the reactions of the reviewers might be a little different from what we had experienced from the field in general. Since this is not the place to argue with our reviewers (if indeed, such a place exists), I shall say only that a review in the *International Journal of Psycho-Analysis* (Krohn 1992) found some merit but was on the whole negative, a review in the *Journal of the American Psychoanalytic Association* (Galatzer-Levy 1994) was more negative, and a review in *Psychoanalytic Books* (Kaufman 1993) was extremely insightful and favorable. Book sales have been disappointing and any hopes we had of winning a great deal of attention quickly have now dissipated.

The field is changing rapidly. Its very existence, some believe, is threatened by changes in health care. Analytic institutes (with some exceptions) are having trouble attracting candidates. A great number of analysts and analytic candidates have become more and more preoccupied with earning a living and have less energy to devote to theoretical niceties. After a while the thought occurs: Is there anyone out there who cares about these matters?

My current state of mind is as follows: working with a different paradigm as I am, I have less interest in the current literature and find that I attend fewer meetings. I feel less involved with the administrative activities of my institute, although I am, if there is any change, more eager to teach, supervise, and analyze candidates. I am alert to opportunities for contact with individuals who might be sympathetic to the schema model; generally, these are individuals who have become dissatisfied with the structural model. I have had intermittent contact with Morton Shane and, through his efforts, have discussed a case presentation at the Institute of Contemporary Psychoanalysis in Los Angeles. I have had a correspondence and exchange of books with Joseph Weiss of San Francisco. Professor Louis Diguer of Laval University in

Quebec, who has done extensive research in psychotherapy, has embraced the schema model; we hope to collaborate on some work. In March 1993, my daughter and I gave a poster presentation on the model at the International Psychoanalytical Association Research Conference in London.

In December 1992 Charles Brenner gave a paper at the meeting of the American Psychoanalytic Association in which he acknowledged the possibility that "the time has come to relinquish the idea that the mind is best understood as consisting of the separate structures id, ego, and superego." This development aroused some hope that a serious challenge to the hegemony of the structural model had occurred and that a real opportunity for a paradigm shift now occurred. However, Brenner has not had much success with his new position, in part I believe because he does not offer a well-thought-out alternative. On November 11, 1994, he and I appeared on the same program at a scientific session of the Philadelphia Association for Psychoanalysis. Clinical material was presented by Gardner Jacobs followed by 15-minute talks by Brenner and myself in which we outlined our theories, taking Jacobs's material as a starting point. The ensuing discussion, in which many members of the audience took part, provided a searching examination of Brenner's replacement model, which consisted of the pleasure principles of compromise formation, and of the schema model. At this meeting in contrast to the past, the schema model was treated with great attention and respect.

REFERENCES

Arlow, J. A. (1963). Conflict, regression, and symptom formation. *International Journal of Psycho-Analysis* 44:12–22.

——— (1969). Unconscious fantasy and disturbance of conscious experience. *Psychoanalytic Quarterly* 38:1–27.

Brenner, C. (1992). The mind as conflict and compromise formation. Paper presented at fall meeting of the American Psychoanalytic Association, December.

Breuer, J., and Freud, S. (1893–1895). Studies on hysteria. *Standard Edition* 2.

Freud, S. (1915). The unconscious. *Standard Edition* 14:166–204.

——— (1923). The ego and the id. *Standard Edition* 19:12–66.

——— (1940). Outline of psycho-analysis. *Standard Edition* 23:144–207.

Galatzer-Levy, R. (1994). Review of *The Schema in Clinical Psychoanalysis*, by J. W. Slap and L. Slap-Shelton. *Journal of the American Psychoanalytic Association* 42:296–301.

Greenacre, P. (1973). The primal scene and the sense of reality. *Psychoanalytic Quarterly* 42:10–41.

Hartmann, H. (1964). *Essays on Ego Psychology*. New York: International Universities Press.

Hartmann, H., Kris, E., and Loewenstein, R. M. (1946). Comments on the formation of psychic structure. In *Psychoanalytic Study of the Child* 2:11–38. New York: International Universities Press.

——— (1949). Notes on the theory of aggression. In *Psychoanalytic Study of the Child* 3/4:9–36. New York: International Universities Press.

Horowitz, M. (1977). Cognitive and interactive aspects of splitting. *American Journal of Psychiatry* 134:549–553.

Kaufman, P. (1993). Review of *The Schema in Clinical Psychoanalysis*, by J. W. Slap and L. Slap-Shelton. *Psychoanalytic Books* 4:506–512.

Klein, G. S. (1976). *Psychoanalytic Theory: An Exploration of Essentials*. New York: International Universities Press.

Krohn, A. (1992). Review of *The Schema in Clinical Psychoanalysis*, by J. W. Slap and L. Slap-Shelton. *International Journal of Psycho-Analysis* 72:780–783.

Kuhn, T. S. (1970). *The Structure of Scientific Revolutions*. Chicago: University of Chicago Press.

Lichtenberg, J., and Slap, J. W. (1973). Notes on the concept of splitting and the defense mechanism of splitting and representations. *Journal of the American Psychoanalytic Association* 21:772–787.

Moscovitch, M. (1979). Information processing and the cerebral hemispheres. In *Handbook of Behavioral Neurobiology, Vol 2: Neuropsychology*, ed. M. S. Gassaniga. New York: Plenum.

Paul, I. H. (1967). *Studies in Remembering*. New York: International Universities Press.

Piaget, J. (1926). *The Language and Thought of the Child*. New York: Basic Books.

Sandler, J. (1983). Reflections on some relations between psychoanalytic concepts and psychoanalytic practice. *International Journal of Psycho-Analysis* 64:34–45.

Schafer, R. (1968). *Aspects of Internalization.* New York: International Universities Press.

Slap, J. W. (1987). Implications for the structural model of Freud's assumptions about perception. *Journal of the American Psychoanalytic Association* 35:629–646.

Slap, J. W., and Slap-Shelton, L. (1991). *The Schema in Clinical Psychoanalysis.* Hillsdale, NJ: Analytic Press.

Waelder, R. (1936). The principle of multiple function: Observations on over-determination. *Psychoanalytic Quarterly* 5:45–62.

——— (1962). Review of *Psychoanalysis, Scientific Method and Philosophy: A Symposium,* ed. S. Hooks. *Journal of the American Psychoanalytic Association* 10:617–637.

10

Psychoanalysis Down Under

Ron Spielman

Living and working in Australia (often called locally "The Lucky Country"—both proudly and wryly), one is aware of being distant and isolated from many of the cauldrons of analytic endeavor in faraway lands.

In addition, the Australian Psychoanalytical Society numbers only some 60 members, most of whom work in three major population centers: Sydney, Melbourne, and Adelaide. I obtained my training with the Sydney Branch of the Society and qualified only ten years ago. This seems such a short time in the analytic time scale. At that time I was the eighth analyst in Sydney—now there are twenty-six. I say this to show that Psychoanalysis is alive and well in Australia! The Society itself has grown from some thirty-five members to sixty-five in the same time span—with some twenty candidates in the Sydney, Melbourne, and Adelaide training programs.

One of the first things I did after getting the invitation to contribute to *More Analysts at Work* was to obtain a copy of *Analysts at Work* (Reppen 1985). (I confidently await, one day, hearing of the publication of *Son of Analyst at Work.*) Although we do have three bookshops in our country that make a practice of obtaining psychoanalytic works, they are often only available a considerable time after the rest of the analytic world has become familiar with them. Thus we all use distributors in the United Kingdom and the United States. I say this to give some indication of the analytic climate in which we work in Australia.

I read *Analysts at Work* in order to get a feel for what Dr. Reppen expected of me. Of the twelve contributors to the earlier volume, all but one were familiar names to me—and the twelfth, Helen Lewis, is an often published author, but in books and journals that I don't think are readily available in Australia. Nevertheless, the twelve are notable contributors to the literature on which we all depend for some measure of companionship in what is, after all, an often lonely form of work. It was fortunate for me that the first two chapters were contributed by two American analysts who had visited Australia recently and whom I had had the pleasure of meeting personally—Giovacchini and Grotstein. This helped me relate to the volume in a more personal way, especially in that both Giovacchini and Grotstein were so generous in sharing their personal experiences of developing and practicing as analysts in the climate of their time. Larsson, Poland, Pulver, Volkan, and Yorke, and, to a lesser extent, Jacobs, Peterfreund, and Thickstun did likewise. Langs chose to describe his theoretical stance.

As Dr. Reppen foreshadowed in his preface, of the twelve analysts, ten were American and two European—one Swedish and one British. This is somewhat of an imbalanced representation of psychoanalysis, which I gather is being redressed in this volume.

The Australian Psychoanalytical Society was sponsored into the International Psychoanalytical Association by the British Society, where a majority of our senior members obtained their training, before our becoming a Component Society and conducting our own training programs. A significant number of senior British analysts have been Visiting Analysts to our Society over the past twenty or so years and have contributed enormously to our development. These analysts have belonged to each of the groups within the British Society—and we have thus benefited from being exposed to the British Society's ability to nurture the different strands of analytic thinking, a feature that has characterized that Society.

In more recent years we have had an increasing number of American analysts, being invited either to our Society or other psychoanalytically committed groups, or making private visits, and exposing us to American psychoanalysis. As most of the Americans we have met in this way have had a significant object relations approach to their work, we have had little difficulty in finding a common dialect of psychoanalysis in which to communicate.

While writing this chapter, I remembered that throughout my training I sensed that I was a little more interested in the American authors than most of my fellow candidates were, and certainly more than most of my teachers were. I was concurrently reading a most sensitive article by Thomas Ogden (1994) in the *International Journal of Psycho-Analysis* in which he wrote of his own psychic work in thinking through the experiences he described having in a case illustration. Ogden spoke of his own feelings about his internal "father/analyst" in working through his understanding of the issues. I suddenly thought about my own "father/analyst"—but to my surprise, it was not my analyst who came first to mind but my "analytic father."

I was introduced to psychoanalysis in a meaningful way when I received psychotherapy supervision, while still working in a state psychiatric hospital, from an American analyst who had come to work in Sydney. It was during the course of nearly five years of supervision that I struggled with (and against) the idea of training as a psychoanalyst. When he finally challenged my resistance to being a patient rather than a trainee, I accepted referral to the analyst who was to become my training analyst. That they both have the same first name no doubt assisted my combining (and splitting) my transference to each of them. Nevertheless, my analytic "paternity" certainly has American influences.

Notwithstanding my own personal experience, all this is to sketch out the type of psychoanalytic climate within which the vast majority of Australian analysts obtained their training and who now work within the framework of object relations informed thinking. In fact, I am sure that when my first supervisor decided to return to America (and "left me" when I was only eight months into my analysis), he left more object-relations oriented analysts than when he arrived.

Having offered this background data, I now speak only for myself—and do not implicate any of my colleagues for any unpardonable deviations from what I was taught.

Larsson's (1985) chapter in *Analysts at Work* mentions the circumstance of working in a country where the government is enlightened enough to permit a significant degree of funding for patients undergoing psychoanalytic treatment. In each patient's case this is a mixed blessing, as we are all aware of the unwelcome intrusion of the "third-party payer." Nevertheless, without this, many who are less well off are benefiting from treatment and would never otherwise have had the opportunity to experience a psychoanalytic approach to treatment. Many readers may bridle at my use of the term *treatment* and its inevitably medical connotations. This is a reality that I accept with all its problems. To some extent the issues are amenable to analysis.

This reality, too, comprises an important element of the psychoanalytic matrix within which I work. Like many other societies, ours is composed of both medical analysts and those with other professional backgrounds. The health-care subsidy of analytic fees is a significant influence on the practice of analysis in Australia, but our professional collegiality mostly transcends this sometimes problematic reality.

So, as a not senior member in my own Society, a not internationally published psychoanalyst, I now proceed to share with you the way I think about being an analyst and, as far as possible, the way I work. My "work" as I conceptualize it comprises a number of areas.

Centrally, of course, my work is my involvement with analysands. Important, if secondary, the privilege of offering supervision and teaching that constitutes a major part of my working week. I also regard working with committees of colleagues on behalf of psychoanalysis an important part of my identity and workload as a psychoanalyst. Yet another aspect of my work I consider of vital importance is conducted "internally"—and that is working on my understanding of psychoanalytic concepts and techniques and their relevance both to my patients and in the broader context.

Writing 100 years after the beginnings of psychoanalysis, and perhaps four or five "generations" of analysts from Freud and his contemporaries, I firmly consider that most of the major original contributions to our field have been made—at least for the time being. I consider it the task of the present members of our profession to consolidate what has been discovered, recognize lessons that have been learned, and attempt to identify what is quintessentially psychoanalysis, freed of personality cults and political agendas. In saying this I am referring more to psychoanalytic practice and technique than psychoanalytic theory.

Poland (1985) in his contribution to *Analysts at Work* commented on hearing an admired teacher say that the longer he worked in the field, the more he came to realize how much people are alike—not much later he said that the longer he continued in the work, the more he came to appreciate how very different each person is from the other. In acknowledging his coming to fundamentally agree with both, Poland speaks of the universality and the uniqueness of each individual's analysis.

It is this reality that characterizes much of the issues with which psychoanalysis must contend. People are unique, but they must struggle with basically similar developmental tasks in their journey from infancy to adulthood. The myriad variables that must be struggled with provide the infinite variety of individuals—but the commonality of underlying issues provides us with a body of clinical experience and theoretical notions without which we would all be flying blind and reinventing the psychoanalytic wheel.

This problem can be condensed into a recognition that we deal with both nomothetic and ideographic aspects of the human condition each time we embark on a psychoanalytic journey with an analysand. Nomothetic aspects are those that we have come to recognize as operating in all human beings, derived by generalizing from those who constitute the collective of analysands to date. (There could, I suppose, be someone, somewhere, who as yet not having graced an analyst's couch could put this to the lie.) Ideographic aspects are those that make each individual unique. I consider the deriving of nomothetic aspects of the human condition to be the legitimate scientific concern of psychoanalysis, while the ideographic aspects are dealt with in essentially a hermeneutic manner, in each unique analytic dyad.

The basic sciences that make up the applied science of meteorology permit a worldwide understanding of the conditions that contribute to the formation of weather patterns under given circumstances. Weather forecasting is notoriously imprecise, yet it serves well enough. Just think of trying to do without it. While a degree of accuracy is attainable in predicting weather patterns on a given day, no amount of knowledge in the field of meteorology, I believe, will ever permit the prediction of the shape of a given cloud.

Similarly, psychoanalysis has accumulated a significant body of experience and knowledge, which permits valid generalizations about the conditions that determine human development and the operation of mental processes. Yet no one will ever be able to account precisely for the shape of the development of a single human being, nor should we be expected to do so.

Taking this argument a step further, I think Poland's coming to agree with the apparent divergence of his teacher's views about individual patients applies as much to analysts themselves. We, too, have much in common, and at the same time are unique in our body of concepts and mode of practice.

In saying this, I do not follow the "anything goes" school of tolerance that some analysts espouse. With Wallerstein (1990), I am concerned about our need to delineate a common ground. Some things *are* psychoanalysis and others clearly, and sometimes not so clearly, are not.

In meeting with analyst colleagues, both locally and at international meetings, I am impressed with the attitudes and concepts that we share, which makes for a feeling of belonging to a common profession. At the same time, some aspects of thinking about psychoanalysis and psychoanalytic practice presented by some analysts at international meetings and in the literature do not sit comfortably with the thoughts of others. Some of this, of course, is part of healthy development in our field; but some of it represents a reluctance to move on with acknowledged developments in the international, as opposed to parochial, community of psychoanalysts or, worse, an insistence on a right to be individualistic and follow one's own star (and if possible recruit followers). Knowing which is which is sometimes difficult, but sometimes is quite clear.

For my part, I consider advances in the conceptualization and utilization of countertransference to be the major development in psychoanalytic theory and technique since Freud. The contribution by British object relations thinkers seems to me to be central in this, while many European, North American, and South American analysts have either independently arrived at similar concepts and practices or have built on those reported in the literature.

Just as the AIDS virus appears to be active throughout the world and permits independently working scientists to come to similar conclusions about it, so too is the human condition universal and open to independent workers genuinely achieving original insights about it. But just as there have been celebrated disputes about "being first" and claiming "ownership" of scientific discoveries (as with the AIDS virus), so too we in psychoanalysis have our celebrated disputes over the originality of ideas. Having some notion of what "being first" or being "*the* one" might involve, we should avoid such unseemly dispute and generously acknowledge originality if newer concepts have been published in the accessible literature. I feel that this has not always been the case.

Getting back to the point, I consider the significant change in the utilization of countertransference to be the major development in psychoanalytic practice and, as a corollary, the importance of the notion of projective identification as the primary mechanism by which the countertransference is mediated.

A second area of fundamental importance to the way I believe modern psychoanalysis should be conducted has to do with the psychoanalytic frame—the setting within which we conduct a psychoanalysis and within which the psychoanalytic process develops and evolves.

This may sound a pious platitude, but I think that adherence to the importance of the frame is not always held as a central aspect of the practice of our profession. Langs (1985), in his chapter in *Analysts at Work,* acknowledges that what he terms "secure frame therapies" (p. 68) involves an ideal set of ground rules, which are always under threat and inevitably broken in every analysis, even with the best of intentions to maintain them.

On the other hand, where deviations from a secure frame are built in to the therapy concerned ("deviant frame therapies"), Langs argues that there is inevitably a set of highly undesirable consequences that mitigate against the development of trust and the development of the sought-after internal psychic structures, that facilitate the individual's acquiring healthier object relationships. I would venture that the vast majority of the time I spend with my analysands and in supervising less experienced colleagues has concerned issues to do with understanding the transference via the countertransference and issues to do with management of the frame. In these two arenas, much of the psychoanalytic work is achieved.

Perhaps it is time to put my money where my mouth is and give some examples.

CASE HISTORY

A woman patient, in her late thirties, has been in analysis for eight years. She presented initially with severe anxiety symptoms, with regular panic attacks that were debilitating and almost made her housebound. She had done quite well at school, yet failed in her attempts to achieve a university degree. Her work record was patchy and at only a basic level, despite her evident intelligence. She had had mainly homosexual relationships, yet had had a four-year relationship with a violent, psychopathic-sounding young man prior to being referred to me for analysis by a therapist who had been seeing the patient once a week, but who had balked at the intensity of the dependency issues encountered even in this abbreviated therapy.

She proved to be a highly motivated analysand, demonstrating her commitment by making the analysis the central concern of her life and organizing her part-time job, her place of living, and, lately, her resumption of university studies so as to facilitate her attending analysis at the times I offered.

Whenever I presented material from this analysis to colleagues in peer clinical seminars, my short-hand way of reminding them of her was to refer to her as my "too-good-to-be-true" patient. By this I was referring to her cooperativeness and willingness to participate in the analytic process—but of course, as my colleagues always reminded me, such behavior can be equally defensive as in the service of the analysis.

Much of the analytic work concerned itself with analyzing her compliance and her rigid and often inflexible manner of ritualizing aspects of the frame—her adhering to "the rules." She was rarely even a minute late and she paid with monotonous regularity—even before I gave her my bill. She initially would come by train and be in the vicinity considerably early to permit arriving *exactly* on time. Later she came by car, but parked at a considerable distance from my rooms. Then she parked in the street where my office is situated and later was able to drive into the premises and park in the space provided for my patients. Needless to say, much of what I have just described was a result of the developments in the transference relationship with me and lived out as she slowly *really* came into analysis—both physically and psychically. This was despite her being so well motivated, as I originally thought.

In eight years of analysis much was talked about in relation to her history and her current relationships with her still intact family of origin and her friends. I firmly consider, however, that the real work, which produced significant changes in her psychic structure and her defensive constellation, was done over issues to do with the frame—issues to do with the manner of her coming to the analysis day by day and her manner of paying my fees (initially she paid by cash for a series of complex reasons, but after some years acquired a checkbook, representing, I thought, a more mature attitude to the handling of money).

With this scant background, let me describe in some detail a significant set of events that occurred.

To facilitate her travel to analysis and the university, she moved from renting accommodations at considerable distance from my office to renting in a nearby suburb. This was the case in up to three separate instances of shared living situations in the same general district.

One weekend, while reading a local newspaper, she saw a real estate advertisement in which my family home was being offered for sale. She came in on Monday morning and said she had seen the ad and experienced a shock. She said she knew approximately where I lived and had confirmed that it was in fact my house by looking it up in the telephone book to see if the details tallied.

After claiming to have recovered from the shock—relatively quickly, she was pleased to say—she thought she would like to know where I was moving to. She surmised, correctly, that the move was occasioned by my children, having completed their university education, leaving home. In spite of her "respect for the boundaries" of the analytic relationship, she had friends who occasionally fed her information about me and my family. Even though she came to understand the destructiveness of this and did attempt to avoid further instances of it, she had been provided with enough information to fuel many fantasies, which did get explored to some extent through the course of the analysis—at least the ones she told me about.

About my moving, she speculated that my wife, who shares the premises where I work, and I would perhaps be moving to more suitable accommodation, as the patient's now-retired professional parents had recently done. She thought we would be staying in the general area in which we had lived and worked. After initially being very "reasonable" about the whole issue, she became more and more strident, insisting on knowing where I was moving.

The next day she came in saying that she had a right to know where I was going to move to and that as she had already known where I lived, this didn't constitute any change in the status quo. Her arguments alternated between the plausible and the irrational. At times it felt to me that the easy way out would be simply to tell her that I was moving to another district, but I resisted this temptation.

An early image developed of me as a balloon floating untethered over the landscape if she couldn't know where I was. She had always coped with my absences by imagining more or less where I might be. The whole of the week was consumed with this issue. I could not recall any other time where such an intense concentration on one issue had occurred. The associated thoughts and fantasies became more and more productive.

However, I began to get irritated by her dogged and unrelenting nagging-away at the issue and her insistence, couched in rationalized and seemingly well-argued terms, on her right to know. She herself came up with the image of an angry child stamping its foot in impotent fury and shouting that she wanted to know.

I interpreted that she wanted to know what was going on behind the door which she felt I was determined to keep closed to her. This brought a return of the balloon imagery, and I suddenly had an image of a pregnant mother pictured as a balloon and recalled that when she was about 14 months old, her mother went to the hospital to have her baby brother. She was cared for by an unfamiliar grandmother at the time and was not taken to see her mother and the baby in the hospital. I ventured the thought that she felt I was the balloon-shaped mother disappearing as a result of activities behind the closed door and that she was enraged at my not letting her know where I was.

She countered with the idea that if she put her mind to it she would be able to find out where I had moved to. She had only to await the appearance of some future telephone directory, which would carry the information she needed. However, what if I decided to have my private telephone number unlisted? This enraged her even more. The fantasy emerged that she would find out regardless of my attempt to prevent her knowing and would leave on my doorstep a box full of shit. Better still, she recalled the scene from the film *The Godfather*, where the man who is the target of Marlon Brando's character's sadism throws back the bedclothes to reveal the severed head of his favorite stallion. That, she said, would make me suffer even more than any attack she could imagine on me—the counterpart of the horse would be a member of my family! She was shocked by the intensity of this fantasy. This was the most vivid experience of the analysis thus far. She could hardly believe that she was capable of saying such a thing.

The following week, the question of the unlisted telephone number again occupied a lot of time. Now, however, it was in the context of my need to protect myself from patients such as herself. She complained that she had been so careful not to intrude on my privacy and now I was going to reward her consideration by hiding my whereabouts from her. This she perceived as a punishment for her.

I suggested that she felt on the one hand that I was frightened of her intense fantasies of wanting to make me suffer for disappearing from her, but on the other hand that she would feel contemptuous of me if I proved to have an unlisted number, which would confirm that this was so. She agreed and went on to talk about wanting me to be a competent analyst who would not make mistakes and needing to feel that I could withstand whatever pressure she put on me to make me fail in my responsibilities to her.

A few weeks later, after a brief holiday break, she began the Monday session wondering whether I might be angry with her. She had had the fantasy during the break that someone had done me some harm and wanted to say to me, "It wasn't me." She then told of a dream, which she said had to do with my moving. She dreamed she had contracted hydatid disease (nowadays a rare parasite transmitted by infected cattle in the country regions in Australia). She'd needed an operation to remove it. She also needed a major dental procedure on her teeth. Her housemate, Jean, was to move from the house and the patient felt very anxious. She equated this with my moving and said she wondered how she could take over the lease on the house. Jean was an older woman (three women shared the house), and it felt as if it was Jean's house and that Jean was like the parent and "in charge," providing stability and security. She talked of their house on the edge of the bushland and again asked where I was moving to. She then offered her own thoughts about the hydatids and the dental procedure and ventured that they represented "bad things inside herself." I suggested that although these thoughts were reasonable, I felt that she was trying to be the grown-up in the house and trying to avoid the feelings of being little and bereft when I was away and moving away. She said it no longer mattered where I was moving to and continued on a familiar theme of my being Jewish and her not. This represented another "shut door" between us that could never be opened. She could rationalize about it, but it never would make any difference. She went on to talk about how much better she was now, and that she no longer had to be like me. She could be herself, could be by herself, and no longer would want to be part of my life. She did however admit to a persistent envy of what went on "behind those doors." After a slight pause, she spoke of having the thought the night before, "Are you [the analyst] really a real person?" She went on to exclaim about my appearing "so perfect," never with any faults or failings, never appearing foolish or vulnerable, and equated this with a small child's view of its parents.

After another pause, she said she should tell me about another dream. It was different. It was about sexuality and aggression. During the break, she had particularly noted her aggression when driving her car. One morning she had driven next to a young man in a new model of small car. She imagined while driving that she was racing against him "psychologically"—she didn't know if he even noticed her. She was desperate to get in front of him in her little old car. After some alternation of position, she finally got in front of him and stayed there. "I won the race. I was triumphant! I didn't speed—I was just quick off the mark. I out maneuvered him." She went on to say that it was nothing dangerous, that this had all occurred in heavy traffic. She was, however, surprised at her competitiveness.

She then said she remembered yet another dream. In this dream she was again driving a car and somehow was half man and half woman. She was interested in a young woman and was trying to impress her. Someone told her she was the best driver they had ever seen. She felt intense pride. This was partly experienced aggressively and partly sexually: she used the word "prowess" to encapsulate the feelings.

She said it was laughable to tell me about a dream such as that. It was so stereotypically male: driving the car like that. What outlets were there for women? In her fantasy world, she said, she often used typically masculine outlets, at least physically. She talked of going to the gym and pushing herself physically. In wondering about her "mixed gender" in the dream, she lamented whether she would ever attain a female identity. (She had in the past year or two been involved with a pleasant-sounding young man, but was having significant difficulty committing to the relationship, especially sexually.)

I chose to take up the competitive theme and said that I thought all this talk of competition was with me and that she wished to triumph over me, but in doing so felt confused as to her feminine feelings of wanting to be with me behind the closed door.

"Compete?" she exclaimed. "I've got other things to do than compete! John [the first and violent boyfriend] used to say I wasn't as competitive as his other girlfriends had been. If you're with someone and supposed to love them, you wouldn't want to triumph over them and grind them into the dirt. I like to be kind and understanding."

I said that it seemed now that she wished to deny what was so obvious in her dream and what she had since talked about.

"No one would like me if I behaved like that. I'd be like my father—only wanting to grind people down. I have to suppress that in relationships, otherwise I hurt people." She went on to talk of perhaps being more in touch with such feelings while I was away. She'd visited her brother and sister-in-law. He had been sounding off as was typical of him. After leaving, she found herself in a similar frame of mind: angry, intolerant, impatient. She likened her brother and her father as having no room for anyone else's sensitivities and sensibilities. "They act it out. I keep it in. Mine is a more acceptable facade—like my mother's. But I'm more than a match for most men! They're pathetic. I could demolish David [the present boyfriend]—but I don't tell him what I think."

"And if you really let go at me?" I asked.

"I think you're more than a match for me. If it came to the crunch, you'd win. So I don't take you on. Anyhow, even if I felt stronger, I'd need to protect you. It's reassuring that I don't have to waste energy protecting you."

"Don't you?" I challenged.

She went on to review the few relationships she had had with men. The current boyfriend she felt she could readily dominate and needed to protect him. The violent boyfriend was physically stronger and frightened her. About another with whom she had had a brief (sadistic-sounding) relationship, she said he had no ordinary feelings and no one could overcome him. He was not a human being.

"I see you as human, though. You're capable of feelings and of being hurt. It's hard to know where love fits into all of this."

"Perhaps it's in struggling with all this anger and competitiveness," I ventured.

"Well . . . you do." she said.

I would now like to explore some of the multitude of issues involved in the above account of the sessions with my patient and to attempt to retrieve some of the thinking that influenced the kind of interpretations I made.

The brief vignette involving her intense reactions to discovering my impending move well illustrates that no matter how well advanced an analysis might appear to be, the analysand is always susceptible to experiencing and being dominated by very primitive feelings, originating in the pregenital period of development. She was shocked by the intensity of these feelings and vividly experienced the struggle between attacking me in order to destroy me and attacking me in order to test my ability to tolerate and withstand her destructive feelings. There is always considerable pressure on the analyst to take the "easy way out" and to collude with a rationalized argument for providing seemingly innocent information, which breaches the psychoanalytic frame.

The attention to one's own fantasies while listening to the patient is a well-recognized mine of valuable information that permits otherwise relatively concealed issues to be accessed. My resonating with the balloon imagery led to my associating to her sibling's birth and the much earlier reported circumstances surrounding it. This permitted my linking the present experience with a past one in a not-too-direct manner that hopefully would lead to her consolidating the connection herself, if it was a valid one to make.

Turning now to the longer account of the session following a break, it seems evident that her response to the break itself was experienced on at least two levels: a pregenital dependent level and a more phallic-striving competitive level. The question about whether the competitive level is itself defensive against the more primitive dependent experience must be asked. Given that this analysis is already of long duration, I considered that a measure of the competitiveness was developmentally appropriate for the stage the analysis had reached.

This question had to be contended with almost immediately in this session. Her making her own interpretation of the dream made me question whether this was an appropriate insight into her own dream or an attempt to master the anxiety of having missed me during the break by being too grown up and having to make her own interpretations and denying her need for me. I opted for a little of each, as I consider that suggesting that the thoughts were reasonable sufficiently acknowledged any appropriate insight, while drawing attention to the issue of being left as being still of considerable importance. Given that much of the first five or so years of the analysis was taken up almost exclusively with issues of dependence and intense reactions to weekends and holiday breaks, I felt that she now in fact was coping with breaks quite well, but the issue of my move had stirred up a specific experience of the disappearance of the mother with the birth of her sibling, thus combining the dependency with the rivalry issues.

She led up to the reporting of the second dream via a series of statements as to how improved she was. She announced that the second dream was to do with "sexuality and aggression."

While there were certainly aggressive and some obvious sexual issues, it seemed to me that the competitiveness overshadowed each of these and that her competitiveness with me was to the fore. I chose to target this in my interpretation. However, because there had been up till now little direct expression of sexual feelings toward me, I felt I had to at least leave some room for her "gender confusion" in the dream and offer an opportunity for her to develop her lament about fully attaining a female identity by linking her rivalry with me and her confusion with the possibility of a need to deny a desire to submit to me sexually (the latter being "ideologically unsound").

Her remark at the end of the second dream about being quick off the mark and outmaneuvering her fantasized rival captured my attention, but I felt I would hold this in mind for the time being.

She took up the rivalry and then attempted to assert her "kind and understanding self." When I interpreted this as defensive, she then appeared to almost blurt out her identification with her father's and brother's angry, intolerant insensitivity to others, ending with an outburst of contempt for most men and her need to protect her present boyfriend from this aspect of herself.

The last few exchanges in the session had to do with another version of the struggle referred to at the end of the brief vignette with which I introduced the clinical material. This is the struggle between destruction and survival of the object.

I consider, with many others, that our psychoanalytic engagement in this struggle—in its myriad incarnations—is one of the major contributions of psychoanalysis toward psychic change in patients with primitive personality disorders. As Winnicott (1969, 1971), among others, has asserted, it is the mother's task to survive her baby's aggressive attacks—just as it is the analyst's task to survive the attacks of the patient. According to Winnicott, love is born out of destructive aggression and hatred.

Winnicott's formulation, couched in more common language, is a paraphrase of the earlier Kleinian—and now object relations—notion that the good object is the object that survives the destructive attacks and toward which reparative efforts are made when the infant "realizes" that the bad (part) object and the good (part) object are the same and need to be integrated into an ambivalently regarded whole object. By careful management of the psychoanalytic setting—within the psychoanalytic frame—opportunities will inevitably arise wherein important transference-countertransference issues, representing significant inner-world conflicts of the patient, can be analyzed. In the experiencing and analysis of these conflicts in the analytic relationship, a closer approach to whole-object experience can often be achieved.

REFERENCES

Langs, R. (1985). The communicative approach of classical psychoanalysis. In *Analysts at Work: Practice, Principles, and Techniques*, ed. J. Reppen, pp. 59–78. Hillsdale, NJ: Analytic Press.

Larsson, B. (1985). An analyst at work in Sweden. In *Analysts at Work: Practice, Principles, and Techniques*, ed. J. Reppen, pp. 79–96. Hillsdale, NJ: Analytic Press.

Ogden, T. H. (1994). The analytical third: working with intersubjective clinical facts. *International Journal of Psycho-Analysis* 75:3–20.

Poland, W. S. (1985). At work. In *Analysts at Work: Practice, Principles, and Techniques*, ed. J. Reppen, pp. 145–164. Hillsdale, NJ: Analytic Press.

Reppen, J., ed. (1985). *Analysts at Work: Practice, Principles, and Techniques.* Hillsdale, NJ: Analytic Press. Reprinted Jason Aronson, 1994.

Wallerstein, R. S. (1990). Psychoanalysis: the common ground. *International Journal of Psycho-Analysis* 71:3–20.

Winnicott, D. W. (1969). The use of an object. *International Journal of Psycho-Analysis* 50:711–716.

——— (1971). The use of an object and relating through identifications. In *Playing and Reality*, pp. 86–94. London: Tavistock.

11

Psychoanalysis, Sexual Life, and Anxiety

Jaime P. Stubrin

I have worked with drug-addicted patients for more than twenty years. As treatments progressed, making possible within them psychoanalytic investigation, I became more aware of the close relationship between the supposed addict "structure" and the supposed "perverse structure." I still had not stopped using the word *perversion.* Later I understood that the word is not a psychoanalytic one. Its origin is related to evil, perversity, corruption. Our patients with addictions, or with sexual behaviors that part from the norm, are far from being related to evil. Psychoanalysis does not consider either goodness or badness.

Saying that someone is perverse is to describe him or her in terms that are degrading and humiliating. In 1974 I wrote a paper, which was later published (Stubrin 1976), in which I connected the structure of perversity with that of the addict. Another paper (Stubrin 1984) was published in Italy in which I also linked drug addiction and perverse structure.

At the time I was still working alone on the subject. In North America, of course, distinguished colleagues were working along the same lines, which I discovered little by little from carefully reviewing the literature.

It was more difficult for them to discover me. Living in South America and publishing in Spanish is a difficult barrier to cross. It was a time when I believed in the existence of a "perverse structure" and had to continue in my search to find it. I was not the only one who believed in it, of course (Baranger et al. 1980, Socarides 1984).

At some moments in my work I believed I was very close to finding, as if it was a matter of a lost link, the famous structure that sustained the psyche of the "perverse" person. The closer I came to this notion the farther I realized I was from it. This was due to various factors: (1) an exaggerated adherence to the concept of the Oedipus complex without including rich conceptualizations about the preoedipal stage, (2) the rigid repetition of concepts of post-Freudian authors, (3) the belief that all people with a different sexuality were ill and were classifiable in the same structural configuration, (4) the all-encompassing idea of the "perversion" concept, (5) the firm belief in the existence of "structures," and (6) a great error in relation to therapeutic objectives.

The points in common that I had found between the drug addict and the people still referred to as perverse were the following:

1. There were in both an immense sensation of interior emptiness, which was experienced as an unmanageable anxiety. The only remedy that appeared capable of calming such destructive anxiety was for the addict the drug and for the perverse a sexual relation that was generally fleeting, anonymous, and with strong pregenital tendencies and promiscuous characteristics. In both cases a vital

risk was always present. I still think that promiscuity is desperation. The drug and/or the partner have an extremely brief tranquilizing effect that reestablishes momentarily a certain libidinal and narcissistic equilibrium.

2. In both cases the analysis permitted me to understand that these people look for the reestablishment of the unification with the mother of the initial symbiosis, therefore resolving, imaginarily, the impaired primitive object relations.
3. It seems clear that both subjects try to repair what was not achieved in the stage of symbiosis and separation-individuation. That repair is found through the fetish or something fetishized that comes to fill a void and to mark, even though momentarily, some kind of border or limit that this kind of person feels to have lost or not achieved—namely, his identity.

For the subject with sexual perturbances the alteration is observed not only in sexual conduct but also in the upheaval in the identity of gender and role, that is, of sexual identity. The fetish, which is something that the subject can create, acts as a transitional object that has failed in the mediating attempt with the mother. I have found in these people that the principal defense mechanism is disavowal (*verleugnung*), and from that perspective the fetish and its "organization" the fetishism are the paradigm of the perversions and what I will call, following McDougall's ideas, "neosexualities," constituting the fetish in the object of desire.

In the introduction to the Spanish edition of McDougall's *Theaters of the Mind* (1987), León Grinberg wrote:

> McDougall prefers "neosexualities" to the sexual perversions, because she maintains that these patients have reinvented human sexuality, changing the goals and the objects and creating a new primary scene. This newly invented sexual theory contains, of course, a great load of anxiety and compulsion. Its central theme is castration, but the "success"

> consists in transforming castration into a carefully controlled play experience. Acts of flagellation, humiliation, etc., are substitutive acts with which one tries to dominate the anguish of castration. [p. 7, my translation]

And McDougall (1985) affirmed:

> It is my contention that neosexualities must deal with a double set of problems, not only those connected with the oedipal conflict but also those belonging to the realm of primitive sexuality—that is, the child's earliest conceptions of the sensual world, with its archaic internal and external stimulations and frustrations. In the enactment of the neosexual scene, the conflicts at both levels must be adroitly disavowed. Neosexualites then serve not only to maintain libidinal homeostasis but narcissistic homeostasis as well. [p. 251]

Happily, my thoughts kept evolving as I learned from my patients. There were also analysts who taught me. The word "perversion" kept losing strength, value, and usefulness. It was actually thanks to Joyce McDougall that I discovered how pejorative and how little psychoanalytic it was. When McDougall asks which acts we designate as perverse and who in reality is perverse, she responds that a pervert is no more than someone that does not make love as other people do. This humane explanation demonstrates to us that the word perversion (as I said earlier) is not in itself a psychoanalytic definition. Thus in looking at its origins one discovers that perversion is not even linked to the sexual and that we have been classifying our patients not with an analytical characterization but a moral one, given that perversion denotes a relation to evil and a (voluntary) desire to do evil.

John Money (1988) in a similar effort coined the term *paraphilia* and defines it thus:

> Paraphilia is defined as a condition occurring in men and women of being compulsively responsive to, and for optimal

> initiation and maintenance of sexuoerotic arousal and the facilitation or attainment of orgasm, obligatively fixated and dependent on an unusual, personally or socially unacceptable stimulus either perceived directly, or in the imagery or ideation of fantasy. [p. 51]

Something similar occurred with the term *structure.* To think this way is to believe that humans are a species of stainless steel robots, that is, unmodifiable. Structure refers to something rigid and not changeable. My work with patients has shown what Robert Stoller (personal communication) thought, that structures were nothing more than metaphors. This clarified the meanings for me. I changed the term structure to the term "organization," which implies greater flexibility and capacity (with possibility) for change.

The word "perversion" ended up relegated to the judicial sphere, that is, to those persons who for important sexual offenses (when basically the other "does not consent") arrive in courts of law. The majority of patients with a different sexuality (different from what?) do not consult us for that reason. Normality is no more than statistical data.

Today homosexuality is a concept that is so widely spoken of and commented upon in all media that it is almost redundant to speak about it. Nevertheless, homosexuals suffer although (apparently) they consult analysts not for that suffering but for situations of any human being (discrimination, the vexations and humiliations of which they are the subjects, etc.). Surprisingly we find many homosexuals whom, in spite of our inability to speak about health and sickness, we would call "healthy."

Needless to say, there are many more homosexuals who do not consult an analyst than who do. Again, those who consult us do so primarily for reasons other than their homosexuality. Considering that 8 percent of the Western population is homosexual, we analysts would have no free time to assist the many who would consult us if it were true that all homosexuals have ailments of their psyche and want treatment.

It is the same for analysts who do not promise changes in

sexual orientation as for those who do; they see many homosexual persons. I belong to the first group of analysts. The therapeutic objective is not to heterosexualize them, that is, not to try to modify their sexual orientation, but to try to see that they live better. No one chooses anything, much less sexual orientation.

As Freud stated, the goal of analysis is simply to develop an ability to love and work and to transform human misery into daily suffering. We analysts have created a stereotype of ourselves when we attempt to explain everything solely from the perspective of the Oedipus complex or from a preoedipal perspective. The work of Margaret Mahler and colleagues (1975) about the difficulty certain persons have in going successfully through the separation–individuation stage, and the concept of the engulfing mother and engulfed child, is of significance as much in our theoretic comprehension of our patients as in the technical considerations we use during psychoanalytic treatment. This implies possible modifications in the frame, very careful interpretations with respect to timing, and, of course, our expectations of what we (and later our patient) will have as a therapeutic objective.

What is the patient like, the one who we would say has a sexual deviancy (I do not refer here to the sexual choice of object)? We analysts have fallen many times into the temptation of establishing theories and statistics based only on the study of patients who come to our offices. That temptation has caused many to write papers in which they explain in a finalistic manner the psychic structure of the so-called sexual deviants. How many "purely deviant" patients does an analyst see to establish a sufficiently encompassing and complete theory? In general it is seldom that someone who has a "very deviant" sexuality consults us for his deviance. He always consults us for other reasons, and many times the discovery of his neosexuality is a discovery made *in* his analysis (Abadi and Stubrin 1980). As the analysis develops, people who in the first interviews relate a "normal" sexuality eventually describe and display a sexuality that is many times profoundly conflictive. In any case, I believe, these patients relate to us *a sexual life of anxiety*.

A distinction must be made because our patients who have

conflictual sexuality that deviates from what "normal" people consider normal and from what analysts tied to Freud (and bound in the Judeo-Christian-Victorian tradition) consider healthy might in their personal relations be extremely successful. They might not only might be successful in their professional lives but also creative. Only in their intimate life (that linked only to what happens in their bedrooms) might they be considered "deviants."

The question becomes complicated because it was thought for a long time that those deviants were marked by sadism (and/or masochism), which would impede a creative life. Reality often shows the contrary and our attitude as analysts is complicated as we see before us subjects with high intellectual, moral, esthetic, and ethical values that confront our own values and prejudices.

Does an analyst have the task or even the right to try to change the sexuality of his patient except in the case of one who may act against his own physical well-being or that of others? What are the characteristics of patients who are homosexual and who consult with us? In general, we will find in them the entire spectrum of the human rainbow. In those whose sexuality is conflictive the affects and attitudes linked to anxiety will rapidly appear.

Socarides mentions a basic anxiety, even though I believe that his error lies in attributing it to all persons who do not have a "normal" sexuality. This basic anxiety, which probably generates conduct and psychic organization, is seen in *compulsive* behavior.

I would define a neosexual person as one who, from the point of view of his sexuality, has a rigid and stable organization, that is, when the desire to have sexual relations is prevented, an intense anxiety that has destructuring characteristics is experienced as a sense of annihilation.

Why does the person look for that kind of sexual relation? Because during it the subject feels he is recovering himself. I insist that the neosexual organization is characterized fundamentally by the presence of compulsive action and ritualized act. During their analysis we analysts must be ready to confront multiple aspects of a psyche that is very complicated. The Oedipus complex and castration anxiety are insufficient concepts to explain those aspects. We must always incorporate into our thinking what comes before Oedipus, the preoedipal, with its archaic and pregenital behaviors.

Neosexualities are constituted by the interweaving of the oedipal with the preoedipal. Current psychoanalytic knowledge prevents us from trying to understand neosexuality by only appealing to the oedipal structure or based only on events of the preoedipal stage. In analysis we can discover disturbance in the organization of the Oedipus complex and even serious alterations in the configuration of the superego. Everyone passes through the oedipal stage (except perhaps primary autistics), each in his or her own way. In all people important events have occurred in the preoedipal stage that are psychologically organizing. Afterwards, this stage will be intertwined with the oedipal and there we find the person who demands help from us.

Who is the person who is asking us for help, what is he like, and what can we do for him? My exposition is limited only to those who consult us as homosexuals, though they do not consult us for their homosexuality. Even though there persists in certain analytical circles the idea that homosexuality is a sickness that must be cured—that is to say that the sexual orientation of the person must be changed—today it is generally accepted that this is not the case. This does not mean, of course, that there are no sick homosexuals, nor does it mean that there are no healthy ones.

Homosexuality is not a psychopathological definition in itself. In general, what we should observe is the basic psychic organization of the subject, what can be disturbed or not and with which we work during the psychoanalysis. Success or failure will be realized only at the end of the process.

In the majority of homosexual patients we find social concerns because of their being homosexual. We could divide these persons in two groups, even though this division resembles medical thinking: (1) homosexuals who have a sick sexuality and homosexuals who have a healthy sexuality. This division is artificial because it is based on the concept of normal, which is only a statistic. A "normal" subject is not one who makes love the way the majority does, and of course this concept is not a psychoanalytical one. At the same time this division is useful for description. In the first category, that is, those persons who have a disturbed sexuality, we include people with the neosexualities and view them from the perspective of their psychic organization. Inside this spectrum of persons we find all kinds of psychic organizations, from the psychotic to the neurotic. If he is psychotic, in general his sexuality will be colored by the alteration that the psychosis itself produces; if he is neurotic we will run into neuroses or borderline pathology. If he is not neurotic or borderline, we will find that he is in the second type of classification. Among people with a sick sexuality, borderline organizations predominate and sexual activity is in general disorganized, with frenetic searching for the sexual partner, with pregenital and promiscuous sexual behaviors (keeping in mind that promiscuity is desperation).

The sexual searching is characterized basically by compulsivity. What does compulsivity mean? That the subject feels an unrestrained desire to have a sexual relation and cannot avoid it, acting as if it were a spring that is released and takes off like a shot in search of sexual satisfaction, much like the addict with a drug (addictive utilization of a subject by another). "In the compulsive neosexual, neither the Super-Ego nor the Ego can be opposed to the strength and the pressure of the command of the unconscious" (Stubrin 1993, p. 125). Joyce McDougall (1985) writes:

> The compulsive, repetitive aspect applies to all addictive sexualities. The person caught in this web of illusion will always choose the magical act, and its painfully compulsive quality, rather than face anxiety and internal persecutors. [p. 280]

She adds:

> From the economic point of view, most neosexual creations have a drug-like quality; they are used to escape from painful

> psychic states and to repair rifts in the feeling or identity as well as to satisfy instinctual impulses. [p. 282]

At the same time, this compulsive sexual action brings these people little contact with reality; they disregard precautions against robbery, attack, blackmail, or jail as well as AIDS. In a men's room a patient who performed fellatio on one man repeated the act on the occupant of the next stall without realizing it was the same person until the man told him.

Compulsive sexual activity always has anxiety as the motor. This anxiety that is unbound, and at the same time unrecognized as such, surges forth in the subject without elaboration and is transformed into an act. Jean Genet (White 1993), who in his writings and biography we would include among the neosexualities, writes: "I was but a prolonged, silent wail" (p. 31, my translation). This affirmation realizes the permanent state of an unbearable amount of anxiety. It is generally uncommon for patients to attribute their sexual behavior to the feeling of anxiety.

More often there appear substitutes, such as the sensation of interior emptiness, a loss of limits, a drop in self-esteem, fear, or ideas of suicide, and it is difficult for him to relate (except through psychoanalysis) his sexual activity and the anxiety he suffers. But as he comes to know himself in treatment there is the possible recognition of anxiety.

Another patient reported that when he felt anxiety, he spent long hours in public restrooms trying to have (and having) sexual relations. We see his anxiety unfolding:

> When I feel anxiety the only thing I can do is go find a groncho,[1] as if to say, "Hey, destroy me." In the restrooms

---

1. In this context the term refers to a somewhat dark-skinned man from a lower social class who has little education and would have homosexual relations for money, either by charging or sometimes robbing. The term *chongo* may also be used.

> everything is impersonal, without affection. When somebody is in the middle of anxiety, he can only have morbid sex, almost fictional, impersonal. Anxiety lowers my defenses and blocks me. It makes me avoid the connection with a human being as such. One does not connect with the other. When you're anxious, then only in bed is there a letting down.

The fantasy of suicide is often implied as an end to the anxiety and also as a "just punishment" (Abadi and Stubrin 1980). In relation to the death drive, it appeared evident in the case of a 22-year-old homosexual with an enormous amount of guilt. He related that he felt so much hatred for himself that he decided to contract AIDS. With that decision he began compulsive sexual behavior, frenetic and promiscuous, and unfortunately achieved his goal. From the moment he began analysis, which is centered fundamentally on his anxiety and guilt, his quality of life improved. His defenses have risen, within reasonable limits, despite his HIV-positive status.

Another patient—located within the neosexualities—whom I call Carlos in *Sexualities and Homosexualities* (Stubrin 1994), said:

> When I have nothing to do and feel empty, the toilet anchors me. Why would I give up the toilets when they are the only passion I have? The toilet itself is a source of arousal, unlike the bed, which has something to do with sadism. The image of myself that I present here is that of an ill person. That's crap! It is irreconcilable with the sensation of being inside, not feeling dissipated. When I am in the toilet, I fall into an oneiric state. In fact, it is like going out to play. I suppose it is the same thing children experience when they go out to play (transitional space; transitional object transformed into a fetish). In fact, the toilet is a soothing place, because I do not experience fear there, and I feel almighty. The game of losing and recovering identity is exciting. When I am outside the toilet, I feel atomized, shattered. [pp. 124–125]

(The patient denies and is incapable of registering the sadism existing in the public restroom.)

> That's my disease; I am aroused by whatever is sordid, clandestine and dangerous. "Home Sweet Home" does not arouse me. I have no doubt that all this is anxiety. In the toilet I am not part of the outside, I am part of myself. The moment I ejaculate, I leave, because I have nothing else to do there. It is a lousy place just to shit or to piss. But before going in, I have the feeling of playing a game. I disguise the place, I remove the dirt from it. Once inside, I do not have the sense of dissipation that I usually feel, and this relieves me. [p. 124]

The death drive helps us as an important piece of information to determine the seriousness of the patient's difficulty. The basic anxiety I have already mentioned is found in all neosexual patients but not in those who, despite having a different sexuality, are not included in neosexuality. The source of anxiety in these neosexual patients is multiple:

1. Many patients tell of having discovered their homosexuality around the ages of 14 to 16 years. According to my experience, the majority remember feeling attracted and inclined to people of the same sex as far back as they can remember. It is not difficult to understand that a boy or girl who becomes homosexual feels different in a world that is basically heterosexual. On the other hand, boys or girls who become heterosexual—even though they will have to confront all the complications of life—will not have difficulties in the area of sexual object choice. It will be enough for a boy to be the progenitor of his own sex. It will seem that life has a marked path for him. He will remember even in nursery school he liked so-and-so, a friend of the other sex. On the other hand, for the homosexual child everything will be more complicated. It will take him a long time

to accept what is happening to him. He will think for a long time that his attraction to boys is only a stage that will soon pass. He will feel odd, strange, and sinful because he will not be able to easily distinguish a pressure that is cultural, social, religious, and parental. Perhaps one of the most salient points is a feeling of having betrayed one's parents. There are no parents who consciously want to have homosexual children.

2. The anxiety generated by social pressure is another source of anxiety. To ignore it would be foolish. We cannot forget our belonging to the Western world marked by Judeo-Christian morality nor can we forget our magnificent ignorance (as psychoanalysts) of the rest of the world and its different codes. So we will note that Judaism and Christianity condemn homosexuality just as Islam does. The child who belongs to that world—which has the force of law—obviously stays outside the faithful flock and outside the law and is in sin, something that of course is not easy to get over. We know that homosexuals have been persecuted and discriminated against for at least 2,000 years. The punishment that comes from the Bible and the pyres of the Holy Inquisition as well as the crematory ovens of the Nazis and contemporary police persecutions is cause enough to unleash intense anxiety with episodes as chronic as they are acute. This is the anxiety that is at the base of all compulsive sexual behavior, in the frenetic search for a fleeting sexual relation, and in promiscuity. We know that the majority of suicides or suicide attempts in adolescents and young adults are committed by homosexuals.

Anxiety is also the generator of homophobia between homosexuals. Self-deprecation, the lowering of self-esteem, resentment, guilt, empty hatred toward themselves, and identification with the aggressor are proof of this.

It is clinically more difficult for me to try to elaborate and subdue the homophobia of homosexuals than that of heterosexuals. Marmor (1980), in defining homophobia, writes:

> It represents a pathological fear of homosexuality, usually based on one of more of the following factors: 1) a deep-seated insecurity concerning one's own sexuality and gender identity, 2) a strong religious indoctrination, or 3) simple ignorance about homosexuals. [p. 19]

For decades analysts set out zealously to heterosexualize their patients. Marmor (1982) writes:

> In a culture such as ours, where being homosexual implies humiliating, ridiculing, and derogative labels, it is surprising that there should be people whose self-image, emotional stability, or feeling are not lowered by the social effects of the manifestation of their tendencies. [p. 472]

Guilt, an ever-present factor in homosexuals because of their being "different" and accused as corrupters, was used by analysts as a "weapon" (for others as a tool) to achieve heterosexualization. We know well that neither guilt nor aggression cures anyone.

To cure what? We are still far from understanding why sexual orientations differ from person to person; even less are we in a position to "cure" someone with deviant sexuality. Perhaps we should accept the idea that homosexual activity is not superimposed on what is heterosexual, just as masculine homosexual activity cannot be superimposed on the feminine. We should not try to explain homosexuality in terms of heterosexuality, just as we would not try to explain femininity in terms of masculinity. Homosexual activity can have some of its own characteristics, which we must respect, investigate, and understand without trying to make our patients fit into a prefabricated mold.

And what must we as analysts do in our daily work? Analyze! But respect the sexual orientation of the patient. Psychoanalysis will finally permit him or her self-respect. I said earlier that we confront two kinds of homosexuals: neosexuals and nonneosexuals. Among those in the first category are the difficult patients. They are the ones in whom anxiety is much stronger and overwhelming. My primary task with them is to systematically analyze the anxiety and its originating motives. We analysts in general know little about how our patients (especially our heterosexual patients) live their sexual lives. They say, "I had magnificent coitus," and we believe them. I am convinced that we must know more about their sexual life, especially if they are neosexuals (as much hetero- as homosexual). Each sexual act in itself is charged with symbolism, and we must discover it because the compulsive act is charged with anxiety. In my experience, the sustained and systematic interpretation of anxiety causes the anxiety to decrease or disappear and may even prompt the disappearance of the compulsive behavior. If what we considered to be a "perverse structure," or at least a rigidly established organization, can possibly be modified to such a degree, it means we are using stereotypical concepts.

I am not trying to include more statistics; I am only relating my experience since it is common to observe that less anxiety promotes less compulsivity. This achievement is an objective in itself.

Transference will develop in these supposedly "deviant" patients—neosexuals and nonneosexuals—according to their basic psychopathology. We will then occupy different roles, such as paternal or maternal, as with any patient. If an erotic transference develops we will have to interpret that as well. Some analysts may have to return to their own analysis to resolve the conflict presented by the transference.

Something similar happens with countertransference. It is an extremely important element that we must take into account and to which we must pay careful attention because it will guide the continuity of treatment. Interpretation from the countertransference is not a confession of our thoughts and feelings, but many times organizes our comprehension and interpretation. In the case of patients with very promiscuous, compulsive, and risky sexual activities, we may feel afraid and anxious about sharing with them because they are including us in their own fears and anguish. Therefore, the analysis of the transference and countertransference is more complex. With "difficult" or severe patients, perhaps, we may have to adjust the classic psychoanalytic frame—as we do with adolescents—to foster an analytical situation and access to the unconscious.

REFERENCES

Abadi, P. D., and Stubrin, J. P. (1980). Estructura perversa: descubrimeniento en el psicoanálisis (Perverse structure: discovery in psychoanalysis). X Congreso Interno y XX Simposium. Asociación Psicoanalítica Argentina.

Baranger, W., Bisi, N., Goldstein, R. Z., et. al. (1980). Perversion. X Congreso Interno y XX Simposium. Asociación Psicoanalítica Argentina.

Mahler, M., Pine, F., and Bergman, A. (1975). *The Psychological Birth of the Human Infant.* New York: Basic Books.

Marmor, J. (1980). Overview: the multiple roots of homosexual behavior. In *Homosexual Behavior: A Modern Reappraisal.* New York: Basic Books.

——— (1982). Homosexuality and disturbances of sexual orientation. In *Comprehensive Textbook of Psychiatry,* ed. A. Freedman, H. Kaplan, and B. Sadock. Baltimore, MD: Williams & Wilkins.

McDougall, J. (1985). *Theaters of the Mind: Illusion and Truth on the Psychoanalytic Stage.* New York: Basic Books.

——— (1987). *Teatros de la mente.* Buenos Aires: Tecnipublicaciones.

Money, J. (1988). *Gay, Straight and In-Between: The Sexology of Erotic Orientation.* New York: Oxford University Press.

Socarides, C. W. (1984). *The Preoedipal Origin and Psychoanalytic Therapy of Sexual Perversions.* Madison, CT: International Universities Press.

Stubrin, J. P. (1976). Drogadicción: identidad y melancolia (Drug addiction: identity and melancholy). *Cuadernos de Psicoanálisis: Organo Oficial de la Asociación Psicoanalítica Mexicana* 9 (2,3).

——— (1984). Tossicodipendenza e struttura perversa: una teoria per la pratica clinica (Drug addiction and perverse structure: a theory for

clinical practice). *Giornale di Neuropsichiatria dell'Eta Evolutiva: Organo Ufficiale della Societa Italiana di Neuropsichiatria Infantile* 4 (1).
——— (1993). La angustia como factor determinante del actuar sexual compulsivo (Anxiety as a determining factor of compulsive sexual action). *Revista de Psicoanálisis* 6.
——— (1994). *Sexualities and Homosexualities.* London: Karnac.
White, E. (1993). *Genet.* New York: Random House.

Index

About the Editor

Joseph Reppen, Ph.D., is editor of *Psychoanalytic Books: A Quarterly Journal of Reviews*; President-Elect of Section 1 of the Division of Psychoanalysis (Div. 39) of the American Psychological Association; Vice President and training analyst of the New York Freudian Society; Fellow of IPTAR; and Senior Member of NPAP. A member of the International Psychoanalytical Association and of the International Association for the History of Psychoanalysis, he is editor and co-editor of numerous books including *Beyond Freud: A Study of Modern Psychoanalytic Theorists* and *Analysts at Work*. Dr. Reppen is on the editorial boards of *Psychoanalytic Review* and *Psychoanalytic Psychology*.